Library World Records

Library World Records

GODFREY OSWALD

McFarland & Company, Inc., Publishers
Jefferson, North Carolina, and London

Unless otherwise noted,
all photographs are from the author's collection.

LIBRARY OF CONGRESS CATALOGUING-IN-PUBLICATION DATA

Oswald, Godfrey, 1966–
Library world records / Godfrey Oswald.
p.   cm.
Includes bibliographical references and index.

ISBN 0-7864-1619-X (softcover : 50# alkaline paper)

1.   Libraries — Miscellanea.   2. Books — Miscellanea.
3. Information resources — Miscellanea.
4. Information services — Miscellanea.   I. Title.
Z721.O79   2004   027 — dc22   2003018521

British Library cataloguing data are available

On the cover (clockwise from top left): the Vatican Library interior
(© Biblioteca Apostolica Vaticana); Mitchell Public Library in Glasgow, Scotland
(courtesy of Mitchell Public Library); the British Library
(©Godfrey Oswald); Al-Qarawiyin University Library, Fez, Morocco
(Moroccan National Tourist Office); the Bibliothèque Nationale, Paris, France;
(©Bibliothèque Nationale de France, Paris)

Manufactured in the United States of America

*McFarland & Company, Inc., Publishers
Box 611, Jefferson, North Carolina 28640
www.mcfarlandpub.com*

To my mom and dad

ACKNOWLEDGMENTS

So many facts about libraries and books were sought during the two year quest to start and finish this book. Inspiration for writing this book actually came from readers of the old 1999 Internet version of *The Book of Library World Records,* who e-mailed wondering if another update was forthcoming and perhaps as a book this time around. For several weeks I contemplated on the pros and cons of embarking on a book version, because of the enormity of the project involved. But realization that a book would be very beneficial galvanized me to start researching in the early months of 2000. Many of the ideas for the initial research focus for the book came in the form of e-mails from around world as far away as Singapore, Alaska, Oman, New Zealand, Cuba, Ghana, South Africa, Brazil, Jamaica, and India to name a few. These e-mails were not just from fellow librarians like myself, but also students, lecturers, and teachers. Just about everyone who heard about the book project on the Internet grapevine and was curious sent in something!

The British Library, the academic libraries of the University of London and City University in London (my alma maters), and several public libraries in London, notably Westminster borough public libraries, have all been indispensable sources of data for the main research, which has resulted in the present volume, *Library World Records.* With the opportunity to travel during the course of finishing the book, visits to the national libraries of France, Germany, Italy, Spain, Switzerland and the Netherlands, as well as several university libraries in these countries, contributed a lot, especially in comparative statistical data. For those libraries I could not visit, their websites provided invaluable starting points for gathering further information.

Special thanks go to the reference libraries and public information centers of several embassies and high commissions in London. In particular the embassies of some member countries of the European Union, as well as the Russian, Israeli, Mexican, Brazilian, Japanese, and Chinese embassies and the South African, Indian, Canadian, Malaysian, Nigerian and Australian High Commissions. They all provided diverse reference sources for the book, to ensure its coverage was international.

I want to say a big thank you to all librarians subscribing to several Internet bulletin boards such as LIS-LINK & LIS-PUB-LIS (part of Jiscmail, and formerly called mailbase) in the U.K. and the American PUBLIB lists (sunsite.berkeley.edu). In particular, my appreciation goes to those who responded to my request for votes on the most fascinating library buildings in the world.

Many photographs used in this book are from libraries, bookstores and universities around the world and I am very grateful for permission to reproduce them in the book.

A personal thank you goes to university student Hee-Jin Song for allowing me to use her laptop in emergencies at short notice.

Finally I want to extend my appreciation to everyone else who has corresponded to me personally by e-mail or has provided me with answers to specific questions I raised or who sent in numerous tips that have helped to fill in the missing gaps for the book.

Godfrey Oswald
(infolibrary@yahoo.co.uk)
Fall 2003

CONTENTS

Acknowledgments   vii
Introduction   1
How to Use the Book   3

World Records for National Libraries

1. Oldest national libraries founded before 1700   5
2. Largest national libraries with over 10 million books   10
3. 5 largest national libraries in the Asia-Pacific region   13
4. 5 largest national libraries in Latin America   15
5. 6 largest national libraries in Africa and the Middle East   16

World Records for Public and Subscription Libraries

6. Largest public libraries with over 5 million books   17
7. 5 largest public libraries in Europe   18
8. 2 largest city public libraries in the U.K.   19
9. 4 largest county public libraries in the U.K.   19
10. Public library with the largest collection of medical books in the U.K.   20
11. Busiest public library   20
12. Busiest public library in the U.K.   20
13. Largest existing circulating library in the U.K.   21
14. 2 largest public libraries in France   21
15. 2 largest public libraries in Germany   22
16. Public libraries with the largest budgets in the U.S.   22
17. States with the largest library budgets in the U.S.   22
18. States with the smallest library budget in the U.S.   22
19. 2 largest public libraries in Asia   23
20. 3 largest public libraries in Latin American   23
21. 2 largest public libraries in the Middle East   23
22. 2 largest public libraries in Africa   23
23. Countries with the largest number of public libraries   24

24. Countries with the largest number of public libraries per capita   25
25. G-8 country with the smallest number of public libraries per capita   25
26. 6 oldest public libraries in Europe   25
27. 3 oldest subscription or commercial circulating libraries in the U.K.   27
28. 10 oldest public libraries in the U.K.   28
29. Oldest public library in Russia   29
30. Oldest public library in Germany   29
31. First subscription library in the U.S.   29
32. 10 oldest public libraries in the U.S.   29
33. 5 oldest public libraries in Latin America   30
34. 5 oldest public libraries in the Caribbean Islands   31
35. Oldest subscription library in Canada   32
36. Oldest public library in Canada   32
37. Oldest subscription library in Asia   32
38. Oldest public libraries in Asia   32
39. Oldest public libraries in Australia   32
40. Oldest public libraries in the Middle East   33
41. Oldest public library in Africa   33
42. First public library commemorative coins of the millennium   33
43. First public library commemorative postage stamp   33

World Records for University and Academic Libraries

44. Largest academic libraries with over 7 million books   34
45. 10 largest university or academic libraries in Europe   37
46. 8 largest university libraries in the U.K.   39
47. 6 largest university libraries in France   40
48. 6 largest university libraries in Germany   40
49. 5 largest university libraries in Italy   41
50. 6 largest university libraries in Austria and Switzerland   42
51. 6 largest university libraries in Spain and Portugal   43
52. 5 largest university libraries in Scandinavia   43
53. 5 largest university libraries in Belgium and the Netherlands   44
54. 2 largest university libraries in Ireland   44
55. 2 largest university libraries in the Vatican City   45
56. 2 largest university libraries in Greece   45
57. 7 largest university libraries in Russia   45
58. 10 largest university libraries in Eastern Europe   46
59. 5 largest university libraries in Canada   47
60. 6 largest university libraries in Japan   47
61. 5 largest university libraries in China   47

62. 15 largest university libraries in the Asia-Pacific region   48
63. 10 largest university libraries in Latin America   48
64. 10 largest university libraries in the Middle East   50
65. 5 largest university libraries in Africa   51
66. 10 oldest university libraries in the world and the Middle East   52
67. Earliest academic library in Europe   53
68. 10 oldest university libraries in Europe   54
69. 5 oldest university libraries in the U.K.   55
70. 5 oldest university libraries in France   55
71. 5 oldest university libraries in Germany   56
72. 5 oldest university libraries in Spain   57
73. 10 oldest university libraries in Eastern Europe   57
74. 12 other significant early university libraries in Western Europe   58
75. 5 oldest university libraries in the Asia-Pacific Region   59
76. 10 oldest university libraries in the Americas   60
77. 5 oldest university libraries in Africa   61

World Records for Specialty Libraries and Archives

78. 6 largest medical libraries   63
79. Largest biomedical and scientific periodicals library   64
80. Oldest dental school library   64
81. Oldest medical school libraries   65
82. Oldest medical school library in the U.S.   65
83. Oldest medical school library in Asia   65
84. Oldest medical school library in the U.K.   65
85. 5 largest medical libraries in the U.K.   66
86. Largest pharmaceutical libraries   66
87. Largest international medical library   66
88. Largest medical library in Scandinavia   66
89. Largest library in Europe on deafness and hearing loss   67
90. Largest library for political science and economics   67
91. Largest library specializing in geography   68
92. Largest library in the Middle East devoted to oil exploration   69
93. Largest engineering libraries   69
94. Largest music library   70
95. Largest poetry library   70
96. Largest film and television library in Europe   70
97. Largest agricultural libraries   71
98. Largest zoological library   71
99. Largest botanical library   71

100. 6 largest military libraries   72
101. Largest library in the U.K. on prison services   72
102. Largest law library   73
103. Largest law libraries in Europe and Asia   73
104. Largest art library   75
105. 2 largest libraries with in Europe specialized collections of books
        on Africa   75
106. Largest astronomy library   75
107. Largest libraries in Europe specializing in education   75
108. Largest social sciences library   76
109. Largest religious libraries   76
110. Oldest library in the U.K. devoted to women   77
111. Largest collection of Shakespeare's printed works   78
112. Oldest national archives   78
113. Oldest national archives in the Americas   79
114. Oldest national archives in the Middle East   79
115. Oldest national archives in Asia   79
116. Oldest national archives in Africa   79

Miscellaneous World Records for Libraries

117. 18 major libraries that have suffered devastating fires or natural disasters   80
118. Library with the most branches worldwide   82
119. Oldest private library in the U.S.   83
120. Most expensive library   83
121. 14 major films that featured libraries   84
122. Some notable people who have worked in libraries or as librarians   85
123. 40 translations of the word "library" around the world   90
124. Earliest libraries   91

World Records for Books, Periodicals and Bookstores

125. 10 oldest existing written works   96
126. Earliest written works in German   107
127. Earliest written works in Mayan   107
128. Earliest written works in Arabic   107
129. Earliest written works in Japanese   108
130. Earliest written works in French   108
131. Earliest written works in Spanish   109
132. Earliest written works in English and Irish   109
133. Earliest written works in Dutch   112
134. Earliest written works from Africa   112

135. Oldest written medical works 114
136. 2 oldest existing books made from paper 114
137. First book printed with movable type 117
138. First book printed in English 119
139. First book printed in English in the U.K. 120
140. First book printed in English in the U.S. 120
141. First book printed in French 121
142. First book printed in Italian 121
143. First book printed in Spanish 121
144. First book printed in Russian 121
145. First books printed in Scandinavia 122
146. First book printed in Irish 122
147. First book printed in Farsi 122
148. First book printed in Hebrew 122
149. First book printed in Hindi 123
150. First book printed in Turkish 123
151. First book printed in Latin America 123
152. First book printed in Africa 123
153. First book printed in Southeast Asia 124
154. Largest collection of books printed before 1501 124
155. 5 earliest dates in copyright 125
156. First regular newspapers 126
157. First printed magazines 126
158. First scholarly or academic journal published in the U.K. 126
159. First law journal 126
160. First medical journal 127
161. First paperbacks 127
162. Earliest professional handbooks for librarians 127
163. Most popular handbook for librarians in the U.S. 127
164. Oldest existing library periodical 128
165. First library serial in the U.S. 128
166. Oldest and largest general reference book in the English language 128
167. Largest general reference book in the French language 128
168. Biggest and smallest books 129
169. Most overdue library book 130
170. Most popular author among library users in the U.K. 130
171. First major book-burning ritual 131
172. 12 most expensive books 132
173. 5 earliest writers of dictionaries in English 134
174. Oldest book museum 134
175. Oldest continuously trading bookstore in Europe 135

176. Oldest existing bookstore — 135
177. First book club — 135
178. Largest bookstore — 135
179. Largest online bookstore — 137
180. Largest online bookstore in Europe — 137
181. Largest online bookstore in Asia — 137
182. Largest online bookstore in Latin America — 137
183. Largest online bookstore in Africa — 138
184. Largest online bookstore in the Middle East — 138
185. Largest bookstores around the world — 138
186. Largest publishers of books — 144
187. Countries with the largest number of books published in more than 10 major local languages — 145
188. Largest annual book fair — 146
189. Largest annual book fair in the U.S. — 146
190. Largest annual book fair in Asia — 146
191. Largest annual book fair in Latin America — 146
192. Largest annual book fair in the Middle East — 147
193. Largest annual book fair in Africa — 147

World Records for Library Buildings

194. Oldest existing library buildings — 148
195. First library building to use extensive electrical lighting — 151
196. 8 tallest library buildings — 152
197. 5 largest library buildings — 154
198. 3 largest university library buildings — 157
199. 4 largest public library buildings — 158
200. Largest scientific and technical library building — 158
201. Most fascinating library buildings — 158
202. 10 most fascinating national library buildings — 159
203. 10 most fascinating university library buildings — 163
204. 10 most fascinating public library buildings — 166
205. 10 other fascinating library buildings — 170

World Records for Library Catalogs, Databases and Technology

206. Oldest library classification scheme — 175
207. Most popular library cataloging principles — 176
208. Largest national library catalog — 176

209. Largest national union library catalog in Europe   177
210. Largest unified university library catalog in the U.S.   177
211. Largest unified university library catalog in the U.K.   177
212. Largest unified library catalog in France   177
213. Largest unified international library catalog   178
214. First computerized library catalog or OPAC   178
215. First library OPAC in the U.S.   179
216. First library OPAC in Europe   179
217. First library OPAC in Australia   179
218. First public library OPAC in the U.K.   179
219. First companies to develop library OPACs   179
220. First library to make use of microfilm   180
221. First major computer database   180
222. First and largest database host   181
223. First database host in France   182
224. First database host in the U.K.   182
225. First database host in Germany   182
226. Largest database host in Russia   182
227. First database host to introduce networked CD-ROM access   183
228. Largest database host in Europe   183
229. Oldest database host in Europe   183
230. Largest database host in Japan   183
231. Largest database host in Scandinavia   184
232. First indexing service   184
233. First citation indexes   184
234. Largest citation index database service   184
235. First major KWIC indexing service   185
236. First table-of-contents database   185
237. First and largest full-text databases   185
238. Largest commercially available microform collection   185
239. Largest electronic information services   186
240. Largest periodicals database   186
241. Largest collection of electronic journals   186
242. First major reference book on CD-ROM   187
243. Oldest electronic newspaper coverage   187
244. Largest producers of newspapers on CD-ROM   187
245. Largest database on the latest books published in English   188
246. Largest company information databases   188
247. Largest database on businesses in the U.S.   189
248. Largest database on companies in the U.K.   189
249. Largest database on companies in Germany   189

250. Largest English language database on companies in Japan   189
251. Largest economics and financial database in Japanese   189
252. Largest business and economics periodicals databases   190
253. Largest collection of U.S. legal databases   190
254. Second largest U.S. legal databases and largest European legal
     databases   190
255. 3 largest U.K. legal databases   190
256. Largest Canadian legal databases   191
257. First and largest biomedical database   191
258. First and largest printed medical indexing service   191
259. Largest biomedical and pharmaceutical database in Europe   191
260. Largest DNA database   192
261. Largest agricultural databases   192
262. Largest biological abstracting and indexing service   193
263. Largest zoological databases   193
264. Largest science and technology database in Asia   193
265. Largest chemical abstracting and indexing service   193
266. Largest engineering abstracting and indexing service   194
267. Largest civil engineering database   194
268. Largest electrical and electronic engineering database   194
269. Largest technical standards database   195
270. Largest database on pulp and paper industries   195
271. Largest database in psychology   195
272. Largest genealogical database   196
273. Largest index to journal articles and documents in education   196
274. Largest bibliographic database on transportation information   196
275. Largest library and information science abstracting and indexing
     service   197
276. First commercial information brokerage   197
277. Most popular stand-alone bibliographic database software   197
278. Largest online information event in the U.K.   197
279. Largest online information event in Germany   198
280. Largest online information event in France   198
281. Largest online information event in the U.S.   198
282. Largest digital images database   198
283. Largest patent databases   199
284. Largest patent database in Europe   199
285. Largest database of U.S. patents   199
286. Largest database on chemical and pharmaceutical patents   200
287. Most popular CD-ROM information retrieval software used in
     libraries to access networked CD-ROM databases   200

288. First major CD-ROM database used in libraries 200
289. Largest search engine 201
290. Largest archives of web pages 201
291. Largest document supply service and inter-lending service 202
292. Largest scientific document supply services 202
293. Largest library network or consortium 203
294. Largest providers of subscription services for libraries 203
295. Oldest providers of subscription services for libraries 203
296. Largest electronic trading services for libraries in the U.K. 204
297. 10 greatest inventions used in libraries today 204

World Records for Library and Information Science Organizations

298. First library school 205
299. Oldest accredited library school in North America 205
300. 5 oldest university library schools in Europe 206
301. Oldest university library school in Asia 206
302. Oldest university library school in the Middle East 206
303. First university in the U.S. to offer an extensive program in
     information science 206
304. First university in the U.K. to offer an extensive program in
     information science 207
305. Top 10 U.S. library schools for the year 2000 208
306. Largest national library association 208
307. Largest and first national library association in Europe 209
308. First national library association in Asia 209
309. First national library association in the Middle East 209
310. Largest national information science association 209
311. Most prestigious award for U.K. and European information
     scientists 210
312. First full-time paid librarian in the U.K. 210
313. 6 libraries with over 800 staff members and their annual budgets 210
314. 212 largest and most important libraries 211
315. 95 oldest libraries 216

Saint Jerome, the Librarian's Patron Saint 219
Godfrey Oswald's 18 Greatest Texts of All Time 220
Bibliography 221
Index 223

Some books are to be tasted, some to be swallowed, and some chewed and digested.
Francis Bacon, British philosopher.

A room without books is like a body without a soul.
Marcus Cicero, Roman politician.

Libraries are the memory of mankind.
Wolfgang von Goethe, German poet.

INTRODUCTION

Have you ever wondered which university in the world has the largest library? Do you know the name of the oldest public libraries in the Americas? In Europe? What year was the first CD-ROM book released? In what year was the first book in the United States printed? When was the first major computer database released? To find the answers to these questions, you could spend days skimming hundreds of reference sources in libraries for this kind of information. Or you might think about the *Guinness Book of World Records*, but it does not cover a lot of information specifically about libraries. However all the answers can be found in this new book.

Library World Records is not just a book about library and book comparisons, it is a remarkable story of libraries and books from the earliest times to present. The hundreds of facts about libraries, periodicals, books and reference databases around the world illustrate just how significantly things have evolved from crude and simple to complex and sophisticated. Necessity, they say, is the mother of invention. From the time humans learned to write, they have not stopped improving the way they communicate their ideas, thoughts, knowledge and inspirations.

The arrangement of specific lists and entries in the book (with regard to geographic area or continent) are in no par-

ticular order of preference, but the following should be noted. A general rule I adopted when organizing specific lists and entries on libraries in the book was to start first with the geographic area with the most numerous libraries (including the largest number of library books) and end with the geographic area with the fewest libraries.

For this arrangement, entries and lists for most libraries in the United States and Europe will appear first, followed by those for libraries in Latin America and Asia, and those for libraries from the Middle East and Africa will appear last.

University and public libraries combined in the West have a greater number of books for each specific country than do libraries in countries from other continents or geographic regions. So there are more lists pertaining to individual countries in the West than the other continents or geographic areas covered in the book.

This arrangement is also used in the lists on World Records for Books, Periodicals and Bookstores. Because Western languages are widely spoken (officially or unofficially) and understood on an international level around the world, there are more entries, for instance, on the oldest books written in Western languages.

Finally I would like to comment on the appearance of many entries and lists on the United Kingdom. Since I live in the U.K., about half of the total time spent in my research for the book was carried out in U.K. libraries, but I tried my best to find other sources for information about libraries and books in countries outside the U.K. in particular and Europe in general. I have tried to ensure that at least on a continental level, facts and figures on major libraries for each continent (Africa, Asia-Pacific region, North and South America etc.) were covered.

If after reading the book, you know of any official or factual information on libraries and books in any country that is missing from this book, please e-mail me (infolibrary@yahoo.co.uk) the details, including the source of the information. Such information will be useful for a future edition of the book.

In the course of writing the book, every effort has been made to ensure accuracy. In particular all dates and total numbers of books are either official, or estimated and verified from several independent and reliable sources. *Library World Records* is for anyone who appreciates the important role libraries have played and continued to play in the development of our modern society.

How to Use the Book

Each separate entry or list within each chapter is given a number to facilitate use of the table of contents. (Exceptions are the last two chapters.) Items within each numbered list are themselves numbered according to their numerical rank. Page numbers are used for the index.

As the book covers mostly world records on libraries, books etc., the word "world" has been omitted for each record entry where applicable, thus the entry "Largest National Libraries" covers the largest national libraries in the world.

But records for national or continental entries, "largest university libraries in France," or "oldest public libraries in Europe" for example, will have the appropriate name of the country or continent.

Where possible, if English is not the official language or one of the official languages of a country, then the name of the national, university or public library in the official language (with transliteration where necessary) is given alongside the English version.

For some entries, additional information has been provided under the heading "*Notes*." These notes will provide either useful background information or additional interesting facts.

WORLD RECORDS FOR NATIONAL LIBRARIES

1.
Oldest National Libraries
Founded Before 1700

For most countries of the world, the number one library is always the national library, which is also a very important cultural institution. For each country the national library normally has a legal right to be given a copy of every book published in that country. For this reason national libraries tend to have large collections. And in some countries the national library is the largest library or the only major library available to the public. Many national libraries around the world began as public libraries such as the national libraries in Russia, India, Argentina, and Bulgaria. In other countries such as Finland, Denmark, Macedonia, Mexico, and Israel, a major university library also functions as the national library. The National Library of Singapore began as a subscription library. In Burma (Myanmar) and the Philippines, the national library also serves as a public library. Some national libraries are the result of an amalgamation of libraries founded much earlier in history, some of which were libraries of the monarchy, religious libraries, or private libraries of public figures.

The Alexandria Library in Egypt, founded around 305 BC by Greek Macedonian king Ptolemy I Soter is probably the earliest significant national library in the world, and undoubtedly the greatest library in existence from the time of Alexandria the Great's Empire to the fall of the Western Roman Empire. Expanded by other kings after Ptolemy I Soter, its first two librarians (great scholars of the day) were Zenodotus of Ephesus (famous for writing a critical review of the works of the mysterious Greek author Homer), and Callimachus, who created a subject catalog of the library's holdings called the *Pinakes*. This catalog was a masterpiece and was composed of over 100 scrolls. One of the goals pursued by the owners of the Alexandria Library was to have a copy of every single book in the world — an ambitious but impossible task given to one of the librarians, a former governor of Athens named Demetrius. King Ptolemy I himself wrote letters to sovereign leaders and statesmen, requesting books by prominent writers, poets, doctors, soothsayers, and people in other important professions. At

The new Alexandria Library in Egypt (courtesy of Ibrahim Nafie, Alexandria Library).

the same time the library sent out literary experts to search the cities of Europe, North Africa and the Asia Minor region for important manuscripts, maps and other items to loot. And being a major harbor at the time, foreign ships passing through Alexandria or moored at the port were thoroughly searched (sometimes with force) for anything significant to add to the library's growing collection. The library did not reach its ultimate goal. Nevertheless at its peak, the library did house over 750,000 parchment and papyrus scrolls, a huge collection for a library of its era. Many of these documents were in several languages, such as ancient Egyptian, Greek, Hebrew and Latin, written by some of the greatest experts of the day in astronomy, medicine, law and science. Famous users of the library included Euclid and Archimedes. The library was destroyed around AD 638 (after existing for almost 1000 years) as Arab armies overran North

Africa, and the circumstances of this destruction has been controversial ever since.

Notes. In 1989 the United Nations Educational, Scientific and Cultural Organization (UNESCO) initiated work to recreate the ancient Alexandria Library as the Bibliotheca Alexandrina. The new Alexandria Library is located near the Alexandria University Faculty of Arts campus, in Shatby, close to the Mediterranean Sea. The completed building, costing over $230 million, now has space for over 4 million books. Many of the books and manuscripts were contributions and donations received from individuals and governments from around the world, and so far the total items in the library are just under 300,000. Bibliotheca Alexandrina opened to the public October 19, 2002.

The following are the oldest national libraries founded before 1700, which exist today.

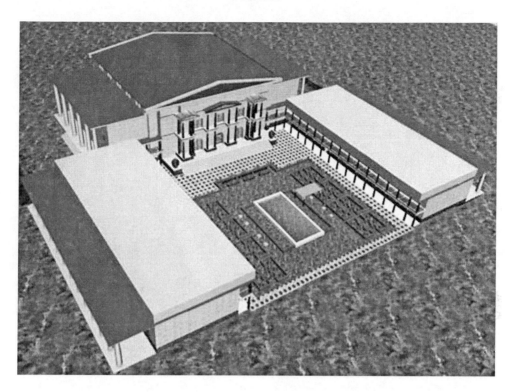

This is how the original Alexandria Library may have looked when it existed more than 2000 years ago (courtesy of UNESCO).

1. National Library of the Czech Republic, Prague (*Národní Knihovně Ceské Republiky*). Founded 1366.

> *Notes. The national library began with a donation of books by King Charles IV. The history of the library is closely related with the foundation of the Charles University in 1348.*

2. National Library of Austria, Vienna (*Österreichische Nationalbibliothek*). 1368.

> *Notes. It was founded from the royal collections of Austrian Dukes (starting with Archduke Albrecht III) as part of the later Imperial Court Library (Kaiserliche Hofbibliothek), during the early period of the Habsburg Dynasty. This royal family ruled Austria from 1278 up to 1918, after the end of the First World War.*

3. Marciana National Library, Venice, Venetian Republic (*Biblioteca Nazionale de Marciana*). 1468.

> *Notes. Cardinal Bessarione started the library with his own collection of important religious manuscripts. The Venetian Republic is now part of Italy, and the library still exists under the same name, a legacy of the time Italy was not a united country, but made of city-states like Genoa and Venice. Today while most countries have one main national library, ten institutions in Italy are given the title of National Library, at Bari, Rome, Florence, Milan, Naples, Palermo, Turin, Venice, Potenza and Cosenza. However those at Rome and Florence are the most prominent.*

4. National Library of France, Paris (*Bibliothèque Nationale de France*). 1480.

The National Library of the Czech Republic in the city of Prague is the oldest national library in the world (courtesy of the National Library of the Czech Republic).

Notes. The legal status of the National Library of France was acquired in 1617, and the library opened for the public in 1735. But actual foundation of the library goes back to 1480 when the library was known as the Bibliothèque du Roi and was part of King Louis XI royal library. A collection of books belonging to King Charles V "the Wise" (a patron of the arts and of learning), and now part of the national library, dates back further to 1368.

5. National Library of Malta, Valetta (*Biblioteka Nazzjonali ta' Malta*). 1555.

Notes. Books belonging to the knights of the Order of St. John of Jerusalem started the library.

6. Bavarian State Library, Munich. Germany (*Bayerische Staatsbibliothek*). 1558.

Notes. Duke Albrecht V founded the library as the Wittelsbach court library during the time Bavaria was a kingdom and Germany was made up of several city-states and then part of the Holy Roman Empire. Today the library is not part of the German national library, but it is one of the largest and most important libraries.

7. National Library of Belgium, Brussels. Royal Library Albert I (*Koninklijke Bibliotheek van België/Bibliothèque Royale de Belgique*). 1559.

Notes. The Dukes of Burgundy laid the foundation for the national library starting with a collection of important manuscripts. Belgium is one of the few countries in Europe that are bilingual, so her libraries tend have two titles; in French and Flemish (Dutch). Books in the li-

The National Library in Rome, one of Italy's 10 national libraries.

braries are in both of these languages as well.

8. National Library of Croatia, Zagreb (*Nacionalna i Sveuèilišna Knjižnica*). 1606.

> *Notes. Jesuits first established the library collections; it is also part of the Zagreb University Library.*

9. National Library of Finland, Helsinki (*Helsingin Yliopiston Kirjasto*). 1640.

> *Notes. It is also forms part of the Helsinki University Library, and was first founded in Turku, the old capital of Finland (formerly called Åbo, when Finland was then part of Sweden). The library moved to Helsinki in 1828 after the Great Fire of Turku.*

10. National Library of Denmark, Copenhagen (*Det Kongelige Bibliotek*). 1653.

> *Notes. King Frederick III originally founded the library. It is also part of the Copenhagen University Library founded in 1482.*

11. National Library of Sweden, Stockholm (*Kungliga Bibliotek*). 1661.

Notes. This national library began as a collection of books originally belonging to the first Swedish king, Gustavus Vasa (Gustavus I). Between 1397 and 1523, Sweden had been part of a political union with Denmark and Norway, but with a Danish monarch (Union of Kalmar). When Sweden left the union in 1523, Norway remained united with Denmark until the 1814 Congress of Vienna ceded it to Sweden.

12. Prussian State Library, Berlin, Germany (*Staatsbibliothek zu Berlin. Preussischer Kulturbesitz*). 1661.

> *Notes. Prussia is now part of Germany and Poland, and the library is now known as the Berlin State Library. Frederick William, ruler of Brandenburg, founded the library. Like the Bavarian State Library, it is not part of the German national library in Frankfurt, but it is one of the three main important libraries in Germany.*

13. National Library of Scotland, Edinburgh. U.K. 1682.

Notes. It was formerly part of the Library of the Faculty of Advocates, which is still in existence, but now as a law library. The separation of the library to become a national library occurred in 1925. The National Library of Scotland (with 6.1 million books) is the third largest library in the U.K., after the British Library and the Bodleian Library at Oxford University.

2.
Largest National Libraries with Over 10 Million Books

When considering the size of a library's collections, only the number of books is taken into account throughout this book; other library materials such as manuscripts, serials (newspapers, journals and so on), microfilms, and maps are disregarded. In 1964 during an UNESCO conference, it was agreed internationally that a book was defined as *a non-periodical printed publication of at least 49 pages.* Many libraries say of their collections that they have so many "items" but this includes all kinds of library materials as well as books.

1. Library of Congress, Washington, D.C. 25 million books. Founded in 1800. The national library with the biggest annual budget, currently about $400 million.

Notes. It was the most expensive library building before the 20th century, when the Jefferson Building, the oldest part of the three buildings that make up the library, opened in 1897 at a cost of $10 million. Storage of its huge collections of books has meant going to extraordinary lengths such as constructing 500 miles of underground rooms beneath the library building. The rate at which the book collection in the Library of Congress has grown in size is staggering. In 1900 it had just over 2 million books. The first full time librarian of the Library of Con-gress was George Watterson in 1815. During the Second World War the original copies of the 18th century Constitution and the Declaration of Independence (engrossed upon parchment), were taken from the Library of Congress to Fort Knox (ordinarily used for storing U.S. gold bullion) in Kentucky for safekeeping. Both documents are today housed in helium-filled glass cases (this time to protect them against decay) in the National Archives building in Washington, D.C. In times of war, revolution or political unrest, other important documents around the world have had similar instances of contingency plans for protection. For instance it is believed that the famous Dead Sea Scrolls found in secret caves were actually hidden there to protect them during the first Jewish revolt that occurred between AD 66 and 70. During the clashes between the Roman army and rebel Jews, it was feared the scrolls would be destroyed if the Romans got hold of them. After Roman emperor Titus put down the rebellion, the scrolls remained hidden and forgotten until a chance discovery in 1947.

2. The British Library, London. 18 million. It is also Europe's largest library.

Notes. Although the British Library was part of the British Museum founded in 1753, it became separate in 1973, and officially different entities in 1998. The British Museum Library itself developed from the Royal Library of King Henry VII. The new British Library building was opened to the public in 1997. Prior to this, the collections of the library were housed in several buildings in central London. There are also two other British national libraries: in Scotland (Edinburgh), founded in 1682, with 6.1 million books, and in Wales (Cardiff), founded in 1911 and with 4 million books.

3. Russian State Library, Moscow (*Rossiskaya Gosudarstvennaya Biblioteka*). 17 million.

> *Notes. With over 42 million items, it is the second largest library in the world (after the Library of Congress), in terms of the number of items held in the library. And with only a million books differentiating it in size from the British Library, sometimes the title of Europe's largest library also goes to the Russian State Library. Formerly called the Lenin State Library of the USSR (until 1991), it was founded in 1924, a few years after Vladimir Ilyich Lenin's October revolution. But the origin of the library goes back to 1828, when it was part of the private collection of Count Nickolai Rumyantsev Library. It was then the first public library in Moscow.*

4. National Library of France, Paris (*Bibliothèque Nationale de France*). 13 million. Third largest in Europe. A new library building opened to the public in 1996, but the library's actual foundation goes back to 1480.

> *Notes. The French national library was the first library to provide full-text access to a great deal of its collections via the Internet. The special catalog called Gallica also provides photographs and illustrations*

from the publication (cover page digital image and/or digital images from inside the publication). Normally a library's catalog only provides bibliographic details of its book collections, so Gallica was a unique deviation from library tradition. It is expected that other national libraries around the world may provide full-text access to some of their collections soon.

5. National Library of Russia, St. Petersburg (*Rossiiskaya Natsionalnaya Biblioteka*). Formerly M.E. Saltykov-Shchedrin State Public Library. 11.8 million.

> *Notes. Empress Catherine the Great founded the library in 1795.*

6. National Library of Germany, Frankfurt, Leipzig and Berlin (*Die Deutsche Bibliothek*). 11.3 million. Founded in 1990 following the merging of the former East German National Library in Leipzig (*Deutsche Bücherei*, founded 1912) with the *Deutsche Bibliothek* in former West Germany (founded 1946). The third location of the national library is in Berlin, where music materials are kept in the *Deutsches Musikarchiv*.

> *Notes. Two other large state libraries also exist in Germany, and are comparable with the national library in Frankfurt. The first one, the Bavarian State Library in Munich, currently holds 8 million books. The other, the Berlin State Library, holds about 9.4 million books. Smaller state libraries also exist in Stuttgart and Dresden.*

7. National Library of Canada, Ottawa (*Bibliothèque Nationale du Canada*). Founded 1953. 10.2 million.

> *Notes. A second national library of Canada also exists in Montreal, as the Bibliothèque Nationale du Québec. The above figure is the total for both libraries.*

Top: Based in London, the British Library is Europe's largest library. *Bottom:* The National Library of France, Paris, at night (©Bibliothèque Nationale de France, Paris).

The National Library of Germany in Frankfurt.

8. Vernadsky National Library of Ukraine, Kiev (*Natsional'na Biblioteka Ukraïny*) 10 million. Founded 1918.

3.
5 Largest National Libraries in the Asia-Pacific Region

1. National Library of Japan, Tokyo (*Kokuritsu Kokkai Toshokan*). Founded 1948. 9.2 million books. Ninth largest national library in the world.

> *Notes. It was originally founded in 1872 during the Meiji period as the Imperial Library or Teikoku Toshokan, but after the end of the Second World War and following adoption of a new constitution, it was renamed Kokuritsu Kokkai Toshokan or Diet Library.*

2. National Library of China, Beijing (*Zhongguo Guojia Tushugan*). Founded 1910. 9 million. Tenth largest national library in the world.

> *Notes. It was previously called the Metropolitan Library of Beijing. A new building for the library was added in 1987.*

3. National Library of Australia, Canberra. Founded 1901. 7.3 million.

> *Notes. It was the first national library to*

Canada's National Library in Ottawa is the second largest in the Americas, after that of the United States (©National Library of Canada, Ottawa).

set up its own website back in 1994. The library played a leading role in the establishment of the National Library of Papua New Guinea, when in 1975 the then Prime Minister of Australia announced its Independence gift to people of Papua New Guinea would be a national library building and its contents. This was possible after consultations with Papua New Guinea leaders. In addition to advising on the design of the building, the National Library of Australia developed the initial collection. By the end of 1977, huge quantities of ordered materials were arriving, signaling the beginning of the huge job of processing books, government publications, films and equipment. A special gift from the National Library of *Australia was Papua New Guinean books, films and maps, some of which were valuable historic items not otherwise available. In 1978, the Australian government formally handed over the keys to the building in Port Moresby.*

4. National Library of India, Calcutta (Kolkata). Founded 1902. 4.5 million.

> ***Notes.*** *The national library is the result of the amalgamation of the Calcutta Public Library founded in 1835, with the Imperial Library in 1903.*

5. National Library of New Zealand, Wellington (*Te Puna Manatauranga O Aotearoa*). Founded 1856. 4.4 million.

Japan's National Library in Tokyo, is the largest in the Asia-Pacific region (©National Library of Japan, Tokyo).

4.
5 Largest National Libraries in Latin America

1. National Library of Mexico, Mexico City (*Biblioteca Nacional de México*). 3.3 million. Founded 1833.

> *Notes. It is also part of the National Autonomous University Library.*

2. National Library of Argentina, Buenos Aires (*Biblioteca Nacional de la República Argentina*). 3 million books. Founded in 1810.

3. National Library of Venezuela, Caracas (*Biblioteca Nacional de Venezuela*). 2.7 million books. Founded 1833.

4. National Library of Cuba, Havana (*Biblioteca Nacional de Cuba*). Havana. 2.6 million. Founded 1901.

5. National Library of Brazil, Rio de Janeiro (*Biblioteca Nacional de Brasil*). 1.8 million books. Founded 1810.

> *Notes. The first collection of books of the National Library of Brazil belonged to the Portuguese royal family, who took the books with them when they fled to Brazil, after Napoleon Bonaparte and his forces invaded Portugal in the late 18th century.*

5.
6 Largest National Libraries in Africa and the Middle East

1. National Library of Israel, Jerusalem. 4 million books. Founded 1925.

> **Notes.** *Also part of the Hebrew University Library.*

2. National Library of Egypt, Cairo (*Dâr el-Kutub Al-Misrîyya*). 2 million. Founded 1870.

> **Notes.** *It began as the royal Khedieval Palace Library belonging to Khedive Ismael.*

3. National Library of Turkey, Ankara. (*Türkiye Milli Kutuphane*). 1.3 million. Founded 1948.

4. National Library of Tunisia, Tunis. 1.2 million. Founded 1845.

5. National Library of South Africa, Pretoria and Cape Town. 1.4 million. The Cape Town branch was founded 1818, while Pretoria branch was founded in 1887.

6. National Library of Algeria, Algiers (*Bibliothèque National d'Algérie*). 960,000. Founded 1835.

WORLD RECORDS FOR PUBLIC AND SUBSCRIPTION LIBRARIES

A public library is usually a library open to the public that is funded by the government. In many cities and towns several branches of a main library may exist in different locations. For instance New York Public Library has over 80 branches in the city. Precursors of public libraries in many countries were called circulating or subscription libraries. Some were part private and part public. Today some subscription libraries have become full public libraries.

6.
Largest public libraries with over 5 million books

Los Angeles and New York are the two cities in the world with the largest combined collection of public library books (all library branches in the city), and the largest annual budgets in the world.

1. New York Public Library, U.S. Has about 12 million books and 84 separate branches. Founded in 1895.

2. Cincinnati & Hamilton County (Ohio) Public Library, U.S. 9.6 million. Founded in 1856.

3. Chicago (Illinois) Public Library, U.S. 9.2 million. Founded in 1873.

*Notes. Because the existing library building did not have enough space for the expanding book collections, a new central library called the Harold Washington Library Center opened to the public in 1991, and it is now the second largest public library building in the world. See list **199**.*

4. Queens Borough Public Library, New York City, U.S. 9.1 million. Founded in 1896.

5. Philadelphia (Pennsylvania) Public Library, U.S. 8.1 million. Founded in 1891.

6. Shanghai Library, China (*Shanghai Tushugan*). 8 million. Founded in 1952.

7. Toronto (Ontario) Public Library, Canada. 7.65 million. Founded in 1884.

> *Notes. It has 9 million items and an annual circulation of 28 million (probably giving it the highest public library circulation numbers in the Americas).*

8. Los Angeles County (California) Public Library, U.S. 7.4 million. Founded in 1912.

9. Boston (Massachusetts) Public Library, U.S. 7.4 million. Founded in 1848.

10. Brooklyn Public Library, New York City, U.S. 6.8 million. Founded in 1897

11. Carnegie Library of Pittsburgh (Pennsylvania), U.S. 6.3 million. Founded 1897.

12. Nanjing Library, China (*Nanjing Tushugan*) 6 million. Founded 1908.

13. Los Angeles (city) Public Library (California), U.S. 5.7 million. Founded in 1872.

14. Houston (Texas) Public Library, U.S. 5.1 million. Founded in 1875.

7.
5 largest public libraries in Europe

1. Mitchell Library, Glasgow, Scotland, U.K. 4.5 million books. Founded in 1874.

2. Birmingham Central Public Library, U.K. 3.3 million. Founded in 1852.

3. Munich City Library, Germany (*Münchner Stadbibliothek*). 3.2 million. Founded 1843.

4. Berlin Central Library, Germany (*Zentral und Landesbibliothek Berlin*). 3.1 million. Founded 1901.

5. Stockholm City, Sweden, and County Library (*Stockholms Stadsbibliotek*). 2.2 million. Founded 1927.

> *Notes. Other major large public libraries in Europe (excluding those in the U. K., Germany and France) and the foundation year are Dublin City Library, Ireland, 2.1 million books, founded in 1884. Rotterdam Municipal Library, Netherlands (Gemeentebibliotheek Rotterdam), 2 million, 1604. Malmö City Library,*

Sweden (Malmö Stadsbibliotek), 2 million. Moscow City Public Library, Russia (Moskva Publichnaya Biblioteca), 1.9 million, 1919. Prague Municipal Library, Czech Republic (Mìstká Knihovně Praha), 1.8 million, 1891. Bucharest City Library, Romania (Biblioteca Municipale Bucureşti), 1.6 million, 1935. Barcelona Public Library, Spain, 1.5 million, 1918. Oslo Deichman Public Library, Norway (Deichmanske Bibliotek), 1.5 million, 1785. Vienna Public Library, Austria (Büchereien Wien), 1.3 million, 1945. Oporto Public Library, Portugal (Biblioteca Publica Municipal Porto), 1.2 million, 1833. Metropolitan Ervin Szabo Library, Budapest, Hungary (Ervin Szabo Könyvtár), 1.2 million, 1904. Warsaw Public Library, Poland (Biblioteka Publiczna Warszawy), 1.2 million, 1907. Antwerp Central Public Library, Belgium (Antwerpen Openbare Bibliotheek), 1 million, 1866. Panizzi Municipal Library, Via Emilia, Italy (Biblioteca Municipale Panizzi), 710,000, 1796.

Mitchell Public Library in Glasgow, Scotland, is the largest in Europe (courtesy of Mitchell Public Library).

8.
2 largest city public libraries in the U.K.

Excluding the Mitchell Library in Glasgow, the two largest city public libraries in the U.K. are Birmingham Central Public Library with 3.3 million books, founded in 1861, and the Liverpool Public Library with 3 million, founded in 1852.

Notes. The combined collection of all the volumes of books in the 32 boroughs that make up Greater London is 4.1 million. The largest ones are Westminster and Barnet borough public libraries.

9.
4 largest county public libraries in the U.K.

1. Hampshire (Winchester) public libraries, 3.8 million books.

2. Kent (Maidstone) public libraries, 3.5 million.

3. Lancashire (Preston) public libraries, 3 million.

4. Essex (Chelmsford) public libraries, 2.8 million.

10.
Public library with the largest
collection of medical books in the U.K.

For several years, the Marylebone branch of Westminster Borough Public Libraries in London had the most extensive stock of medical books available for reference work in a U.K. public library. In the late 1990s its entire stock was, however, relocated and distributed to agencies in a better position to maintain the collection. Some major medical reference materials do remain in the library.

11.
Busiest public library

New York Public library in the United States is the busiest in the world, receiving over 10 million visitors a year and having over 3 million registered members.

12.
Busiest public library in the U.K.

Using the standard set by the U.K. Chartered Institute of Public Finance & Accounting or CIPFA, which is the national body responsible for the collection of data on public and local authority services, Birmingham Central Public Library currently receives 1.5 million visits per year (just under 7,000 a day). This makes it the most visited public library in the U.K.

Notes. Opened in 1977, the Georges Pompidou Center's state-of-the-art multimedia Public Information Library or BPI (Bibliothèque Publique d'Information) always seems to draw record number of crowds, with at least with 14,000 people a day (or 5 million a year) visiting the library. This figure is about half the total number of people who visited the New York Public Library. If it isn't the free access without membership cards that attracts the crowds or the 1,800 reading desks, 450,000 books, 2,600 periodicals, and 2,400 videos, then it's the yearly Festival of Reality, dedicated to documentary and ethnological film.

The Georges Pompidou Center, a.k.a. "ocean liner" or "Beaubourg" has the most visited public library in Paris, and probably in Europe.

13.
Largest existing circulating library in the U.K.

The London Library, set up in 1841 by Thomas Caryle, today has about 650,000 books.

14.
2 largest public libraries in France

Lyons Municipal Library (*Bibliothèque Municipale de Lyon*) founded in 1527 presently has over 2 million books, while Bordeaux Municipal Library (*Bibliothèque Municipale de Bordeaux*) has about 1.2 million books. It was founded in 1740.

Notes. The combined book collection of public libraries in Paris (including the Georges Pompidou Center Library) is just over 4 million volumes. The largest is the Paris City Library (Bibliothèque de la Ville de Paris).

15.
2 largest public libraries in Germany

Munich City Library in Germany (*Münchner Stadbibliothek*) has over 3.2 million books. It was established in 1843. Hamburg Public Library (*Hamburger Öffentliche Bucherhallen*) owns about 2.6 million books. It was founded in 1899.

Notes. There are several public libraries in the German capital Berlin, most beginning with the title Stadtbibliothek. The Berlin Central Library (Zentral und Landesbibliothek Berlin) is the largest.

16.
Public libraries with the largest budgets in the U.S.

New York Public Library had a budget of $97 million in 2001. It is also the largest single public library budget in the world. Chicago Public Library ($80 million); Los Angeles County Public Library ($68 million) and Queens Borough Public Library ($60 million) all trail behind.

17.
States with the largest library budgets in the U.S.

Public libraries (1,077) in the state of New York shared a budget of over $700 million in 2001. This was followed by California public libraries (1,039) which received $655 million in public funding.

18.
States with the smallest library budget in the U.S.

In 2001, the State of North Dakota public libraries (88) received about $8 million from public funds.

19.
2 largest public libraries in Asia

1. Shanghai Library, China (*Shanghai Tushugan*). 8 million. Founded in 1952.

2. Nanjing Library, China (*Nanjing Tushugan*). 6 million. Founded 1908.

> **Notes.** *In addition to the above two, China has several large public provincial libraries with over 2 million books. The largest Asian public library outside China, is the Delhi Public library in New Delhi, India. It was founded in 1951, and has about 1.5 million books. The three largest public libraries in Japan are the Tokyo Metropolitan Central Library, with 1.4 million books; the Aichi Prefectural Library in Nagoya, holding just over 990,000 books and the Osaka Prefectural Library with over 900,000. The largest public library in South Korea is the Pusan Civil Library with about 850,000 books. It was founded in 1968.*

20.
3 largest public libraries in Latin America

1. São Paulo Municipal Library *(Biblioteca Municipal Mario de Andrade)*, Brazil. 630,000 books. Founded in 1925.

2. Mexico Public Library, Mexico City (*Biblioteca de México*). 510,000. Founded in 1949.

3. Rio Grande Public Library, Brazil (*Biblioteca Rio Grandense*). 450,000. Founded in 1846.

> **Notes.** *Public libraries in many Latin American countries such as Argentina are known as popular libraries.*

21.
2 largest public libraries in the Middle East

Tel Aviv Central Public Library (*Shaar Zion*). Founded 1958. 950,000 books. Jerusalem City Public Library founded 1961. 810,000 books. Both located in Israel.

22.
2 largest public libraries in Africa

Johannesburg Public Library. 1.7 million. Founded in 1959. Cape Town City Library, it was founded in 1947 with 1.2 million books. Both are in South Africa.

> **Notes.** *The Cape Provincial Library Ser-*

Cape Town City Library, South Africa, is located within the Cape Town City Hall (courtesy of Cape Town City Library, South Africa).

vice of South Africa based in Cape Town has over 200 affiliated public libraries

and over 70 depot libraries giving a total collection of over 5 million books.

23.
Countries with the largest number of public libraries

In 2001, Russia had more than 35,100 public and government funded libraries, followed by the U.S. with over 16,000 public libraries.

Notes. By the end of 2000, Russia had a total of almost 64,500 libraries, making it the country with the largest number of libraries in the world. The American Library Association estimated that there are more public libraries in the U.S. than McDonald's restaurants. The large number of sophisticated public libraries in the U.S. can sometimes mean public libraries

are subject to surveillance by the same government agencies. For instance in the 1980s, during the Ronald Reagan administration and at the height of the Cold War, the FBI under its Library Awareness Program tried to recruit public librarians in the U.S. as freelance agents to help in identifying "suspicious" use of library materials in U.S. public libraries. But after a few months of fierce opposition from the American Library Association, the FBI finally abandoned the idea. But in a further case of Big Brother, in October 2001, the U.S. Congress passed the PATRIOT Act. This law which among other things, allows the FBI to serve search warrants to public libraries, to enable them to access the confidential records of targeted library users under suspicion of being involved in terrorism.

Once again the American Library Association is fighting the law, because while the law can be beneficial in investigating terrorism, it can be abused and infringes privacy.

24.
Countries with the largest number of public libraries per capita

The U.K. has more than 7,000 libraries for a population of 60 million. Norway has over 1000 public libraries for a population of 4.5 million, while Finland has over 2700 public libraries for a population of 5 million

Notes. *In Europe having a large number of public libraries can be translated to mean that the country has a large number of avid book readers. A survey in 2002 showed that the largest numbers of book readers in Europe are in the U.K., Finland and Sweden. All three have the largest number of public libraries in Europe per capita. Not surprisingly the most enthusiastic book readers in the world are in the U.S., while it is Iceland that has the world's highest literacy rate.*

25.
G-8 country with the smallest number of public libraries per capita

Japan only has about 2100 libraries for a population of over 120 million. Traditionally, the Japanese do not borrow books from publicly funded libraries. One reason for the small number of public libraries was that the cultural idea of public libraries became significant only after the Second World War, when legislation was passed to begin the establishment of public libraries in Japan. And every April 30 (the date when the library bill became law) is celebrated as "Public Library Day."

26.
6 oldest public libraries in Europe

The Pisistratus Public Library in ancient Athens, Greece, was set up by Greek scholars circa 540 BC. The library was later destroyed when soldiers of the Roman

Empire overran Greece. The first Roman public library was set up in 40 BC by Gaius Asinius Pollio, the Roman general, historian and poet.

The following are the 6 oldest existing major public libraries in Europe.

1. Vatican Library, Rome, Vatican City (*Biblioteca Apostolica Vaticana*). It was founded in AD 1451 by Pope Nicholas V, but the original founding date actually goes back to the 14th century. At this time the construction of the library in Rome was interrupted by the removal of the popes from Italy to France, when Pope Clement V (French Archbishop of Bordeaux) moved the papal court from Rome to Avignon in 1305, the event called the "Babylonian Captivity." The Vatican Library was completed when the popes returned to Rome in 1377 with the initiative of Pope Gregory XI. However the problems of having the papacy in the two cities continued with the election of rival popes ("The Great Schism"), until 1417, when Rome was once again the official seat of the Vatican. The Avignon papal library, the largest library in Europe in the 14th century, still exists today in France.

2. Lyons Municipal Library, France (*Bibliothèque Municipale de Lyon*). 1527.

3. Laurentian Library, Florence, Italy (*Biblioteca Medice Laurenziana*). 1571.

4. Rotterdam Municipal Library, the Netherlands (*Gemeentebibliotheek Rotterdam*). 1604.

5. Ambrosian Library, Milan, Italy (*Biblioteca Ambrosiana*). 1609.

Notes. *The library contains the largest collection of Leonardo da Vinci's notebooks, collectively called the Codex Atlanticus.*

6. Mazarin Library, Paris, France (*Bibliothèque Mazarine*). 1643.

Notes. *Several European libraries with some sort of public library function were founded in the 16th century, influenced by the invention of printing and/or the Reformation. These included the German Magdeburg Public Library in 1525, and the Swiss Bern Public Library in 1528. The Vatican Archives, containing the "state papers" of the Vatican as a civil and ecclesiastical government, are distinct from the Vatican Library. By the 15th century the Vatican Library was the largest library in world, until university libraries in Europe began to expand their libraries, with the influence of both the Renaissance and the invention of printing. Troops of Napoleon Bonaparte once raided the Vatican Library and the Vatican Archives and transferred several priceless manuscripts (many related to the Inquisition, which were subsequently lost) back to Paris, only to be returned after the 1815 Congress of Vienna. As the Vatican library is a manuscript library, many important historical non-paper manuscripts, such the Codex Vaticanus, a 4th century AD Greek Bible, are still preserved in the library, alongside books printed before 1501 (i.e. incunabula). One interesting collection of items in the Vatican Library are the several personal letters written by statesmen over the centuries. One such collection is the love letters written in 1536 by English King Henry VIII to his new lover Anne Boleyn before he married her, one of the six wives he had in all.*

The Vatican Library, in Rome, is Europe's oldest existing public library (©Biblioteca Apostolica Vaticana).

27.
3 oldest subscription or commercial circulating libraries in the U.K.

Prior to the creation of free public libraries in the U.K., it was common for members of the public to subscribe to commercial circulating libraries. The largest of these libraries were based in London. There were more than fifty such circulating libraries in the U.K. by 1750. By the end of the century such circulating libraries were widespread. In 1801 it was estimated that there were no fewer than a thousand such libraries. Three candidates for the title of U.K.'s oldest subscription libraries are:

1. Chetham Library, Manchester, England. 1653.

> *Notes.* Even though it started out originally as a subscription library, it is often referred to as the oldest public library in the English-speaking world.

2. Edinburgh Circulating Library, Scotland. 1725.

3. Linen Hall Library in Belfast, Northern Ireland. 1788.

> *Notes.* The London Library, a private subscription library formed in 1841, is the

most important surviving subscription library remaining in the capital. Its collection includes several 19th century books on literature. The first library to

act as a public library in Ireland was the Marsh Public Library in Dublin, founded in 1701 by Irish Archbishop, Narcissus Marsh.

28.
10 oldest public libraries in the U.K.

Officially public libraries in the U.K. came into being with the passing of the 1850 U.K. Public Library Act. Both Canterbury and Warrington public library (below) users had to pay a small admission fee of around 1*d* to the library before they could use the library, so technically Salford Public library below is the oldest public library in the U.K. The British Museum Library, founded in 1753, was actually a public library, but it is today one of the U.K.'s national libraries, the British Library.

1. Canterbury Public Library. 1847.

2. Warrington Public Library. 1848.
    Notes. Records show that it was founded in November 1848 under the 1845 U.K. Museums Act, 2 years before the 1850 U.K. Public Library Act. It is nevertheless officially the first public library in the England.

3. Salford Public Library. 1849.

4. Norwich Public Library. 1850.
    Notes. It was formerly a subscription library, then renamed Norwich Public Library in 1850, when it became the first public library to adopt the 1850 U.K. Public Library Act.

5. Winchester Public Library. 1851

6. Liverpool Public Library. 1852.

7. Manchester Public Library. 1853.

8. Bolton Public Library. 1854.

9. Oxford Public Library. 1855.

Joint 10.
    Kidderminster Public Library and Cambridge Public Library. 1856.
    Several libraries (not circulating or subscription libraries) were already in existence before the 1850 U.K. public library Act. They were not necessarily open to everyone (e.g., some were barred to women and children or the working class, and they were not necessarily all free). The oldest of these founded before the 1700s were:

1. Norwich City Library, England. It opened in 1608 as a public library, but it only stocked theological books and publications.

2. Innerpeffray Library in Crieff, Perthshire, Scotland. 1680. Founded by David Drummond, 3rd Lord Maddertie.

3. Kirkwell Library, Orkney, Scotland. 1683.

4. Leignton Library, Dunblane, Scotland.

1688. In 1734 it was reconstituted as a public library.

Notes. *The oldest and only residential library in the U.K. was founded in 1889. Its book collections grew from a donation of books by the 19th century Prime Minister William Gladstone. The library is named St. Deiniol's and includes a hostel. Today it has over 200,000 books. Based in Hawarden in Flintshire, readers pay an annual subscription fee.*

29.
Oldest public library in Russia

M.E. Saltykov-Shchedrin State Public Library (later National Library of Russia), founded 1795 by Empress Catherine the Great, in St. Petersburg.

30.
Oldest public library in Germany

The first German public libraries (*Volksbibliotheken*) were established in 1840 in Berlin.

31.
First subscription library in the U.S.

Library Company of Philadelphia. Set up by Benjamin Franklin in 1732.

Notes. *The Franklin Public Library, in Wrentham, Massachusetts, named in honor of Benjamin Franklin, is America's first lending library, having been established in 1778. The oldest subscription library in the U.S. in continuous service is Darby Library Company, since 1743.*

32.
10 oldest public libraries in the U.S.

1. Peterboro Public Library, New Hampshire. Founded 1833.

2. Buffalo & Erie County Public Library, New York. 1836.

3. New Orleans Public Library, Louisiana. 1843.

4. Boston Public Library, Massachusetts. 1848.

Boston Public Library is the first true tax-supported public library in the United States (courtesy of the Boston Public Library).

Notes *Boston Public was the first true tax-supported public library in the U.S. because Peterboro, New Orleans, and Buffalo & Erie, initially all charged an admission fee. Boston Public Library was also the first public library to allow people to borrow books.*

5. Cincinnati & Hamilton County Public Library, Ohio. 1856.

6. Cleveland Public Library, Ohio. 1869.

7. Los Angeles Public Library, California. 1872.

8. Chicago Public Library, Illinois. 1873.

9. Houston Public Library, Texas. 1875.

10. Pasadena Central Public Library, California. 1882.

33.
5 oldest public libraries in Latin America

1. Santa Fe Public Library, Bogotá, Colombia (*Biblioteca Pública Santa Fe*). Founded 1777.

2. Buenos Aires Public Library, Argentina

(*Biblioteca Buenos Aires*). 1812. Later became the Argentine National Library in 1884.

3. Oaxaca Public Library, Mexico (*Biblioteca Pública Oaxaca*). 1826.

The Houston Public Library in the state of Texas was founded 39 years after Texas became independent from Mexico in 1836 (courtesy of Andrea Lapsley, Houston Public Library).

4. Chihuahua Public Library Mexico (*Biblioteca Pública Chihuahua*). 1829.

5. La Paz Municipal Library Bolivia (*Biblioteca Municipal Mariscal Andres de Santa Cruz*). 1838.

34.
5 oldest public libraries in the Caribbean Islands

1. Dominican Public Library, Santo Domingo, Dominican Republic (*Biblioteca Dominicana*). Founded 1729.

2. Nassau Public Library, The Bahamas. 1847.

3. Bridgetown Public Library, Barbados. 1851.

4. Port of Spain Public Library, Trinidad and Tobago. 1851.

5. Carnegie Public Library, San Juan, Puerto Rico. 1916.

35.
Oldest subscription library in Canada

Quebec City Library (*Bibliothèque de Québec*) was set up in 1779 by Governor Frederick Haldimand. It stocked books in both French and English.

36.
Oldest public library in Canada

Toronto Public Library (*Bibliothèque Publique de Toronto*) was founded in 1884. Since Quebec City Library is now a public library, Toronto Public Library is regarded as the second oldest public library today.

37.
Oldest subscription library in Asia

Penang Library, Malaysia was founded in 1817 by the British colonial government. It is now part of the Penang Public Library Corporation *(Perbadanan Perpustakaan Awam Pinang)*.

Notes. Sir Stamford Raffles, the founder of Singapore was also instrumental to the founding of the Raffles Subscription Library in 1823, which later became the National Library of Singapore.

38.
Oldest public libraries in Asia

Hardayal Municipal Public Library, New Delhi, India was established in 1862. While in Japan, the Kyoto Public Library (*Kyoto Koukai Toshokan*), was founded in 1873.

39.
Oldest public libraries in Australia

Melbourne Public Library was founded 1853 and Brisbane Public Library in 1896. The oldest Australian subscription library was the Sydney Subscription Library, founded in 1826. It is now known as the State Library of New South Wales.

40.
Oldest public libraries in the Middle East

Koprulu Library established in Istanbul, Turkey, in 1678 with public funds, while the Beyazit State Library, also in Istanbul, was opened in 1884.

41.
Oldest public library in Africa

Luanda Municipal Library, Angola (*Biblioteca Municipal*). It was founded in 1873 by the Portuguese colonial government.

Notes. The first African public library act, to legalize the role of public libraries in sub–Saharan Africa was the 1948 Ghana Library Board Act. Subscription libraries in South Africa were first set up in 1838; many later became public libraries.

42.
First public library commemorative coins of the millennium

In 2000, the Royal Mint in Llantrisant, which makes all the coins used in the U.K., celebrated the 150th anniversary of the U.K. Public Library Act by issuing a special 50 pence coin.

Notes. In 2000 the U.S. Mint in Washington, D.C., issued two special commemorative coins. Both of the coins are honoring the Library of Congress. One of them was a beautiful ten dollar bimetallic (platinum and gold) coin, the first ever issued by the U.S. One side of the coin shows the hand of Minerva raising the torch of learning over the dome of the Jefferson Building. The other commemorative coin was a silver one dollar coin, the first such commemorative U.S. coin of the millennium.

43.
First public library commemorative postage stamp

The New York Public Library in the U.S. was the first public library to be featured on a postage stamp, issued in 1920.

Notes. The National Postal Museum Library and Research Center has over 40,000 books and manuscripts, making it the world's largest philatelic and postal history library facilities. The Smithsonian Institution Libraries operates the library. The postage stamp itself was invented in 1840, with the introduction of the "Penny Black" in 1840 in London, U.K.

WORLD RECORDS
FOR UNIVERSITY AND
ACADEMIC LIBRARIES

Yet the reverence for size continues. The library that has the most books is likely to be regarded as ipso facto, the best.

Herman Fussler, U.S. academic librarian. 1949.

Universities can be made up of several campuses, either in the same city or in different cities. For instance, the University of California has branches in 9 cities in the state, but each one is a university in its own right. It follows that a university may have several libraries in different buildings and locations. It is common for even a single-campus university library to have a central collection and other collections divided among different faculties and departments. Hence all numbers of books given below are the total in aggregate of books in all libraries of each specific university listed, including departmental and faculty libraries. When considering lists for the oldest university libraries, where the actual opening date of the library is not known, the foundation date of the university is used. But bear in mind that some university libraries may actually open on the same day a university is officially opened (in many cases after the foundation date), or after the university is opened, in this case from a few months to a few years. Some of the earliest universities had no building dedicated to a library; for instance the U.K.'s Oxford University in the 13th century kept its book collection in St. Mary's Church nearby until the 14th century.

44.
Largest academic libraries
with over 7 million books

1. Harvard University Library, Cambridge, Massachusetts, U.S. Has 13.6 million books. Founded in 1636 with 300 books bequeathed to the university by John Harvard. Also the oldest university library in the U.S. Apart from Cambridge, Harvard University also has libraries in Boston, Washington, D.C., and Florence,

The Romanian Academy Library is the largest library of an academy in Europe, after the Russian Academy of Sciences Library (courtesy of Romanian Academy Library, Bucharest).

Italy. Altogether there are just over 90 Harvard University libraries.

> **Notes.** *The Harvard University student population currently numbers about 19,600 students. In comparison, the State University of New York, the largest university in the U.S., has over 250,000 students. Its largest library, at Buffalo campus, contains about 3.2 million books. The first full-time librarian at Harvard was Solomon Stoddard in 1643.*

2. Russian Academy of Sciences Library, St. Petersburg, Russia (*Biblioteka Rossiskaya Akademii Nauk*). 10 million. Founded in 1714 by Peter I.

> **Notes.** *It is the first state-owned public library of Russia.*

3. Yale University Library, New Haven, Connecticut, U.S. 9.9 million. Founded in 1701.

4. Romanian Academy Library (*Bib-lioteca Academiei Române*), Bucharest, Romania. Founded in 1866. 8.9 million.

> **Notes.** *Technically this is one of Romania's three national libraries.*

5. University of Illinois Library, Urbana-Champaign, U.S. 8.6 million. Founded in 1867. Third largest U.S. university library, after Harvard and Yale.

6. University of California Library, Berkeley, U.S. 8.4 million. Founded in 1868.

> **Notes.** *The MELVYL catalog (the combined University of California and State University libraries union catalog), is larger than the Harvard University library catalog.*

7. Lomonosov State University Library, Moscow, Russia *(Nauchnaia Biblioteka Universiteta Lomonosova)*. 8 million. Founded in 1756.

> **Notes.** *It is also called the Maxim Gorky*

Like the Harvard University Library, Yale University book collections are spread over several separate libraries. This one is the Sterling Memorial Library (courtesy of Michael Marsland, Yale University).

Research Library of the Moscow State University. It was for several years the only major library in the 18th century available to the public in Russia, till the M.E. Saltykov-Shchedrin State Public Library (later National Library of Russia) was founded 1795 by Empress Catherine the Great in St. Petersburg.

8. Tokyo University Library, Japan (*Tokyo Daigaku Toshokan*). 7.7 million. Founded 1893.

9. University of Texas Library, Austin, founded in 1839, and the University of California Library, Los Angeles, founded in 1919. Both in the U.S. 7.2 million.

10. University of Michigan, Ann Arbor. 7.1 million. Founded 1838.

11. Stanford University Library, California, U.S. 7 million. Founded 1892.

12. Columbia University Library, New York City. 7 million. Founded 1784.

13. Ukrainian National Academy of Sciences, Vernadsky Central Scientific Library, Kiev. 7 million. Founded 1919.

Notes. One of the librarians of Columbia University Library, Melvil Dewey is famous for inventing the popular Dewey Decimal System for classifying books and also founding the first library school in the world. There are so many university libraries in the U.S. with over 3 million volumes that most belong to organizations that help to support these libraries either financially or in a professional capacity to help develop the library. Two major organizations are the Association of Research Libraries and the Association of College and Research Libraries.

45.
10 largest university or academic libraries in Europe

1. Russian Academy of Sciences Library. (See list **44**).

2. Romanian Academy Library. (See list **44**).

3. Ukrainian National Academy of Sciences. (See list **44**).

4. Lomonosov State University Library. (See list **44**).

5. Bodleian Library, Oxford University, U.K. Founded in 1602. 6.5 million books.

Notes. The main library of U.K.'s largest university, the University of London (excluding the Open University), i.e. the University of London Library at Senate House, had about 1.7 million books and 80,000 students in 2001 compared to Oxford University's 18,000 students. However the combined collections of all the London University individual libraries are just slightly smaller than the Bodleian. In 1602 Thomas James became the first full time librarian for Oxford University. By the end of the 17th century most of the books in the Bodleian were in Latin, with only a handful in English. It was not until the end of the 19th century that the number of books in English exceeded those in Latin.

6. Berlin Free University Library, Germany (*Bibliothek der Freie Universität Berlin*). Founded in 1952. 6.4 million.

Notes. The other and much older Berlin University (called Humboldt University to avoid confusion in names) was founded in 1810. But its allegiance with Communism (since it was in the former East Germany), led several non-communist academics to leave the Humboldt University and found the Berlin Free University.

7. The University of Paris Library, France (*Bibliothèque de l'Université Paris*). Has a combined book collection of 6.3 million books. Founded 1230.

Notes. The University of Paris is made up of 13 separate universities, all given names with Roman numerals I to XIII. For instance the library of Paris University V is called Bibliothèque de l'Université Paris V. The University of Paris also has the 4th largest student population, after the State University of New York, in the U.S., Calcutta (Kolkata) University, in India, and Mexico National Autonomous University, Mexico City. All four universities had over 250,000 students in the year 2000.

8. Cambridge University Library, U.K. 5.8 million. Founded 1347.

The Bodleian Library is the largest academic library in the United Kingdom.

Notes. Apart from having the U.K.'s second largest university library, Cambridge University is also the richest university in the U.K., worth over $2 billion and with an annual turnover of $300 million.

Oxford and Cambridge university libraries. First library founded in the early 19th century. The libraries of King's College and University College are the largest.

9. University of London Libraries, U.K. Combined collection of about 5.4 million books. Third largest in the U.K., after

10. Zhdanov State University Library, St. Petersburg, Russia. Founded in 1819. It currently has about 5.1 million books.

Berlin Free University has the largest academic library in Germany (© Union-Picture.de).

Notes. Its official name is St. Petersburg University. It was originally founded in the 18th century. The most memorable moment in the history of the university library occurred during the Second World War. While many of the staff and students had been evacuated, other librarians and university staff stayed on to defend the university against the Nazis during the 900-day siege of St. Petersburg (Leningrad). Ivan Pavlov, who made famous psychological experiments with dogs that earned him a Nobel Prize, was a regular user of the university library, as a student reading chemistry and physiology in the 19th century.

46.
8 largest university libraries in the U.K.

1. Bodleian Library, Oxford University. (See list 45.)

2. Cambridge University Library. (See list 45.)

3. University of London Libraries. (See list 45.)

4. John Rylands University Library, Manchester. 4.8 million books. Founded in 1900.

5. Edinburgh University Library. 2.7 million. Founded 1580.

Notes. Charles Darwin, who revolutionized our understanding of evolution, did not have sufficient time to use the library as he spent a little over a year at Edinburgh University studying medicine before dropping out in 1827. Things looked bleak for Darwin until when he went to Cambridge for theological studies, and while there befriended a botany professor. It was this academic who recommended Darwin for the post of naturalist for the exploration of South America by a British navy ship. On his return Darwin would publish a book about his extraordinary voyage and the rest is history.

6. Leeds University Library, 2.5 million. Founded 1874.

7. Birmingham University Library. 2.3 million. Founded 1880.

8. Glasgow University Library, 1.6 million. Founded 1450.

> **Notes.** *U.K.'s first 24 hour academic library is at Bath University. The round-the-clock library service began in 1996. Bookworms and workaholics will find the service a great way to spend an all-nighter brainstorming. For those who begin to fall asleep in the early hours of the morning, a softbound book will be a good substitute for a pillow.*

47.
6 largest university libraries in France

1. The University of Paris Library. (See list **45**).

2. Strasbourg National University Library (*Bibliothèque Nationale et Universitaire de Strasbourg*). Founded in 1540. 4.5 million books.

3. Montpellier University Library (*Bibliothèque de l'Université de Montpellier*). Founded in the 1240. 3.3 million.

4. Lyons University Library (*Bibliothèque de l'Université de Lyon*). 2.4 million. Founded 1970.

5. Toulouse University Library (*Bibliothèque de l'Université de Toulouse*). 2.1 million. Founded 1292

6. Aix-Marseille University Library (Provence University), Marseille and Aix-en-Provence (*Bibliothèque de l'Université d'Aix-Marseille*). 1.9 million. Founded 1413.

48.
6 largest university libraries in Germany

1. Berlin Free University Library. (See list **45**).

2. Hanover Technical University Library (*Bibliothek der Hanover Technische Universität*). 4.8 million books. Founded 1831.

3. Martin Luther University Library, Halle-Wittenberg (*Bibliothek der Martin*

Luther Universität). Founded in 1502. 4.6 million.

4. Leipzig University Library (*Universitätbibliothek Leipzig*). 4.5 million. Founded 1409.

> ***Notes.*** *Wolfgan von Goethe, the famous German poet, as a student borrowed books from the Leipzig University Library.*

5. George Augustus University Library, Göttingen (*Bibliothek der Georg-August Universität).* 4.1 million. Founded in 1737.

Notes. *It was founded by King George II of Britain and entrusted with the task to act as the German national library for the eighteenth century.*

Joint 6th. Dresden Technical University Library (*Universitätbibliothek Dresden).* Founded in 1828. Frankfurt University Library. Founded in 1511. (*Universitätbibliothek Frankfurt am Main).* Both 4 million.

> ***Notes.*** *For most of the 1800s, a university library in Germany was run by a university professor, but each was later headed by a full time librarian.*

49.
5 largest university libraries in Italy

1. Florence University Library (*Biblioteca Università degli Studi di Firenze).* Founded in 1321. 4 million books.

2. Rome University Library (*Biblioteca*

Università degli Studi di Roma "La Spienza"). Founded in 1304. 2.9 million.

> ***Notes.*** *It also has the 2nd largest student population in Europe, after the University of Paris in France.*

La Spienza University Library in Rome (courtesy of Stefania Sepuylcri, Rome University).

3. Turin University Library (*Biblioteca Università degli Studi di Torino*). 2.6 million. Founded 1404.

4. Bologna University Library (*Biblioteca Università degli Studi di Bologna*). 1.8 million. Founded 1088.

5. Milan University Library (*Biblioteca Università degli Studi di Milano*). 1.3 million Founded 1923.

50.
6 largest university libraries in Austria and Switzerland

1. Vienna University Library, Austria (*Universitätbibliothek Wien*). 4 million books. Founded 1365.

2. Swiss Federal Institute of Technology Library, Zürich (*Bibliothek Eidgenössiche*

Technische Hochschule Zürich). 3.3 million. Founded 1855.

3. Graz University Library, Austria (*Universitätbibliothek Graz*). 3 million. Founded 1586.

The Swiss Federal Institute of Technology Library has one of the largest patent libraries in Europe. Albert Einstein graduated from here in 1900, and went on to the Swiss patent office in Bern (courtesy of Bildarchiv ETH-Bibliothek, Zürich).

4. Basel University Library, Switzerland (*Universitätbibliothek Basel*). 2.6 million. Founded 1460.

5. Bern University Library, Switzerland (*Universitätbibliothek Bern*). 2 million. Founded 1528.

6. Zürich University Library, Switzerland (*Universitätbibliothek Zürich*). 1.8 million. Founded 1523.

> **Notes.** *It was here in 1905 that Albert Einstein obtained his Ph.D. for the first of several published scientific papers in a German physics journal, which eventually led to the famous paper on theory of relativity.*

51.
6 largest university libraries in Spain and Portugal

1. Madrid Autonomous University Library. Spain (*Biblioteca de la Universidad Nacional Autónoma de Madrid*). Founded in 1510. 2.7 million books.

2. Complutense University Library, Madrid, Spain (*Biblioteca de la Universidad Complutense de Madrid*). Founded in 1293. 2 million.

3. Coimbra University Library, Portugal (*Biblioteca Universidade de Coimbra*). 2 million. Founded 1290.

> **Notes.** *The university was originally* founded in Lisbon, before it moved to Coimbra in 1537.

4. Saragossa University Library, Spain (*Biblioteca de la Universidad de Zaragoza*). Founded in 1480. 1.8 million.

5. Barcelona University Library, Spain (*Biblioteca de la Universitat de Barcelona*). 1.6 million. Founded 1430.

6. Navarre University Library, Pamplona, Spain (*Biblioteca de la Universidad de Navarra*). 1.3 million. Founded 1952.

52.
5 largest university libraries in Scandinavia

1. Copenhagen University Library, Denmark (*Bibliotek Københavns Universitet*). 1482. 4.6 million books.

> **Notes.** *It is also forms part of the National Library of Denmark. Copenhagen University Library was once open only to professors, but students enrolled at the university were only finally allowed to borrow books from 1789. A famous relic at the library is a British cannonball,* part of the British bombardment that destroyed parts of the university in 1807, during the war between Denmark and the U.K. Ironically one of the books of the library hit by the cannonball was titled Defender of Peace.

2. Oslo University Library, Norway (*Universitetet Bibliotek i Oslo*). 4.5 million. Founded 1811.

Notes. Until 1948, it was the only university library in Norway.

3. Lund University Library, Sweden (*Bibliotek Lunds Universitet*). 4.1 million. Founded 1671.

4. Helsinki University Library, Finland (*Helsingin yliopisto Kirjasto*). 2.8 million. Founded 1640.

> *Notes. It is also part of the National Library of Finland.*

5. Stockholm University Library, Sweden (*Bibliotek Stockholm Universitet*). 2.5 million. Founded 1878.

53.

5 largest university libraries in Belgium and the Netherlands

1. Leuven Catholic University Library (*Katholieke Universiteitbibliotheek Leuven*). Leuven, Belgium. 3.6 million. Founded 1425.

> *Notes. The above university is in the Flemish speaking part of Belgium. There is another university in the French speaking part of Belgium, called Louvain Catholic University (Université Catholique de Louvain), and located in the city of Louvain-la-Neuve. It has about 2 million books. Both universities were originally one, founded in 1425 by Pope Martin V, but were split up in 1968. The central library was established in 1627.*

2. Utrecht University Library, Netherlands (*Universiteitbibliotheek Utrecht*). 4.2 million. Founded 1584.

3. Amsterdam University Library, Netherlands (*Universiteitbibliotheek Amsterdam*). 4 million books. Founded 1578.

4. Leiden State University Library, Netherlands (*Universiteitbibliotheek Leiden*). 2.4 million. Founded 1575.

5. Brussels Free University Library, Belgium (*Bibliothèque de l'Université Libre de Bruxelles*). 1.6 million. Founded 1834.

> *Notes. In 1970 the university was split into Flemish and French universities. Liège University Library, founded in 1816, has about the same number of books.*

54.

2 largest university libraries in Ireland

1. Trinity College, Dublin University Library. 2.9 million books. Founded 1592.

2. National University of Ireland Library, Dublin, Cork, Maynooth and Galway. 2 million. Founded 1840s and 1850s.

> *Notes. Trinity College Library receives by law a copy of every book published in the U.K. This began in 1801 (when Ireland was then part of the U.K.), and has continued long after Ireland gained its Independence. The other five legal deposit*

libraries in the U.K. entitled to receive, free of charge, a copy of every single book produced in the U.K. are: Bodleian Library (Oxford University), Cambridge University Library, the national libraries of Scotland and Wales, and the British Library.

55.
2 largest university libraries in the Vatican City

1. Pontifical Gregorian University Library. Rome (*Biblioteca Pontificia Università Gregoriana*). 1.3 million books. Founded 1553.

> **Notes.** *Because Latin is one of the six languages of instruction, its library has the largest collection of academic books in Latin, after those in the library of St.* *Thomas Aquinas Pontifical University Library.*

2. Pontifical Lateranese University Library, Rome (*Biblioteca Pontificia Università Lateranese*). 810,000. Founded 1937.

56.
2 largest university libraries in Greece

1. Aristotle University of Thessaloniki Library (*Bibliotheke Aristoteleio Panepistimio Thessalonikus*). 2 million books. Founded 1927. 2. National and Kapodistrian University Library. Athens (*Bibliotheke Athinisin Ethnikon Kai Kapodistriakon Panepistimio*). 1.2 million. Founded 1837.

57.
7 largest university libraries in Russia

1. Lomonosov State University Library. (See list **44**.)

2. Zhdanov State University Library. (See list **45**.)

3. Kazan State University Library. 4.9 million books. Founded 1804.

> **Notes.** *V.I. Lenin was a famous user of the library in the late 1880s. He graduated with a first-class degree in law from the university.*

4. Irkutsk University Library. 4 million. Founded 1918.

5. Tomsk State University Library. 3.5 million. Founded 1888.

6. Saratov State University Library. 3 million. Founded 1901.

7. Rostov State University Library. 2.8 million. Founded 1915.

58.
10 largest university libraries in Eastern Europe

N.B.: this list excludes libraries in Russia.

1. Vilnius University Library, Lithuania (*Biblioteka Universitas Vilnensis*). 5.2 million books. Founded in 1579.

   Notes. *The library remained closed for almost 100 years, when the university was shut down by the Russian government in 1832.*

2. Jagiellonian University Library, Kraków, Poland (*Biblioteka Universytet Jagielloński*). 3.9 million. Founded 1364.

   Notes. *The most famous user of the library in the 15th century was Nicolaus Copernicus as a student from 1491. He also studied at Italy's Bologna and Padua universities. His book on astronomy upset many scholars and the Vatican (who banned it). His publishers eventually printed the book, but only after adding a clever preface to exonerate them from criticism.*

3. Mickiewicz University Library, Poznań, Poland (*Biblioteka Universytet im Adama Mickiewicza w Poznaniu*). 3.5 million. Founded 1919.

4. Cluj-Napoca Lucian Blaga University Central Library, Romania (*Biblioteca Centrală Universitatea Lucian Blaga*). 3.5 million. Founded 1872.

5. Odessa University Library, Ukraine. 3.3 million. Founded 1807.

6. Charles University Library, Prague, Czech Republic (*Knihovně Univerzita Karlova v Praze*). 3.3 million. Founded 1348.

7. Tartu University Library, Estonia. 3.2 million. Founded in 1802.

   Notes. *During the 19th century, students caught stealing books from the library were punished by being locked up in a building at Tartu University that is today called the Student's Lock-Up Museum.*

8. Tbilisi State University Library, Georgia. 3.2 million. (*Universitätsbibliothek Tbilisi*). Founded 1918.

9. Bucharest University Library, Romania (*Biblioteca Universitatea Bucureşti*). 2.5 million. Founded 1694.

10. St. Clement Ohridski National and University Library. Bitola and Skopje, Macedonia (*Sveti Kliment Ohridski Narodna i Univerzitetska Biblioteka*). 1.9 million. Founded 1944.

    Notes. *The university library is also part of the National Library of Macedonia.*

59.
5 largest university libraries in Canada

1. Toronto University Library. Founded 1827. 6.2 million books.

2. McGill University Library, Montreal (*Bibliothèque de l'Université Montréal*) Founded 1821. 4.5 million.

3. Waterloo University Library. Founded 1961. 3.3 million.

4. British Columbia University Library, Vancouver. 3 million. Founded 1908.

5. Alberta University Library. Edmonton. 2.9 million. Founded 1906.

60.
6 largest university libraries in Japan

1. Tokyo University Library. (See list **44**.)

2. Kyoto University Library (*Kyoto Daigaku Toshokan*). Founded 1899. 5.5 million books.

3. Waseda University Library, Tokyo (*Waseda Daigaku Toshokan*). 4.3 million. Founded 1882.

4. Kyushu University Library, Fukuoku (*Kyushu Daigaku Toshokan*). Founded 1889. 3.6 million.

5. Hokkaido University Library, Sapporo (*Hokkaido Daigaku Toshokan*). 3 million. Founded 1876.

6. Kobe University Library (*Kobe Daigaku Toshokan*). 2.9 million. Founded 1949.

61.
5 largest university libraries in China

1. Beijing University Library (*Peking Daxue Tushugan*). Founded 1902. 6.5 million books.

> *Notes. The most famous name associated with the library is Mao Zedong (Mao Tse-tung). The Chinese leader was not a student of the university, but an assistant librarian.*

2. Nanjing University Library (*Nanjing Daxue Tushugan*). Founded 1908. 6.3 million.

3. Chinese Academy of Sciences Library, Beijing. 4.7 million. Founded 1951.

> *Notes. The official name of the library (adopted in 1985) is the Documentation and Information Center of the Chinese Academy of Sciences or DICCAS.*

4. Fudan University Library, Shanghai (*Fudan Daxue Tushugan*). 3.5 million. Founded 1918.

5. Nankai University Library, Tianjin. 2.3 million. (*Nankai Daxue Tushugan*). Founded 1919.

62.
15 largest university libraries in the Asia-Pacific Region

N.B.: this list excludes libraries in Japan and China. See lists **60** and **61**.

1. Sydney University Library, Australia. 4.3 million books. Founded 1852.

2. Melbourne University Library, Australia. 3 million. Founded 1853.

3. Seoul National University Library, South Korea. 2.5 million. Founded 1946

4. Malaya University Library, Kuala Lumpur, Malaysia *(Perpustakaan Universiti Malaya).* 2.2 million. Founded 1957.

5. New South Wales University Library, Sydney, Australia. 2.2 million. Founded 1948.

6. Australian National University Library. Canberra. 1.9 million. Founded 1946.

7. Queensland University Library, Brisbane, Australia. 1.7 million. Founded 1910.

8. Yonsei University Library, Seoul, South Korea. 1.6 million. Founded 1915.

Joint 9. Adelaide University Library, Australia. Founded 1874. And the Chinese University of Hong Kong Library (*Xianggang Zhongwen Daxue Tushugan*). Founded 1963. Both 1.5 million.

10. Auckland University Library. New Zealand. Founded 1883. 1.4 million.

11. Singapore National University Library. 1.36 million. Founded 1946

12. Taiwan National University Library, Taipei. 1.32 million. Founded 1928

13. New Delhi University Library, India. 1.2 million. Founded 1922.

14. Monash University Library, Clayton. Australia. 1 million. Founded 1958.

15. Philippines University Library, Quezon City, Metro Manila. 985 000. Founded 1908.

63.
10 largest university libraries in Latin America

1. Buenos Aires University Library, Argentina. (*Biblioteca de la Universidad de* *Buenos Aires*). 4 million books. Founded 1821.

The Federal University of Pernambuco Central Library, in Recife, is the largest academic library in Northern Brazil.

2. São Paulo Federal University Library, Brazil (*Biblioteca de la Universidade Federal de São Paulo*). 3.7 million. Founded 1934.

3. Mexico National Autonomous University Library, Mexico City (*Biblioteca de la Universidad Nacional Autónoma de México*). 3.3 million. Founded 1555.

> **Notes.** *Also forms part of the National Library of Mexico.*

4. Rio de Janeiro Federal University Library, Brazil (*Biblioteca Universidade de Rio de Janeiro*). 2 million. Founded 1920

5. Guadalajara University Library, Mexico (*Biblioteca de la Universidad de Guadalajara*). 1.2 million. Founded 1752.

6. La Plata National University Library, Argentina (*Biblioteca de la Nacional Universidad de La Plata*). 810,000. Founded 1905.

7. Tamaulipas Autonomous University Library, Victoria City (*Biblioteca de la Universidad de Tamaulipas*). Mexico. 710,000. Founded 1956.

8. Puebla Autonomous University Library, Mexico (*Biblioteca de la Universidad de Puebla*). 630,000. Founded 1578.

9. Pernambuco Federal University Central Library, Recife, Brazil (*Biblioteca Central da Universidade Federal de Pernambuco*). 600,000. Founded 1946.

10. Minas Gerais Federal University Library, Belo Horizonte, Brazil (*Biblioteca Federal de Minas Gerais Universidade*). 550,000. Founded 1927.

Israel's Hebrew University of Jerusalem is the largest library in the Middle East (courtesy of Hebrew University of Jerusalem, Israel).

64.
10 largest university libraries in the Middle East

1. Hebrew University Library Jerusalem, Israel *(Bet Ha-Sefarim Ha Leummi Weha-Universitai)*. Founded 1892. 4 million books.

> **Notes.** *Also part of Israel's National Library and the Berman National Medical Library, and is officially called the Jewish National and University Library.*

2. Cairo University Library, Egypt. 1.8 million. 1908

3. Haifa University Library, Israel. 1.3 million. Founded 1963.

4. Tehran University Library Iran. 1.3 million. Founded 1949.

5. King Saud University Library, Riyadh, Saudi Arabia. 1.2 million. Founded in 1960.

6. Tel Aviv University Library, Israel. 810,000. Founded 1953.

7. Israel Institute of Technology Library, Haifa. 960,000. Founded 1912.

8. Islamic University of Imam Muhammad Ibn Saud Library, Riyadh, Saudi Arabia. 700,000. Founded 1974.

9. Ben Gurion University Library, Negev, Israel. 730,000. Founded 1966.

10. American University Library, Beirut, Lebanon. 630 000. Founded in 1866.

Notes. Prior to the 1991 Gulf War, Baghdad University Library, the largest in Iraq, had about 700, 000 books.

65.
5 largest university libraries in Africa

1. South Africa University Library, Pretoria. 1.7 million books. Founded 1873. (Cairo University Library has more books, but is listed under Middle East university libraries.)

2. Cape Town University Library, South Africa. Founded in 1829. 1.5 million.

3. Witwatersrand University Library, Johannesburg, South Africa. 1.2 million. Founded 1922

4. Pretoria University Library, South Africa. 1.1 million. Founded 1908.

5. University of Algiers Library, Algiers.

University of South Africa, Pretoria (courtesy of University of South Africa Library, Archives and Special Collections).

760,000. (*Bibliothèque de l'Université d'Alger*). Founded 1880.

> **Notes.** *About a half a dozen more South African academic libraries have large collections with over, or approaching 500,000 books. The five nearest sub-Saharan African academic libraries that have over half a million books are Ghana*

University Balme Library, Accra (founded in 1948), Ibadan University Library, Nigeria (1948), Zimbabwe University Library, Harare (1955), Zambia University Library, Lusaka (1963), and the University of Nigeria Library, Nnsuka, Nigeria, (1964).

66.
10 oldest university libraries in the world and the Middle East

1. Al-Qarawiyin University Library, Fez, Morocco. (*Bibliothèque de l'Université El-Qaraouiyin*). Founded circa AD 859.

> **Notes.** *This university is not to be confused with Al-Akhawayn University in the city of Ifrane, close to Fez. Fatima Feheri, a wealthy woman who came to Morocco from Tunisia, founded the library as part of the Al-Qarawiyin Mosque. It was not uncommon to find a big library in mosques throughout the Islamic world. Mosque libraries are called vakif libraries in Turkey. A number of educational institutes that qualify to be called universities predate Al-Qarawiyin. The very first university in the world was probably the Buddhist Takshila University, established in the ancient city of Takshila (in the former kingdom of Gandhara), in the western part of India around 600 BC, but it vanished centuries later, and very little is known about its library collection today. The second earliest universities to be established in the world after Takshila University are the old Alexandria University in Egypt, and the Academy and Lyceum in Greece, all three having been established in the 4th century BC. The only one in*

existence anymore is Alexandria University, which was re-founded in 1938. Gondishapur University in Iran (once a leading medical university in Persia) dates back to the 3rd century AD (circa 270), although it no longer exists. Many of the preserved ancient medical texts from the university's library are good examples of pre–Islamic medical knowledge in the Middle East. Nalanda University and Vikramshila University, both Buddhist universities, located in what is today the State of Bihar, in India, were founded circa AD 414 and AD 760 respectively. They were well known centers of Buddhist education for scholars from all over Asia, and their large library collections contained some of the important Buddhist texts of the day. Both universities are no longer in existence, having been completely destroyed by Muslim armies in the 13th century. Finally in Hanoi today, there is a building known as the Temple of Literature, built in AD 1076. It is credited as being the first national university of Vietnam. The library contains early Buddhist texts. In 1483 another national university was built. The present National University of Vietnam, which has campuses in both Hanoi and Ho Chi Minh City, was founded in 1993 by an amalgamation of several institutes of higher learning.

2. Al-Azhar University Library, Cairo, Egypt. AD 985.

> **Notes.** This university library also began as a mosque library, and is largest library in Egypt, after the national library and Cairo University library.

3. Al-Nizamiyah University Library, Baghdad, Iraq. AD 1070.

> **Notes.** The university was founded by Vizier Nizam al-Mulk (Vizier of the first Turkish Seljuck sultan). Open to scholars from all over the Muslim world, the university was one of the prominent Islamic centers of education also known as Madrasahs and Masjids. The capture of Baghdad by Hulagu Khan in 1258 following the Mongolian invasion of Arab lands partially destroyed the university library. Tamerlane (Timur "The Lame"), later inflicted further devastation on many libraries of the Madrasahs and Masjids, when he conquered Baghdad and Damascus in 1392. During the period of the Turkish Ottoman Empire, the concept of Madrasahs was continued and many well-stocked libraries were founded. The first major library of the Madrasahs open to the public (with funding from charitable organizations) was the Koprulu Library established by Grand Vizier Koprulu Ahmet Pasha in Istanbul in 1678.

4. Hacettepe University Library, Ankara, Turkey (Hacettepe Üniversitesi Kütüphane). 1206.

5. Istanbul (Constantinople) University Library, Turkey (Istanbul Üniversitesi Kütüphane). 1455.

> **Notes.** The university was believed to have been founded as Constantinople University by Theodosius II, during the time Constantinople was part of the Eastern Roman Byzantine Empire around AD 430, and re-founded after Constantinople fell to the Turkish Ottoman Empire led by Sultan Mehmet in 1453.

6. Istanbul Technical University Library, Turkey (Istanbul Teknik Üniversitesi Kütüphane). 1773.

7. Jesuit University of St. Joseph Library, Beirut, Lebanon (Bibliothèque de l'Université Saint-Joseph). 1846

8. American University Library, Beirut, Lebanon (Bibliothèque de l'Université Américain) 1866.

9. Hebrew University Library Jerusalem, Israel. 1892

10. Gordon Memorial University Library, Khartoum. Sudan. 1902.

67.
Earliest academic library in Europe

Aristotle's Peripatetic School Library in the Lyceum was set circa 335 BC in Athens, Greece. Famous Romans such as

Marcus Cicero later made use of the library.

> **Notes.** Higher education in ancient Greece

began in Athens at the Academy, established in about 387 BC by Plato, and together with the Lyceum offered advanced study of philosophy. Subsequent schools of philoso- *phy, modelled upon Plato's, were also called academies; this term was eventually used to indicate any institution of higher education or the faculty of such an institution.*

68.
10 oldest university libraries in Europe

The history of European academic libraries begins with the founding of libraries in monasteries in the Middle Ages. When the Western Roman Empire fell in AD 476, much learning and reading was restricted to the libraries in monasteries where monks such as St. Benedict encouraged the importance of reading manuscripts. Example of these early 6th and 7th century monastic libraries include those of Saint Gallen in Switzerland, Jarrow in the U.K., Fulda in Germany, Luxeuil in France, and Monte Cassino in Italy. From the early 11th century libraries in cathedrals began to replace libraries in monasteries as centers for learning. But unlike monastic libraries, the libraries in cathedrals and cathedral schools were designed for educational rather than inspirational and religious reading. Scholars believe universities grew out of cathedral schools. Some well-known cathedral libraries were at York in the U.K., Rouen in France, Hildesheim in Germany, and Barcelona in Spain.

Coupled with the fact that from the Middle Ages, education was firmly established in monasteries and cathedrals and lectures were theological in content, many pre-Renaissance European university libraries, were run by theological librarians such as monks and scribes. It is thus sometimes difficult to differentiate a library set up purely for religious studies

and one for academic studies, which included theology. Prior to the 17th century, book and manuscript collecting in Europe was mainly a royal, religious or private pursuit. By the early 17th century many princes, churchmen, and wealthy collectors were organizing their collections with the help of librarians and then opening their collections to the scholarly public. The following are the oldest university libraries in Europe.

1. Bologna University Library, Italy (*Biblioteca Università degli Studi di Bologna*). Founded AD 1088.

2. Padua University Library, Italy (*Biblioteca Università degli Studi di Padova*). 1122.

   Notes. *It has the oldest existing university library building in Italy.*

3. Modena University Library, Italy (*Biblioteca Università degli Studi di Modena*). 1160.

4. Vicenza University Library, Italy (*Biblioteca Università degli Studi di Vicenza*). 1204.

5. Palencia University Library, Spain (*Biblioteca de la Universidad de Palencia*). 1210.

6. Salamanca University Library. Spain (*Biblioteca de la Universidade de Salamanca*). 1218.

7. University of Paris Sorbonne Library, France (*Bibliothèque de l'Université de Paris*). 1230.

8. Montpellier University Library, France (*Bibliothèque de l'Université de Montpellier*). 1240.

9. Perugia University Library, Italy (*Biblioteca Università degli Studi di Perugia*). 1243.

10. Siena University Library, Italy (*Biblioteca Università degli Studi di Siena*). 1245.

69.
5 oldest university libraries in the U.K.

1. Cambridge University Library. Founded 1347. The university was originally founded in the 13th century. Peterhouse College Library was the first in 1302.

2. St. Andrews University Library. 1410.

3. Glasgow University Library. 1451.

4. Aberdeen University Library. 1494.

5. Edinburgh University Library. 1580.

> *Notes. Oxford University Library was originally founded in 1320 by the Bishop of Worcester, but troops of King Edward VI destroyed the library in AD 1550. The library was re-founded 1602 by James Bodley and called the Bodleian Library. The library of Eton College, near London, the oldest public school in the U.K. (founded by King Henry VI), dates back to 1440.*

70.
5 oldest university libraries in France

1. University of Paris Library (*Bibliothèque de l'Université de Paris*). Founded 1230.

2. Montpellier University Library (*Bibliothèque de l'Université de Montpellier*). 1240.

3. Toulouse University Library (*Bibliothèque de l'Université de Toulouse*). 1292.

4. Orleans University Library (*Bibliothèque de l'Université d'Orléans*). 1306.

5. Grenoble University Library (*Bibliothèque de l'Université de Grenoble*). 1339.

71.
5 oldest university libraries in Germany

1. Rupert-Charles University Library, Heidelberg (*Ruprecht-Karls Universitätbibliothek Heidelberg*). Founded 1386.

> *Notes. In 1623, as an appreciation for financial help given to Maximilian, the Duke of Bavaria by Pope Gregory XV, in his religious conflict with Protestants, during the Thirty Years War, a generous gift was sent to the pope. The gift was in the form of 3,000 manuscripts and 4000 books from the Heidelberg University Library (The Palatina Library), which were donated to the Vatican Library in Rome. About 200 years later some were returned for political reasons.*

2. Cologne University Library (*Universitätbibliothek Köln*). 1388.

3. Erfurt University Library (*Universitätbibliothek Erfurt*). 1392.

> *Notes. Martin Luther, who began the Reformation in the Roman Catholic Church, graduated from here in 1505 with a Ph.D. in law*

4. Wurzburg University Library (*Universitätbibliothek Würzburg*). 1402

5. Leipzig University Library (*Universitätbibliothek Leipzig*). 1409.

Cologne's university library is the second oldest in Germany.

72.
5 oldest university libraries in Spain

1. Palencia University Library (*Biblioteca de la Universidad de Palencia*). Founded 1210.

    Notes. Because of a decline of university functions, with staff leaving for the more popular Salamanca University, the entire library collections of Palencia University were transferred to Valladolid and Salamanca university libraries at the end of the 13th century, and the university closed down.

2. Salamanca University Library (*Biblioteca de la Universidad de Salamanca*). 1218.

    Notes. Christopher Columbus consulted the university library before embarking

on his famous voyage in 1492, and on his return gave several lectures here on his discoveries in the Americas, (which he mistakenly thought were in Asia).

3. Valladolid University Library (*Biblioteca de la Universidad de Valladolid*). 1290.

4. Complutense University Library, Madrid (*Biblioteca de la Universidad Complutense de Madrid*). 1293.

5. Valencia University Library (*Biblioteca de la Universitate de Valencia*). 1298.

73.
10 oldest university libraries in Eastern Europe

1. Charles University Library, Prague (*Knihovně Univerzita Karlova v Praze*). Czech Republic. Founded 1348.

2. Jagiellonian University Library, Kraków (*Biblioteka Universytet Jagielloński*). Poland. 1364.

3. Pécs University Library, Hungary (*Könyvtár Pécsi Egyetem*). 1367.

4. Palacky University Library. Olomouc (*Knihovně Univerzita Palackèho v Olomouchi*). Czech Republic. 1566

5. Vilnius University Library (*Biblioteka Universitas Vilnensis*). Lithuania. 1570.

5. Edward Kardelja University Library,

Ljubljana (*Edvarda Kardelja Knjižnica Univerza v Ljubljani*). Slovenia. 1595.

7. Eotvos Lorand University Library (*Könyvtár Eötvös Loránd Egyetem*). Budapest, Hungary. 1635.

8. Ivan Franko State University Library, Lvov, Ukraine. 1661.

9. Zagreb National and University Library (*Nacionalna i Sveučilišna Knjižnica u Zagrebu*). Croatia. 1669.

10. Bucharest University Library, Romania (*Biblioteca Universitatea Bucureşti*). 1694.

    Notes. Königsberg University was founded in 1544, but it was destroyed in

Lithuania's Vilnius University Library is the oldest in the Baltic states (courtesy of Vilnius University, Lithuania).

the Second World War. A new university called Kaliningrad University was opened in 1967. Kaliningrad region is a Russian territory between Lithuania and *Poland; in historic times it was part of the German enclave of East Prussia, and its main city Königsberg is today's Kalingrad City.*

74.
12 other significant early university libraries in Western Europe

1. Coimbra University Library, Portugal (*Biblioteca Universidade de Coimbra*). Founded 1290.

2. Lisbon University Library, Portugal (*Biblioteca Universidade de Lisboa*). 1291.

3. Vienna University Library, Austria (*Universitätbibliothek Wien*). 1365

4. Louvain (Leuven) Catholic University Library, Belgium (*Katholieke Universiteitbibliotheek Leuven / Université Catholique de Louvain*). 1425.

5. Basel University Library, Switzerland (*Universitätbibliothek Basel*). 1460.

6. Uppsala University Library, Sweden (*Bibliotek Uppsala Universitet*). 1477.

7. Copenhagen University Library, Denmark (*Bibliotek Københavns Universitet*). 1482.

8. Zürich University Library, Switzerland (*Universitätbibliothek Zürich*). 1523.

9. Bern University Library, Switzerland (*Universitätbibliothek Bern*). 1528.

10. Pontifical Gregorian University Library. Rome. Vatican City (*Biblioteca Pontifica Università Gregoriana*). 1553.

11. Leiden State University Library, the Netherlands (*Universiteitbibliotheek Leiden*). 1575.

12. Amsterdam University Library, the Netherlands (*Universiteitbibliotheek Amsterdam*). 1578.

75.
5 oldest university libraries in the Asia-Pacific Region

1. Pontifical Santo Tomás University Library, Manila, the Philippines. Founded 1611.

Notes. Another Filipino university library, San Carlos University Library in Cebu City was founded in 1595, but it

Sydney University Library, oldest in Australia. This is the Fischer Library (courtesy of Sydney University Library, Australia).

gained university status in 1948, after being closed in 1769 when Jesuits were expelled from the Philippines, and reopening in 1783.

2. Ryukoku University Library, Kyoto, Japan (*Ryukoku Daigaku Toshokan*). 1639.

3. Sydney University Library, Australia. 1850.

Joint 4th. Calcutta (Kolkata), Bombay (Mumbai), and Madras university libraries (all in India), and Padjadjaran University Library, Bandung, Indonesia (*Perpustakaan Universitas Padjadrajan*). 1857.

5. Keio University Library, Tokyo, Japan (*Keio Daigaku Toshokan*). 1858.

76.
10 oldest university libraries in the Americas

1. Santo Domingo Autonomous University Library, Dominican Republic (*Biblioteca de la Universidad Autónoma de Santo Domingo*). Founded in 1538.

> **Notes.** *The present library building dates from 1927. Not surprisingly Santo Domingo, founded in 1496, is the oldest city in the Americas founded by European explorers. Its cathedral has the tomb of Christopher Columbus, although the Seville Cathedral in Spain also claims it has the remains of the great explorer.*

2. St. Nicholas of Hidalgo Michoacan University Library, Morelia, Mexico (*Biblioteca de la Universidad Michoacana de San Nicolás de Hidalgo*). 1549.

3. Mexico National Autonomous University Library, Mexico City, Mexico (*Biblioteca de la Universidad Nacional Autónoma de México*). 1551.

> **Notes.** *Spanish King Charles I (Holy Roman Emperor Charles V) founded the University. It was closed in 1810, during the Mexican War of Independence. Reopening in 1910, eventually its library be-*

coming part of the National Library of Mexico.

4. San Marcos National University Library, Lima, Peru (*Biblioteca de la Universidad Nacional Mayor de San Marcos*). 1552.

5. Quito Central University Library, Ecuador (*Biblioteca Universidad Central de Ecuador*). 1586.

6. Puebla Autonomous University Library, Mexico (*Biblioteca de la Universidad Authonoma de Puebla*). 1598.

7. Córdoba National University Library, Argentina (*Biblioteca de la Universidad Nacional de Córdoba*). 1615.

8. Yucatan University Library, Mexico (*Biblioteca de la Universidad de Yucatan*). 1624.

9. San Francisco Xavier Royal Pontifical University Library, Sucre, Bolivia (*Biblioteca de la Universidad Real y Pontificia de San Francisco Xavier*). 1625.

10. Jesuit College Library, Quebec, Canada (*Bibliothèque de l'Université Jesuit*). 1635.

> *Notes.* Technically Jesuit College is not a full university; the oldest university in Canada is St. Mary's University in Halifax, which was founded in 1803. The oldest U.S. university library is Harvard University Library in Cambridge, Massachusetts, founded in 1636. The second oldest university library is William & Mary College, in Williamsburg, Virginia, in 1693. However the very first academic library to be established in the U.S. was a library set up in 1620, in Henrico, Virginia (just after the Pilgrims on board the ship Mayflower landed in Plymouth). A gift from Thomas Burgrave, this library was part of an early abortive plan to set up a college in Virginia. Most Brazilian universities were founded in the 20th century, but the oldest university is the Pelotas Federal University, founded in 1883.

77.
5 oldest university libraries in Africa

N.B.: This list excludes libraries in Morocco and Egypt. See list **66**.

1. Fourah Bay College Library, Free Town (Sierra Leone University). Founded 1828 by the British Church Missionary Society.

Fourah Bay College in Free Town is the oldest academic institution in sub–Saharan Africa. This photograph shows one of the earlier college buildings (housing the library), which was destroyed in 1997 during the civil war. A new building was constructed a few years later (courtesy of L.N. M'Jamtusie, Fourah Bay College Library).

2. Cape Town University, South Africa. 1829.

3. Monrovia University Library, Liberia. 1851.

4. Orange Free State University Library, Bloemfontein, South Africa. 1855.

5. University of Algiers Library, Algiers (*Bibliothèque de l'Université d'Alger*). 1880.

> **Notes.** *The earliest university library founded in sub–Saharan Africa was* probably that of Sankore University in Timbuktu (Tombouctou), in modern day Mali. It was an Islamic university set up in the 15th century by King Mansa Musa, when Timbuktu (originally founded by the Berber Tuaregs from North Africa in the 11th century) was part of the Malian Empire and the later Songhai Empire. The university was destroyed in 1593 by an invasion of Spanish mercenary forces employed by Morocco, and the extensive library manuscripts were transported back to Moroccan libraries.

WORLD RECORDS FOR SPECIALTY LIBRARIES AND ARCIHVES

Special libraries are libraries that devote their book collections to one or more specialized subjects such as medicine, law, humanities and business. As such they are more likely to be found in companies, in research institutes or other scholarly bodies, or government-funded libraries. Very few are open to members of the public, as they are primarily for company staff or researchers and members of a research institute.

78.
6 largest medical libraries

1. National Library of Medicine, Bethesda, Maryland, U.S. Has over 5 million medical books and over 6500 different medical serials. Founded in 1836 as the Library of the Surgeon-General's Office, it is located on the campus of the National Institutes of Health, which has its own medical library.

2. Russian State Medical Library, Moscow. 3.9 million. Founded in 1923.

3. German National Library for Medicine, Cologne (*Deutsche Zentralbibliothek fuer Medzin*). 1.3 million. Founded in 1969.

3. Harvard University Medical School Library, Cambridge, Massachusetts, U.S.

Also known as Francis Countway Medical Library. 1.1 million. It was founded in 1960.

4. New York Academy of Medicine Library, U.S. 810,200. Founded in 1847.
> *Notes. It is the largest public medical library in the world.*

5. Yale University Medical School Library, New Haven, Connecticut, U.S. 430,000. Also known as the Harvey Cushing / John Whitney Medical Library.
> *Notes. There are also several large national medical libraries in Europe (which are distinct from the main national library). Prominent among them are the ones in Rome, Italy; Paris, France; and Prague, the Czech Republic. The Russian*

The National Library of Medicine at Bethesda, outside Washington, D.C. (courtesy of the National Library of Medicine).

Central Epidemiology Institute, in Moscow has over 4 million volumes but this figure may include not just books, but *also medical reports, microforms, manuscripts and other publications.*

79.
Largest biomedical and scientific periodicals library

The Canada Institute for Scientific and Technical Information, founded in 1924 in Ottawa, has a huge serial collection of over 16,000 journals and more than 2 million technical reports. It functions as a Canada's national science library and also has about 4.3 million books on science, technology and allied subjects.

80.
Oldest dental school library

University of Maryland Dental School Library in Baltimore, U.S., was founded in 1842.

Notes. *The world's largest dental library is the American Dental Association Library* *in Chicago, Illinois, U.S. It was founded in 1859 and has over 40,000 books on dentistry and 16,000 dental and medical journals. The British Dental Association Library in London, is the largest dental library in Europe, with over 12,000 books.*

81.
Oldest medical school libraries

In Italy, Florence Medical School Library (*Biblioteca Scuola Medica Firenze*) was founded in 1287, while the Salerno Medical School Library (*Biblioteca Scuola Medica Salernitana*), was established in 13th century. In France, Montpellier University Medical School Library was set up in the 14th century.

82.
Oldest medical school library in the U.S.

Pennsylvania University Medical School Library, Philadelphia, U.S., was opened in 1775. And in 1788, the library of the College of Physicians of Philadelphia (CPP) was founded.

83.
Oldest medical school library in Asia

In 1845 Panaji Medical School Library was set up in Goa, a Portuguese colony till 1961, and now a state in India. Today it is now part of Goa University.

84.
Oldest medical school library in the U.K.

London Hospital Medical Library was founded in 1786. It is now part of London University Queen Mary's School of Medicine and Dentistry Library in London. The Royal College of Surgeons Library in Edinburgh was founded in 1505, and the Royal College of Physicians Library in London was founded in 1518, However both are not exactly medical schools, but institutes for qualified surgeons and physicians. However both have the oldest medical libraries in the U.K.

85.
5 largest medical libraries in the U.K.

1. Royal College of Surgeons Libraries, London (founded 1800), and Edinburgh (founded 1505).

2. Royal College of Physicians Libraries, London (founded 1518), and Edinburgh (founded 1681).

3. Royal Society of Medicine Library. London. Founded 1805.

4. National Institute of Medical Research Library. London. Founded 1920.

5. British Medical Association Nuffield Library. London. Founded in 1832.

The combined library collection of these five is over 1,950,600 medical books and over 7000 different medical serials.

Notes. There are plans to establish a university for training National Health Service staff in the U.K. in about 2003. It will be called the National Health University, and possess one of the most modern and sophisticated medical libraries in the world.

86.
Largest pharmaceutical libraries

Based in New York, Pfizer, the world's largest pharmaceutical company (known for the drug Viagra) also has the largest pharmaceutical library with over 130,000 titles on subjects such as pharmacy, biochemistry, organic chemistry and pharmacology. In the U.K., Boots Pharmaceutical Research Library in Nottingham has over 70,000 books, while books in GlaxoSmithKline libraries in the U.K. and overseas total over 95,000.

87.
Largest international medical library

The library of the World Health Organization Library in Geneva, Switzerland has a collection of over 150,000 medical books, and is open to medical researchers and academics from around the world.

88.
Largest medical library in Scandinavia

Karolinska Institute Library (*Karolinska Institutet Bibliotek*), based in Stockholm, Sweden, contains more than 210,000 medical books and about 900 medical serials.

Notes. *The Institute is involved in awarding the annual Nobel Prize in physiology & medicine.*

89.
Largest library in Europe on deafness and hearing loss

The Royal National Institute for the Deaf Library in London, U.K., which is part of the University College Library also in London, stocks more than 10,000 books, devoted to deafness, hard of hearing and electronic gadgets to improve hearing.

90.
Largest library for political science and economics

The library of the Kiel Institute of World Economics, at the Kiel University in Germany is the largest in the world with over 2.6 million books and over 10,000 periodicals on all aspects of economics. The library of the London School of Economics and Political Science (part of London University), the second largest in Europe, currently has more than 1 million books and some 28,000 journals. Sidney Webb founded the library in 1896 as the British Library of Political and Economic Science. The library is the editorial office of the International Bibliography of the Social Sciences, and also has extensive archives on world economics dating from the 19th century.

The famous London School of Economics.

91.
Largest library specializing in geography

The American Geographical Society Library has over 130,000 books. It is based at the University of Wisconsin–Milwaukee Golda Meir Library. Its library holdings extend back as far as second generation vellum copies of the famous 15th century Rome edition of Greek genius Claudius Ptolemy's eight-volume atlas *Geographia*. This manuscript had been originally completed in AD 150 at the Alexandria Library in Egypt. The oldest original map in the collection is a world map dating from 1452 and compiled in Italian by the Venetian cartographer Giovanni Leardo.

Notes. The Geographia (also known as Cosmographia) was the explorer's bible for more than 1000 years after it was completed. Famous 15th and 16th century sailors such as Christopher Columbus, Vasco da Gama and Ferdinand Magellan used the book as a guide for planning their overseas explorations. A mistake in Ptolemy's geographic calculations on the size of the oceans contributed to Columbus' believing he was in Asia when in fact he was in the Americas. During the Middle Ages while Europe was fighting with the Arabs in the Crusades, they began looking for the manuscript when it suddenly disappeared and seemed lost forever. But all along the Arabs had been quietly looking after the Geographia after it had apparently been stolen. Europe was able to recover a copy of the original Geographia when a member of the Italian nobility, the Strozzi family, of Florence, obtained a perfect copy in Constantinople (Istanbul) in 1407. Taken back to Italy it caused a sensation, and to ensure it was not lost again, several further copies of the Geographia were made and promptly translated from Greek into Latin and several other languages for scholars and university libraries all over Europe. Some of the earliest copies were obtained by the Vatican Library in Rome in 1478 and are on display today, but the copy at the Nancy City Library in France dates from 1427 and is the oldest surviving copy today. The Arabs probably were the first to use knowledge gained from the Geographia, to explore the New World. A Chinese manuscript known as the Sung Document (so called because it was written during the time of the Chinese Sung Dynasty between AD 960 and 1279) provides fascinating details of a voyage made in 1178 by Arab sailors from the Philippines to the Americas. This was more than 300 years before the voyage of Christopher Columbus. The Arab sailors traveled from southern Philippines across the Pacific Ocean and landed on the coast of what is now California, a land the Chinese called Mu-Lan-Pi, then made a return journey to the Philippines. Some of the Chinese sailors in the Philippines who were lucky enough to travel with the Arab sailors, sent word of the feat back to Canton (Guangzhou) the same year, where the Sung Document originated. The problem was the Arab sailors made no further voyages to follow up the 1178 voyage, nor did Chinese sailors. And when the Portuguese and Prince Henry "the Navigator" began the Iberian age of overseas explorations in the 15th century that eventually lead to the voyage of Columbus, none of them had ever heard of the Sung Document. Hence like the insignificance of Leif Erikson and the Norwegian Viking landings in the Americas (Newfoundland) around AD 1000, Columbus remains the official discoverer *of the New World in 1492. And credit to the crossing of the huge Pacific Ocean, starting from either east of Asia or west of the Americas, goes to Ferdinand Magellan's three-month voyage of 1521. Marco Polo, the Italian traveler, visited extensively China in the 13th century, but there is no mention of the Sung Document in his famous story about his travels (see entry **101**). Had Columbus or any other European explorers known about the Sung Document, the history of the Americas would have been very different.*

92.
Largest library in the Middle East devoted to oil exploration

With the Middle East having very large petroleum deposits, many libraries there have important book collections on oil exploration and refining. The King Fahd University of Petroleum and Minerals Library in Dhahran, Saudi Arabia (founded 1963), is the largest of its kind in the Middle East and currently has over 380,000 books covering chemical engineering and petroleum production among others.

Notes. *The university was established by the well-known former Saudi Oil Minister Sheik Ahmed Yamani with the help of the Massachusetts Institute of Technology, Princeton University and the American University in Beirut, Lebanon.*

93.
Largest engineering libraries

The Department of Electrical and Computer Engineering library at the University of Illinois in the U.S. (Grainger Engineering Library Information Center) has the largest university engineering library in the Americas. There are currently over 300,000 books. The university also has the largest chemistry library in the world. The largest mechanical engineering library in the world is the library of the American Society for Mechanical Engineers or ASME (founded in 1880 in New York), with about 200,000 books. The largest electrical engineering library in the world belongs to the IEEE (Institute of Electrical and Electronic Engineering).

Set up in 1884, it has over 220,000 books. The IEEE, based in Piscataway, New Jersey, in the U.S., also publishes about 35% of the total books in the world on electronics and electrical and computer engineering. Established in 1820, the Institution of Civil Engineers Library in London, U.K., has the largest library for civil and structural engineers in Europe, housing some 100,000 titles.

Notes. *The libraries of the five major engineering societies in the world (outside Europe) comprising the IEEE, the ASME, the ASCE (American Society for Civil Engineers), the AIME (American Institute for Mechanical engineers) and the*

AIchE (American Institute for Chemical Engineers) founded the Engineering Societies Library or ESL in 1915. The combined collections of the ESL, which has been based at the Linda Hall Library in Kansas City since 1995, number over 600,000 volumes. This makes the Linda Hall Library the largest (privately-funded) engineering and technology library in the world.

94.
Largest music library

The U.S. Library of Congress Music Division, Washington, D.C., founded in 1897, has about 1.4 million books all on all aspects of music. It also has the largest collection of sound recordings in the world. The British Library's National Sound Archive has over 1 million disks and over 150,000 tape recordings of sounds. This is the largest such collection in Europe.

95.
Largest poetry library

Founded in 1953, the Poetry Library in London, U.K., is the largest of its kind in the world devoted to modern poetry, with over 80,000 books.

96.
Largest film and television library in Europe

The British Film Institute Library in London provides access to over 40,000 books on film and television in English and fifteen or more other languages. In addition it holds 5000 periodical titles, dating back to the earliest years of cinema in the 19th century. The British Broadcasting Corporation (BBC) Library in London has the largest audio-visual library collection in Europe.

Notes. The University of California, Los Angeles, has the largest collection of film and television programs in a university (the earliest is from the year 1890), this is not surprising as the university is close to Hollywood. The world's largest collection of U.S. and foreign produced films are in the U.S. Library of Congress. It includes the oldest existing motion picture, made by Thomas Edison in the 1890s.

97.
Largest agricultural libraries

The U.S. National Agricultural Library, in Washington, D.C., which is part of the agricultural research service of the U.S. Department of Agriculture, has more than 2.7 million books. It was founded in 1862. The Russia Central Scientific Agricultural Library, in Moscow (*Rossiskaya Akademiya Selskokhozyaistvennyjk Nauk*) has almost 2 million books and periodicals. It was founded in 1930. The largest agricultural library in Western Europe is the David Lubin Memorial Library, which is based at the headquarters of the UN Food and Agricultural Organization in Rome Italy. The library currently has over 350,000 volumes, and was founded in 1952. The largest agricultural library in Asia is the library of the Chinese Academy of Agricultural Science (CAAD). Established in 1957 in Beijing, it has over 310,000 books.

98.
Largest zoological library

The Zoological Society of London Library in the U.K. has over 200,000 books and is the largest of its kind in the world. This is also the largest library in a zoo, as the Zoological Society of London Library is based in the famous London Zoo. The largest library on aquatic sciences and fisheries in Europe is the National Marine Biological Library, in Plymouth, U.K. Founded 1887, the library has over 14,000 books.

99.
Largest botanical library

The library of the New York Botanical Gardens in the U.S. (called the LuEsther T. Mertz Library) possesses more than 300,000 books. The largest library on plant and horticulture in the Europe is the Royal Botanical Gardens Library, Kew, London, U.K. The library contains over as about 75,000 books and 4,000 periodicals. It was set up in 1852.

100.
6 largest military libraries

1. Library of the Central House of the Russian Army, Moscow, Russia, 4 million books. Formerly called Library of the Central House of the Soviet Army (up to 1991).

2. The combined collections of the three U.S. military academies at West Point in New York, Annapolis in Maryland (Naval Academy) and Colorado Springs in Colorado (Air Force Academy). 3.2 million.

3. Air University Library, Maxwell Air Force Base, Alabama, U.S. 2.6 million. Founded in 1946.

4. National Defense University Library, Fort McNair, Washington, D.C. 500,000. Founded in 1982.

5. Royal Military Academy, Sandhurst, Library, Camberley, U.K. 321, 000.

Notes. The Royal Military Academy, Sandhurst, was formed in 1947 as the successor to the Royal Military Academy, Woolwich, founded in 1741, and the Royal Military College, Sandhurst, founded in 1801. Established in 1875, the Institution of Royal Engineering Library in Brompton Barracks, Chatham, has over 40,000 books on military engineering. The Joint Services Command and Staff College Library in Shrivenham is the second largest military library in the U.K.

6. Royal Military College Library (*Bibliothèque Ecole Militaire*), Paris, France. 180,000. Founded in 1751.

Notes. Napoleon Bonaparte made good use of books at the library of the Royal Military College Library in Paris while he was a student there. He completed his military training in 1784, and was commissioned as a second lieutenant.

101.
Largest library in the U.K. on prison services

The Prison Service College Library in Wakefield has over 210,000 books on penology, criminology etc. The library also holds official prison reports for the U.K. going back to 1835.

Notes. The three largest prison libraries in the U.K. are at Wandsworth, Liverpool and Brixton prisons. A library is a legal statutory requirement in the U.K.'s 139 prisons. The oldest prison libraries in

Europe date back to the 13th century, most notably those in the Italian city states of Genoa, Venice and Florence. Adolf Hitler, Miguel de Cervantes, Wole Soyenka, Walter Ralegh, Daniel Defoe, Jawaharlal Nehru, Oscar Wilde and Marco Polo are among famous and infamous people who made good use of prison libraries in their countries to write bestsellers while incarcerated. Here is a brief look at Marco Polo's fantastic book:

Marco Polo was the famous Italian traveler who took 24 years visiting Asia and meeting rulers such as the Mongol leader Kabulai Khan. He was probably the first European to witness block-printing of documents on paper during his travels to China in the 13th century. Having invented paper, the Chinese took the first step in inventing printing by developing what is called block-printing in the 6th century, (the precursor to the printing technique invented by Gutenberg in the 15th century). At this time block-printing was unknown in Europe, even when the secrets of making paper finally reached Europe late in the 12th century. Among other "firsts" attributable to Marco Polo are that he was the first European to see paper money (the first European paper money was issued in Sweden in 1661), paper playing cards, and libraries with books made from paper. After his travels in Asia, he returned to Venice and dictated the story of his travels while a prisoner in Genoa to a fellow inmate who was a writer. His book, The Travels of Marco Polo, *became a best-seller in medieval Europe, but there were some people who were skeptical and called him "Marco Milione," and his book* Il Milione *or* The Million Lies, *because the story of his travels was too fantastic to be true. To his skeptics, Marco Polo said the memorable words, "I have only told half of what I saw!"*

102.
Largest law library

Harvard University Law Library was founded in 1817, the same year as the law school. It is the world's largest law library, with about 2.5 million law books, manuscripts and other library items such as legal gazettes and periodicals, and is also the oldest university law library in the U.S.

Notes. *The U.S. Library of Congress in Washington, D.C., is the second largest law library in the world, as it has more than 2 million law books. Columbia University Law Library is the third largest in the U.S. The largest law library on the Internet is www.lawresearch.com, which has over 1 million legal Internet resources. The largest law library in Canada is York University's Osgoode Hall Law School Library. It was founded in 1889 and its collections total over 400,000 books. This also makes it the largest law library of the Commonwealth countries.*

103.
Largest law libraries in Europe and Asia

The largest law library in France is the Cujas Library (*Bibliothèque Cujas*) which is part of the Sorbonne University of Paris. There are over 130,000 books in the library.

In the U.K. apart from the British

For several years Lincoln's Inn Law Library in London chained its valuable law books to the shelves.

Library's law collection, the 15th century Lincoln's Inn Law Library in London (oldest of the four Inns of Court law libraries for U.K. lawyers), has about 180,200 law books. Oxford University Bodleian Law Library has the largest collection of academic law books in the U.K. (200,000 titles).

The largest law library in Asia is China's Tsinghua University Law School Library in Beijing. It currently holds just over 110,000 books

Notes. *So valuable were the majority of law books in Lincoln's Inn Law Library that they were all secured by chains in the library until 1771. In fact before the use of electronic tags hidden in books to prevent their being stolen from libraries and bookstores, several European libraries such as the Leiden State University in the Netherlands and Hereford Cathedral Library in the U.K. used chains fastened to their books. The problem was you could not take a book and read it in your "favorite corner" in the library. Today several books at Hereford Cathedral Library are still in chains.*

104.
Largest art library

Based in New York, the Avery Architectural and Fine Arts Library is the largest in the world with more than 250,000 books and about 1,300 periodicals. Established in 1890, its book collection is diverse, encompassing architecture, art history, painting, sculpture, graphic arts, and archaeology. The National Art Library in London is the largest in Europe with over 170,000 books and manuscripts.

105.
2 largest libraries in Europe with
specialized collections of books on Africa

1. London University School of African and Oriental Studies or SOAS, U.K. Founded in 1920 its library has over 850,000 books and 4,500 periodicals, as well as extensive collections of archives and manuscripts written in African and Asian languages.

2. Belgian Ministry of Foreign Affairs African Library (*Bibliothèque Africaine*), Brussels. It has over 480,000 books, and was developed from a collection started by King Leoplod II in the 1860s.

106.
Largest astronomy library

The United States Naval Observatory in Washington, D.C., has over 100,000 books on all topics of astronomy including space exploration and astrophysics. It was established in 1830.

107.
Largest libraries in Europe
specializing in education

Comenius Library (*Comenius-Bücherei*), founded 1871 in Leipzig, Germany has over a 460,000 books on education and teaching on all levels. Founded in 1902, the Institute of Education Library (part of London University) has over 300,000 books and more than 2000 periodicals. The largest government library devoted to education is the U.S. National Library of Education in Washington, D.C. It was founded in 1878.

108.
Largest social sciences library

The Russian Academy of Sciences Institute for Scientific Information on Social Sciences Library in Moscow, better known by the acronym INION (*Insitut Nauchnoi Informatsii po Obshchestvennym Naukam*) has over 3.6 million books. It was founded in 1918.

Notes. The London School of Economics and Political Science has the second largest collection of books on social sciences in Europe.

109.
Largest religious libraries

CHRISTIANITY

Established in 1969 the Flora Lamson Hewlett Library in Berkeley, California, has over 500,000 books on Christianity. It is part of the Graduate Theological Union. Based in New York, the American Bible Association presently has about 44,000 books, including the largest collection of ancient and modern copies of the Bible in several languages. The largest Christian library in Europe is in the St. Gallen Monastery in eastern Switzerland. The library, called *Stiftsbibliothek*, contains over 100,000 books and the monastery, which dates back to the 7th century AD, is the premiere tourist attraction in the city of St. Gallen and a UNESCO Heritage site.

Notes. The first important Christian library is believed to be the one founded in Jerusalem by Bishop Alexander in AD 250. Pope Damascus (4th century AD) and Pope Agapetus (6th century AD) founded the earliest Roman Christian libraries in Rome. With the fragmentation of the Western Roman Empire, the Benedictines and friars in monastic libraries preserved the collections of these libraries across the whole of Europe. The largest

publisher of books on Christianity in the world is Thomas Nelson, based in Nashville, Tennessee, U.S.

ISLAM

The largest non-academic Islamic libraries are in the Al-Mutawakki Mosque, Samarra, Iraq; Shah Faisal Mosque Library in Islamabad, Pakistan; and the Suleymaniye Mosque in Istanbul, Turkey. Hartford Seminary Library probably has the largest Islamic library in the U.S. The collections include hundreds of rare Arabic and Islamic manuscripts and a collection of thousands of books and other materials from the personal library of D. B. Macdonald, at one time the premier Arabist in the U.S. The Hartford Seminary is also one of the largest official U.S. repositories for all materials published in the Middle East.

BUDDHISM

The library of the Sakya Buddhist Monastery in Shigate, Tibet, is the largest in the world with over 46,000 books, including thousands of *sutras* (teachings and discourses of the Buddha). The monastery itself was originally founded in AD 1073 by Khon Konchog Gyalpo.

Judaism

The largest Jewish libraries in the world are the Hebrew University Library, Jerusalem, Israel, the Jewish Theological Seminary of America Library in New York, the *Bibliothèque de Alliance Israélite Universelle,* Paris, France, and the Budapest Synagogue Library in Hungary.

110.
Oldest library in the U.K. devoted to women

The Women's Library, with over 60,000 volumes, based in London's Whitechapel, was founded in 1927, when it was located in London Guildhall University. The library collection include books on past and present famous women who have made important contributions to U.K. society, and is the most extensive of such a collection in the U.K.

Notes. The only women's lending library in the U.K. is the Glasgow Women's Library.

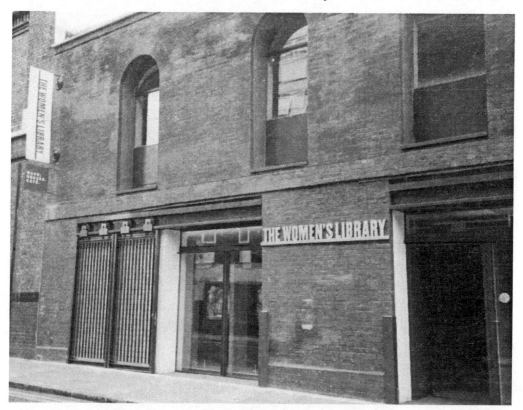

The Women's Library has the most extensive collection of women's history in the United Kingdom.

111.
Largest collection of
Shakespeare's printed works

The Folger Shakespeare Library, founded in 1930 in Washington, D.C., has more than 300,000 books. Henry Clay Folger, who had an intellectual passion for buying rare books on Shakespeare, founded the library.

112.
Oldest national archives

The growth of archives for the preservation of state and commercial documents started in Europe during the late Renaissance period. The Vatican Archives in Rome (*Archivio Segreto Vaticano*) dates back to 1611 (some archives however date further back to the 4th century AD collections of Pope Damascus), while the Swedish Chancery Archives was set up in 1618. However, Europe's first modern state archives was the French National Archives (*Archives Nationales de France*), established in 1789. It was also the first to use microfilm to archive documents.

The French National Archives in Paris.

Notes. One of the holdings in the Vatican Archives most sought after by scholars are the files pertaining to the Inquisition, which were not available for research until 1998, when the Vatican Archives permitted limited access to the Inquisition files.

113.
Oldest national archives in the Americas

The National Archives of Argentina was set up in Buenos Aires in 1821.

Notes. The National Archives of Mexico dates back to 1790, but was not officially opened until 1900.

114.
Oldest national archives in the Middle East

The National Archives of Egypt has been in existence since 1828.

115.
Oldest national archives in Asia

The National Archives of India was set up in 1891.

116.
Oldest national archives in Africa

This appears to be the National Archives of Angola, set up by the Portuguese colonial government in 1654 (an earlier smaller archive had been founded in 1603, but was destroyed by the Dutch in 1641). In the 1970s a new archive was established after Angola gained independence.

MISCELLANEOUS WORLD RECORDS FOR LIBRARIES

117.
18 major libraries that have suffered devastating fires or natural disasters

1. Alexandria Library, Egypt. The collection of 750,000 parchment and papyrus scrolls of the greatest library of the ancient world was destroyed with fire by an Arab army led by Arab general Amr Ibn-al-As in AD 638 on the orders of Caliph Omar I in Mecca, after surviving two earlier devastating fires. Caliph Omar was said to have justified the burning of the library by quoting the famous words, *if the writings of the Greeks in the library agree with the Koran they are unnecessary and need not be preserved, but if they disagree they are blasphemy and will be destroyed...* So either way the Alexandria Library lost out and was thus destroyed. One of two other earlier fires to devastate the library was started by Julius Caesar in 47 BC, when he got involved in a political struggle between Queen Cleopatra and her younger brother Ptolemy XIII. A brand new Alexandria library was opened in 2002.

2. Harvard University Library, Cambridge, Massachusetts. Suffered a devastating fire in 1764, which destroyed over 90% of its collection of books (it was the largest library in the original 13 colonies in the 17th and 18th century at that time). Luckily donations rebuilt the library to its original size in just two years. The British, in charge of the colonies, did not start the fire, as it would be another 12 years before the American Revolution. Today Harvard University Library is the largest university library in the world.

3. U.S. Library of Congress, Washington, D.C. It was burnt down in 1814 by British forces during a brief war between the U.S. and the U.K. over Canada and the sea trade. And in 1851, another fire caused by a faulty chimney flue destroyed over 30,000 books.

4. Lomonosov State University Library, Moscow, Russia. In 1812 as the invading army of Napoleon Bonaparte from France marched onto Moscow, locals there set fire to the city, and in the ensuing inferno the university library was among buildings obliterated. Even when the library was rebuilt, it was further damaged dur-

ing the Second World War. But its collections were again rapidly rebuilt at such a pace that today it is the largest university library in Europe.

5. Russian Academy of Sciences Library, St. Petersburg, Russia. The largest fire to damage a major library in the 20th century happened here in February 1988. Nearly 2 million books were destroyed as well as a third of the newspaper holdings.

6. National library of Finland, Helsinki. When this library was based in the old Finnish capital of Turku (Åbo), as the Helsinki University Library, much of it was destroyed by fire in 1827. The library was moved to Helsinki in 1828 and rebuilt from scratch.

7. British Library, London. Over 250,000 books were lost in 1941 during the Second World War, when German incendiary bombs started fires that forced the library to close until 1946.

8. Belize libraries. In 1931 an unnamed hurricane wrecked devastating havoc by destroying all libraries in this central American state.

9. Louvain (Leuven) Catholic University Library, Belgium. The library was destroyed completely twice as a result of the two World Wars, first in 1914, and the second time in 1940, in both instances due to invasion by the German army. As a result the university library had to be rebuilt twice.

10. National Library of Algeria, Algiers. It was rebuilt in 1962, after a huge fire set by French colonial troops destroyed the library.

11. Hamburg University Speersort Library, Germany. Totally destroyed during the Second World War. It was one of several large German libraries to suffer devastation in the war, which included the Berlin State Library and the Bavarian State Library.

12. Copenhagen University Library, Denmark. It was rebuilt from scratch, when its entire collection was destroyed in the fire of 1728 in Copenhagen.

13. National Library of Sarajevo. Bosnia — Herzegovina. The library (which dates back to the time Sarajevo was part of the Austria-Hungarian Empire) was razed to the ground by Bosnian-Serb forces during the 1992–1995 civil war, which forces also destroyed the library of the Oriental Institute containing irreplaceable rare manuscripts.

14. National Library of Cambodia. Phnom Penh. Troops of Pol Pot's Khmer Rouge forces wrecked the library in 1975, forcing it to close until 1980, when Vietnamese troops (who invaded Cambodia in 1978) drove the Khmer Rouge out of the country's urban areas.

15. Ambrosian Library, Milan, Italy. During the liberation of Italy by Allied forces during the Second World War, the library was severely damaged by fire, and a large number of rare manuscripts were lost forever.

16. Chicago Public Library. U.S. In 1871 the Great Chicago Fire destroyed what was the predecessor of the Chicago Public Library, a subscription library. This older Chicago library was not huge, (its total book collections was under 50,000 at

the time). But the destruction of the library was what gave rise to the founding of the Chicago Public Library in 1873. Because appeals for donation of books by descendants of Chicagoans living in Europe, who heard news about the fire, caused so many donated books to be to be sent to Chicago, legislators in the city had to pass an Act to establishing the Chicago Public Library.

17. Bucharest University Library, Romania. During the 1989 Romanian revolution, the central library was completely destroyed. Following the overthrow of the communist regime, the library was later rebuilt.

18. Heidelberg University Library was Germany's oldest university library, containing some of the most treasured manuscripts outside of Italy during the Renaissance. The library was totally destroyed during the War of the Palatine Succession in 1693.

Notes. Today libraries destroyed by natural disasters (or accidentally or deliberately such as in times of war) can get extra help in reconstruction with generous funds made available from both UNESCO and the World Bank. Thousands of books were destroyed at the Loreto College Library in Darjeeling, India, in 2001, not this time by fire or man, but by dozens of hungry langur monkeys, who were after the food in the student's lunch boxes. Local wildlife officials could not capture the monkeys without upsetting the worshippers at the nearby Hindu Mahakal Temple, who love feeding the monkeys, and see them as sacred and as having a symbolic relationship with the temple.

118.
Library with the most branches worldwide

The British Council, the U.K.'s international organization for educational and cultural relations, has over 1441 libraries and information centers in 110

The British Council, with headquarters in London, has more library branches around the world than any other organization.

countries. The largest library is in Bombay in India.

> *Notes.* Several countries around the world have similar organizations for promoting educational and cultural activities in foreign countries. Most notable are the Institut Français of France, which has over 150 branches in more than 50 countries, and the Goethe-Institut of Germany, which has over 128 branches in 76 countries. Both have over 600 libraries attached to these organizations.

119.
Oldest private library in the U.S.

The Boston Athenaeum was set up in 1807, from a need for a library to store the collections of the Anthology Society. Its huge collection of books (today, over a half a million) made it the largest private library in the U.S. It is now a subscription library, and yearly membership is available to members of the public.

> *Notes.* In Europe private libraries were already well established from the Middle Ages, and most had religious books, such as the 14th century library of Richard de Bury, Bishop of Durham in the U.K. In 1990, the FBI charged a man from Minnesota with the theft of over 30,000 books from 140 university libraries in the U.S. When the FBI raided his home, they were astonished to find that the haul of stolen books had filled 14 rooms, resembling a large legitimate private library.

120.
Most expensive library

The U.S. National Security Agency (NSA) library based at Fort George Mead in Maryland is believed to be more secure than the CIA, Israeli Mossad, British MI6, French DGSE, and former Russian KGB libraries, in terms of the huge cost of implementing high-tech security devices and computer systems. These include the world's most sophisticated voice recognition systems, as well as retinal and finger print digital scanners, in addition to body heat, body movement, and sound digital sensors (as seen in the spy films *Sneakers, Enemy of the State* and *Mission Impossible*). The NSA Library collections include several PC terminals linking to a Cray supercomputer system (used especially for code breaking work), extremely sensitive and classified intelligence publications as well as the best books written on cryptology (cryptography and cryptoanalysis), bugging devices and eavesdropping. The huge audio-visual collection includes hundreds of dossiers with (National Reconnaissance Office) Keyhole KH-12, and Lacrosse-3 spy satellite photographs and 3-dimensional imagery. The library budget has been estimated at $900 million per annum (based on the 1997 Freedom of Information Act law suit filed by Steven Aftergood, director of the Federation of American Scientists Project on

U.S. Government Secrecy). This is the largest annual library budget anywhere in the world (and is larger than the annual budgets of many third world countries in Africa and the Caribbean). The second largest annual library budget in the world is that of the U.S. Library of Congress, at $400 million per annum. Among university libraries, Harvard has the largest annual budget, with over $140 million. New York Public Library has an annual budget of $97 million. For more library budgets see also list **313**—"6 libraries with over 800 staff members and their annual budgets."

121.
14 major films major that featured libraries

Hollywood and other national film industries around the world are not exactly obsessed with making a blockbuster movie featuring lots of library scenes, but many libraries did get to star in major films! Here of 14 of them.

The Day of the Jackal (1973). Edward Fox (as Jackal, an assassin hired by a French paramilitary organization) pays a visit to the newspaper section of the British Library, looking for information as part of his plot to assassinate Charles de Gaulle. Based on a novel by British author Fredrick Forsyth.

Carrie (1976). Sissy Spacek is shown in a high school library searching for books on paranormal telekinetic powers, which she possesses. Based on a novel by U.S. author Stephen King.

Escape from Alcatraz (1979). Clint Eastwood (incarcerated in the notorious Alcatraz Island Prison) is seen very busy each day at the impregnable island's prison library.

War Games (1983). California State Library books on computers interests Matthew Broderick (a teenage whiz kid), who almost starts the Third World War after hacking into the Pentagon computer systems.

Ghostbusters (1984). Los Angeles Public Library gets an unscheduled visit by a bunch of scary ghosts. Who ya gonna call?

Wings of Desire (1987). This German film features Bruno Graz and Peter Falk at the Berlin State Library in Germany.

Fatal Attraction (1987). A passionate but deadly love affair is confessed quietly by Michael Douglas to his lawyer in a law firm's library; it is hoped no one overheard him.

Indiana Jones and the Last Crusade (1989). Harrison Ford, as Indiana Jones, the world's greatest archaeologist, digs a big hole in a library in Venice, Italy (making a lot of noise in the process), to reveal a secret passage and some ancient secrets.

The Pelican Brief (1993). A law library is used by Julia Roberts in her efforts to solve a high level conspiracy against judges.

Goldeneye (1995). Trigger-happy KGB guards in a Russian library shoot at Pierce Brosman and a beautiful girl, and in the ensuing confrontation, many books get destroyed. Based on the James Bond novel by British writer Ian Fleming.

City of Angels (1998). The movie shows scenes in the San Francisco Public Library, with Nicholas Cage in a rendezvous with angels.

Mercury Rising (1998). FBI agent Bruce Willis uses a public library computer to locate the whereabouts of e-mails that seem to come from the super secret National Security Agency.

The Ninth Gate (1999). Johnny Depp (a rare book expert) is seen visiting libraries in Europe looking for follow-ups and leads to locating copies of a book about occultism and demons.

Harry Potter and the Philosopher's Stone (2001). David Radcliffe (the orphaned son of wizards) is shown looking for information in Oxford University's Bodleian Library. Based on J.K. Rowling's popular children's story books. The film was released in the U.S. as *Harry Potter and the Sorcerer's Stone*.

Other films with some scenes of libraries are: *You're a Big Boy Now* (1966), New York Public Library; *The Graduate* (1967), University of Southern California's Doheny Library; *Foul Play* (1978), Pasadena Public Library; *Sakara no Sono* (a.k.a. *The Cherry Orchard*, 1981), Fukagawa Library, Tokyo; *Twelve Monkeys* (1995), Philadelphia Public Library, Ridgeway branch; *Robo Cop* (1997), Dallas Public Library; *Mr. Magoo* (1997),

Vancouver Public Library, Canada; *Double Jeopardy* (1999), Vancouver Public Library, Canada; *Charlie's Angels* (2000), Huntington Library, San Marino, California; *Cadaverous* (2000), New York University's Bobst Library; *Sweetest Thing* (2002), Huntington Library, San Marino, California; and *Red Dragon* (2002), the Library of Congress, Washington D.C.

Notes. Not everything we see in cinemas or on television that depicts libraries or librarians has a happy ending. In the summer of 1996, a new advertisement for Packard Bell computers in the U.S. cause an outrage among librarians. Designed by Saatchi and Saatchi, the advertisement seemed to portray libraries as scary dark places with spiders creeping out of dusty books and a skinhead as a librarian uttering the dreaded "keep quiet" sound, "shhh..." It suggested that those looking for information were better off using a Packard Bell computer to access information sources at home, such as via the Internet, than visiting the local library. The slogan for the advertisement was, Wouldn't you rather be at home? After a couple of runs, the advertisement was eventually withdrawn to the relief of librarians, who no doubt saw it as the worst advertisement made depicting libraries.

122.
Some notable people who have worked in libraries or as librarians

Over the centuries, hundreds of famous people, and some infamous, have been involved in library work or worked for a while as librarians. Below are some.

Al-Khwarizmi. This 9th century Arab mathematician, who invented *Al-Jabr* (Algebra), worked as a librarian in the famous library of Abbassid Caliph Al-

The Assryian King Assurbanipal was involved in the expanion of the famous Nineveh Library.

Mamun, in Baghdad, also known as the House of Wisdom. Latinization of Al-Khwarizmi was the origin for the word algorithm.

Allesandi Arturo, Chilean president, worked at the National Library of Chile in the 1940s.

Jalalal-Din Akbar. The Mughal sultan of India organized a rather meticulous library in 1605. Among other things he helped catalog all the books in his library and stored them in arrangements, such as by author or calligrapher, and by language, such as Hindi, Greek, Arabic and Persian.

Avicenna. This well known Arab physician, also know as Ibn Sina, classified medical books in a Baghdad library in the 11th century AD, making them easier to find by the Arab doctors of the day who used the library.

Ashurbanipal (Assurbanipal), Assyrian King, helped developed the famous Nineveh library in the 600s BC. He was also involved in organizing the catalog in cuneiform script.

Karl Ernst von Baer, Estonian zoology professor and a founding father of developmental biology, was appointed librarian of the Russian Academy of Sciences library, St. Petersburg, in 1843.

John Billings was the U.S. surgeon instrumental in the development of the U.S. National Library of Medicine's *Index Medicus* medical journal abstracting services, which evolved into today's MEDLINE database.

St. Benedict. This Italian monk was also a librarian for the Monte Cassino monastery, near Rome, from AD 510. He was famous for his *Benedictine Rules,* which stipulate that everyone should have time to study in a library. (A translation of the rules by Dom Justin McCann in 1961 was the winner of an award for best English language translation.)

Alfredo Baquerizo worked at a public library in Ecuador, and later became president of the country in the early 1900s.

Baybars I. This famous Mamluk sultan of Egypt and Syria established the Al-Zahiriyah Library in Damascus.

Hector Berlioz, French composer, was employed as librarian at the Paris Conservatoire (a school of music) in 1838.

Jorge Luis Borges, Argentine author, was a librarian at the National Library of Argentina in the 1940s.

Federico Borromeo. This bishop of Milan founded the Ambrosian Library in Milan around 1609. It later became Italy's first public library.

Laura Bush. The current U.S. first lady, who has a master of library science degree from the University of Texas, worked as a librarian at Houston Public Library, Dawson Elementary School Library and Dallas Public Library.

Giovanni Casanova. This Italian adventurer in 1785 began a 13-year career as a librarian for Count von Waldstein in the chateau of Dux in Bohemia, Czech Republic.

Charlemagne. Also known as Charles the Great, this French king and first Holy Roman Emperor set up in AD 800 the Aachen palace library and helped expand it into a major library of the time.

Mihail Eminescu. This Romanian poet worked in the 1870s as a librarian at the Iaşi (Jassy) University Library.

Fredrich Engels, German philosopher, was appointed librarian at the Schiller-Anstalt library in the late 19th century.

Eratosthenes. This prominent ancient Greek geographer was a chief librarian at the Alexandria library in ancient Egypt, around the 2nd century BC. Significantly, all the librarians at the Alexandria Library were scholars, such as poets, critics, and grammarians. They included Zenodotus, the writer; Aristophanes, the grammarian; Callimachus, the poet who wrote the 120 volumes of Greek bibliography (a famous catalog of the library called *Pinakes*); and the only female librarian, the Platonist philosopher named Hypatia (see below).

Abigail Powers Fillmore, first wife of Millard Fillmore, president of the United States from 1850 to 1853, established the first White House Library.

Notes. U.S. presidents since Rutherford B. Hayes have had libraries named after them. These presidential libraries are more museums and archives than libraries because they mostly contain official documents related to the president's term in office. They are administered by the U.S. National Archives and Records Administration. Before Rutherford B. Hayes, outgoing presidents took their official papers with them, and some ended up in university or state libraries.

Benjamin Franklin, U.S. politician and inventor, helped set up the first subscription library and library serial in the U.S., in the 1730s.

Johann Wolfgang von Goethe, German poet, supervised the Jena University library in Germany between 1817 and 1832.

Notes. Another famous name associated with Jena University is Karl Marx, who received his Ph.D. in 1841. But he wrote the first volume of the classic book Das Kapital *(known as the Bible of the working classes) in London in 1867, making use of the British Library for much of his research.*

J. Edgar Hoover. This U.S. law enforcement officer, lawyer and first FBI director worked as a cataloger at the U.S. Library of Congress.

Notes. J. Edgar Hoover once ordered the FBI to carry out clandestine surveillance on many writers suspected of "un-American activities." Those targeted included Ernest Hemingway, for whom the FBI had a huge dossier, Sinclair Lewis and Allen Ginsberg,

David Hume, Scottish philosopher and historian, worked as a librarian at the Library of the Faculty of Advocates Edinburgh (National Library of Scotland) from 1757.

Hypatia. She was a well-known ancient Greek philosopher and mathematician alongside Plato and Plotinus. She worked for some time as a librarian at the Alexandria Library in ancient Egypt.

Immanuel Kant, German philosopher, in the middle 1700s was assistant librarian at Königsberg Castle library (now in modern day Kaliningrad).

Lao-Tzu, Chinese philosopher and founder of Taoism, was a librarian in a Henan province library in the 6th century BC, perhaps the first official librarian in China.

Philip Larkin, British poet, was also a librarian at Hull University Library, U.K.

Gottfried von Leibniz. This German philosopher and mathematician worked as a librarian in the law courts of Hanover from 1676 and later as a librarian of the duke of Braunschweig-Lüneburg. He is often considered the greatest librarian of his generation.

Mahmud I, Turkish Ottoman sultan, founded many libraries in the 18th century, such as the Faith Library, and the Ayasofya Library built in Ayasofya Mosque in St. Sophia, which is a masterpiece of Ottoman architecture.

Notes. During the Ottoman era, several other sultans founded libraries in Constantinople (Istanbul), such as Sultan Ahmet and Sultan Süleyman the Magnificent, who set up the famous library of the Süleymaniye Mosque, the largest mosque in Istanbul. Most of these libraries were situated among a collection of buildings composed of a mosque, a medrese (high school of theological studies), a primary school, a hospital, and a kitchen for the poor. The mosque libraries were also called vakif libraries and the very first official vakif library in Istanbul was set up in 1459. In Istanbul today, the Topkapi Museum Library contains many Islamic manuscripts collected by sultans, generals, and other officials of the Ottoman Empire since 1452.

Archibold Macleish, poet and assistant U.S. Secretary of State, was employed as head librarian at the U.S. Library of Congress between 1939 and 1944, an appointment that did not meet the approval of the American Library Association because he lacked the appropriate graduate degree.

Mazarin, French cardinal and a first minister to Louis XIII, founded the Mazarin Library in Paris in 1643. He employed Gabriel Naudé as its first librarian. The Library was originally set up in the Hôtel Tubeuf in Paris, eventual home for the French National Library.

Golda Meir. The former Prime Minister of Israel had earlier worked as a public librarian in the U.S. city of Milwaukee, Wisconsin.

Pope Nicholas V. A former librarian to Cosimo de' Medici (involved in setting up Italy's famous Laurentian Library), he began to build up the Vatican Library in the Vatican City in 1451.

Antonio Panizzi. This famous Italian lawyer and politician worked at the British library in the 19th century.

Philip II, King of Spain (Felipe II),

in 1563 set up the famous Escorial Library northwest of Madrid, which today has one of the best collections of Arabic manuscripts in Europe.

Notes. Among the rare Arabic manuscripts in the library is the oldest handwritten book on paper in Europe, dating from AD 1009. The Escorial Library owns some of its rare Arabic books to the lucky chance interception by Spanish ships of a small vessel in the Mediterranean Sea carrying the entire private library of important handwritten books belonging to Sharif Zaydan, sultan of Morocco. He was fleeing Spain, after Spanish Christians were gradually recapturing many cities ruled by the Moors.

Pope Pius XI. Before becoming Pope in 1922, he worked for many years in the Ambrosian Library in Milan, Italy, as chief librarian. He also helped to reorganize the Vatican Library collections in Rome. Several other popes have worked in the Vatican Library or in other libraries such as those in monasteries.

Joseph Priestley. This British chemist, who isolated many gases, including oxygen, worked as a librarian for the 2nd Earl of Shelburne, William Petty Fitzmaurice (British statesman and Prime Minister), in 1772.

Ptolemy I, Greek Macedonian general and king of Egypt, founded the famous Alexandria Library.

Henry Pu Yi. This last Chinese emperor of the Qing Dynasty in the 1960s worked as a librarian in Beijing. The story of his life was made into a successful film *The Last Emperor* in 1988.

Rama V of Chakri, King of Thailand, founded the National Library of Thailand in 1905. His palace was the first home for the library.

Count Nikolai Rumyantsev. This Russian politician's library became part of the Russian State Library.

Alexander Solzhenitsyn, Russian novelist, dramatist and poet, became a prison librarian in the infamous gulag run by Joseph Stalin.

Ainsworth Spofford, U.S. journalist, author and co-founded of UNESCO, helped develop the U.S. Library of Congress in the early 20th century.

August Strindberg, Swedish playwright and novelist, was a library assistant at the Royal Library in Stockholm, Sweden, in the late 1870s.

Marcus Trajan, Roman emperor in AD 98–117, founded the largest library in the Roman Empire.

Mao Tse-tung (Mao Zedong), Chinese leader, worked at the Beijing University Library from 1918 as an assistant to the chief librarian, who happened to be Li Ta-chao, founder of the Chinese Communist Party.

Oscar Wilde. During his time spent in Reading Prison, this British writer looked after the prison library. Among his responsibilities was taking books to other prisoners and repairing books damaged by them.

123.
40 translations of the word "library" around the world

Latin	Libraria
*Greek	Bibliotheke
Esperanto	Biblioteko / Librejo
English	Library
Spanish	Biblioteca
Italian	Biblioteca
Portuguese	Biblioteca
Romanian	Biblioteca
French	Bibliothèque
German	Bibliothek
Dutch	Bibliotheek
Swedish	Bibliotek
Icelandic	Bibliotek
Norwegian	Bibliotek
Danish	Bibliotek
*Hebrew	Bibliotek
*Russian	Biblioteka
Polish	Biblioteka
*Ukrainian	Biblioteka
*Serbian	Biblioteka
Irish	Leabharlanna
Finnish	Kirjasto
Hungarian	Könyvtár
Turkish	Kütüphane
Czech	Knihovně
Croatian	Knjižnica
*Arabic	Maktaba
*Farsi	Ketab-khaneh
*Hindi	Pustakalaya
*Bengali	Granthagar
*Urdu	Qutab-khana

*Japanese	Toshokan
*Chinese	Tushugan
*Korean	Tosogwan
Malaysian	Perpustakaan
Indonesian	Perpustakaan
*Thai	Hongsamud
Filipino	Aklatan
Swahili	Maktaba
Igbo	Ulo Akwukwo

*Indicates transliteration from non-Roman alphabet. The most common word for a library in Europe is derived from the Greek word for library, but apparently English is the only major language that uses the Latin word. In Arabic a bookstore is also called Maktaba and a library can also be called *Dâr el-Kutub* or "house of books." Finnish is the only Scandinavian language that is not an Indo-European language, hence the difference in the word for library.

Notes. *The French word for library is Bibliothèque, but the French word for bookstore is librairie. So it can sometimes cause confusion to an English-speaking tourist who mistakenly reads the sign on a bookstore to mean a public library. The Spanish word for bookstore is librería, but it can also be spelled as liberia, which in English can be confused for Liberia, an African country.*

124.
Earliest libraries

Necessity they say is the mother of Invention. It was the invention of writing that led to the need to store written documents for later use and research by others. Thus the credit to starting up the first library goes to the ancient Sumerians, who lived in the southern part of ancient Mesopotamia, now in modern-day Iraq, notably at the town of Warka where the first clay tablets have been uncovered. They devised an early form of writing, the cuneiform system, around 3500 BC. The Sumerians began to store and organize collections of their written documents (clay tablets), as "libraries" around 2700 BC. Some of the clay tablets in these 4300 year old libraries were small enough to be held in the hand.

Libraries were also set up in several other ancient civilizations apart from the Sumerians. The following are some of the other early significant libraries of the world that were founded before AD 1000. Almost all of them no longer exist, except for some preserved ruins.

Babylonia. Borsippa Library was founded 1700 BC by King Hammurabi. It is probably the second earliest significant library to be founded in ancient times after the ones set up by the Sumerians. The most important and famous book (clay tablet) was King Hammurabi's *Code of Laws*, and it is now preserved at the Louvre Museum in Paris, France.

Ancient Egypt. The most important library established by the pharaohs was the Ramses II library, in Thebes. It was founded circa 1250 BC, and its collections were composed entirely of papyrus scrolls, inscribed with hieroglyphics and hieratic script.

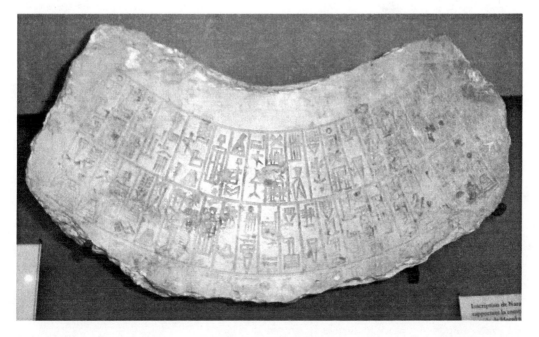

Sumerian clay tablets.

Assyria. The Nineveh Library (near modern day Mosul in northern Iraq), originally started by King Sennacherib, was developed fully around 650 BC by King Ashurbanipal (Assurbanipal). The library had over 20,000 clay tablets and was the greatest library in Assyria.

Ancient China. Several major ancient libraries were in existence in China from 500 BC. The first known Chinese librarian was the philosopher Lao-Tzu, who was appointed keeper of the royal historical records (written on silk, bamboo and wood) of the libraries of the Zhous (Chou) Dynasty rulers, in about 550 BC. The libraries were situated in the modern day Chinese province of Henan.

Ancient Greece. The three earliest and greatest libraries of the ancient Greek world were among the world's best. The Alexandria Library was founded 305 BC by King Ptolemy I Soter (after Greek Macedonian King Alexander the Great

The most important library in ancient Egypt was the one founded by Ramses II in 1250 BC.

conquered Egypt). The Serapeum Library in the temple of Serapis was founded 230 BC, while the Pergamum Library near present-day Smyrna (Izmir), Turkey, was founded 175 BC by Attalus I and Eumenes II.

Notes. With Alexandria, in ancient Egypt, the principal market for buying and selling papyrus, the ancient Greek scribes obtained their papyrus from Alexandria via the port of Byblos (which gave its name to the Bible). Following an embargo on the export of papyrus from ancient Egypt by King Ptolemy Philadelphus, the price of papyrus became expensive. So starting from about 6 BC the use of parchment, made typically from the skin of calf, goat, and sheep (which had been used in insignificant amounts since 300 BC alongside papyrus), in manuscript production was encouraged at the Pergamum Library and elsewhere in ancient Greece. Later on, vellum (which was made from specially prepared calf skin) was introduced However several Greek scholars still made papyrus rolls until the 14th century AD. The Pergamum Library was actually used as a romantic gift. Although the romance between Roman general Marc Anthony (Marcus Antonius) and Queen Cleopatra ended in tragedy, as William Shakespeare reminds us, the romance did involve one of the most expensive romantic gifts ever given for centuries before the fall of the Roman Empire, when Marc Anthony raided the Pergamum Library and gave Cleopatra its entire contents of over 200,000 parchment and papyrus scrolls books. Since this library was the main rival to the greatest library in existence then, the equally famous Alexandria Library in Egypt, the Pergamum Library col-

lections was probably worth a huge amount in today's money. Sadly the library was completely destroyed in the 3rd century AD.

Western Roman Empire. When ancient Greece became part of the expanding infant Roman Empire around 146 BC, all of its important libraries became Roman libraries. The most important library was the Ulpian Library, founded by Marcus Trajan in AD 114 in Rome. Among the important manuscripts stored in Roman libraries are the *Rylands Papyrus* and the *Codex Vaticanus.* The only Roman library that has survived the ages is the Piso Library, set up by Lucius Calpunrius circa AD 20 in the ancient city of Herculaneum, close to Pompeii. Although the eruption of the volcano Mount Vesuvius in AD 79 destroyed the library, it was discovered among the volcanic ash ruins of Herculaneum in 1754. Hundreds of preserved Piso Library papyrus and parchment scrolls, some just lumps of charcoal, can be seen today at the National Archaeological Museum in Naples, Italy.

Eastern Roman Empire. The Eastern Roman (Byzantine) Empire was carved out of the Roman Empire in AD 285 by Emperor Diocletian. Emperor Constantine the Great (who converted to Christianity in AD 311), founded the Byzantium Imperial Library in 332 in Constantinople (which he founded in 330 and is now called Istanbul in Turkey). The library rose to contain some of the most important Christian manuscripts (in parchment, vellum and papyrus) of the day, with many written in Greek, the official language of the Byzantine Empire. Much of the collection of Christian manuscripts was made possible from the late 4th century AD when Theodosius I the Great encouraged Christianity as a state religion of the Roman Empire, and put an end to pagan worship. The Byzantium Imperial Library was destroyed in the 13th century, when the armies of the 4th crusade invaded Constantinople.

Islamic Empire. The earliest significant Islamic libraries were founded during the time of the Abbasid Caliphate in Baghdad from about AD 750, when the first mosques when built. Some important manuscripts of these libraries (usually situated in a building in a mosque) included Arabic translations of important Indian texts such as *Panchatantra* and *Siddhanta.* During the ninth century, the famous library of Abbassid Caliph Al-Mamun, in Baghdad, also known as the House of Wisdom or *Bayt al-Hikmah,* had important translation departments. Here language scholars such as Hunayn ibn Ishaq translated texts dating from the civilizations of the Assyrians and Babylonians to those in Greek, Persian and Sanskrit, into Arabic. Donations from Byzantine Emperor Leo III were among the many sources for classical Greek texts. Other important Islamic libraries were founded in later caliphates, such as those of the Fatimids in Cairo, and the Saladin's Ayyubid Caliphate of the 12th century. The library of Caliph Al-Hakem II in Córdoba was the largest library in Islamic Spain, with over 500,000 manuscripts. Library books were stored not just in buildings. The 10th century Grand Vizier of Persia (now Iran), known as Abdul Kassem Ismael, was such a prolific bookworm that he took his entire library collection of over 100,000 books wherever he went with him. Employing over 500 camels, which carried the books in an alphabetic order. He probably set up the first major mobile library in history.

Notes. When the Moorish city of Toledo in Spain was captured by Christian Europe in 1085, its libraries, which contained many important scientific and medical texts of the Greek and Roman era as well as Arabic translations, changed hands. Using Jews in Spain as translators for the Arabic texts (because both Arabic and Hebrew languages have similar origins as well as scripts), all of the manuscripts in the libraries were translated into Latin at what was the famous Toledo translation school. Many indigenous Arabic texts, as well as those originally translated from classical Greek texts, were then translated into Latin. As every city and town of Islamic Spain was retaken, their library collection was translated into Latin, and this continued until 1492 when Granada, the last Moorish state, was captured, thus ending over 700 years of Arab colonization that began in AD 711. It is believed that the fall of Toledo and the opening of its many libraries to European scholars of the day was one of the contributing factors (along with the knowledge gained from manuscripts written during the Greek and Roman periods which were brought back by the crusaders from Byzantium in the 13th century) to the revival of intellectual learning in Christian Europe prior to the Renaissance. Among the many benefits introduced by the work of the translation school at Toledo was the adoption of Arabic numerals and the symbol zero, an Arabic word.

For a list of the oldest existing libraries today see entry **315**.

World Records for Books, Periodicals and Bookstores

Evidence suggests that Neanderthals 170,000 years ago almost certainly could not speak in a primitive form of language because the arrangement of their larynxes prevented full vocalization. Communication no doubt took place by other means such as hand gestures and grunts and shouts. Modern humans (*Homo sapiens sapiens*), who appeared about 120,000 years ago (first in Africa, then later in the Asia-Pacific region, Europe and the Americas), fared much better. Their larynxes were well developed for speech. Hence the earliest forms of modern human language probably began about 90,000 years ago, but it would probably have been many thousands of years later before humans attempted any form of handwriting.

Before humans invented writing, they first drew pictures. The oldest radiocarbon-dated cave paintings in the world go back to 50,000 BC. Sumerian was the language of perhaps the first civilization in the world (based in what is now modern day Iraq), and it was spoken extensively around 6000 BC. Then from about 3500 BC, or over 5000 years ago, people finally began writing.

Prior to the invention of paper, clay tablets were used as writing materials in ancient Sumer, Babylonia and Assyria and the later civilizations that overran these. While the ancient Egyptians, Greeks and Romans used papyrus in addition to clay, later on, parchment and vellum were the chief materials used in Europe and the Middle East, replacing papyrus. In some instances tablets dipped in wax were used as well. Silk, bamboo, bones, bronze and linen were the main writing materials in China, Korea, and many other East Asian cultures that had written forms of their languages before the arrival of paper. On the Indian subcontinent and in Southeast Asia, lontar leaves, tree barks such as birch bark, palm leaves as well as bamboo were used as writing materials. Across the Atlantic in the Americas, before the arrival of Columbus, for ancient civilizations such as the Maya, Moche, and Aztec, the chief materials for writing were stone, wood, and deerskin.

Following the invention of writing, three writing systems were eventually developed over the centuries:

1. Alphabetic writing systems were used for languages such as Arabic, Latin, English, Greek, Russian, Hebrew, Malay, and Korean.

2. Syllabic writing systems (known as syllabaries or pseudo-alphabets) were used on the Indian subcontinent and in East Asia for languages such as Hindi, Khmer, Bengali, Burmese, Javanese (Indonesia), Thai, Tibetan, and Tamil (Sri Lanka), as well as some non–Asian languages such as Amharic.

3. Pictographic, logographic and ideographic writing systems were first used for Sumerian cuneiforms and ancient Egyptian and Mayan hieroglyphics, and ideograms are used today in China and Japan.

Today there are more than 6000 languages and some 53 scripts. The Khmer (Cambodian) script is the largest with 74 letters, 39 vowels, 10 digits, and 14 other punctuation marks. One of the Melanesian languages of the Solomon Islands in the Pacific Ocean called Rotokas has the shortest alphabet, with only 11 letters. Modern Chinese script com-monly uses just over 8,000 ideograms (but the total number of ideograms in existence is between 40,000 and 50,000). A Japanese child must learn about 2,000 Chinese ideograms, or *Kanji*, as well as two Japanese phonetic scripts, *Hiragana* and *Katakana*, both with about 45 symbols. All three make up the Japanese script. A Roman alphabet (for use in transliteration) was introduced in Japan in 1981 and called *Romanjii*, and another in 1958 for the Chinese, called *Pinyin*. The Korean script is not an ideographic one but a full alphabet using modified symbols adapted from Chinese script. Korean script has two Roman alphabetic systems, the McCune-Reischauer System and the Korean Ministry of Education System.

Notes. *In March 2001, an international forum was hosted in Baghdad by the Iraqi government to celebrate the 5000th birthday of the invention of writing.*

125.
10 oldest existing written works

The following are major inscriptions, manuscripts and text fragments from around the world. Most date from well before AD 1, and are thus thousands of years old. Since radiocarbon dating and other criteria for determining age cannot always guarantee precise dates, approximations or rough estimates are a way to get round this.

1. Sumer, Babylonia and Assyria. Clay tablets from Sumer (in southern Mesopotamia, near the Tigris and Euphrates valley of present-day Iraq), inscribed in Sumerian cuneiform writing, are dated from circa 3500 BC, and are thus about 5500 years old. Some of these tablets were discovered by French archaeologists in 1877 at the ancient town of Lagash (now Telloh in southern Iraq). Many museums around the world, such as the Louvre in Paris, display many fragments from these ancient clay tablets, including the oldest storybooks such as *The Epic of Gilgamesh* (the biblical story of Noah and the great flood) and *The Lord of Aratta*. A number of scripts based on the Sumerian cunei - form appeared later on, notably the Elamite script. Fragments of clay tablets

found at Suse (Susa), the capital of the ancient kingdom of Elam, in south-western modern Iran, were dated at 2900 BC. When the Sumer civilization declined, it was taken over by the civilizations of Babylonia and Assyria. Several 4200-year-old cuneiform clay tablets inscribed in Akkadian, the language of ancient Babylonia and Assyria dating from about 2650 BC, have been uncovered. Like the clay tablets from Sumer, museums today also display many fragments of these ancient clay tablets from Babylonia and Assyria. Later on in time, the Hittites, (originally from parts of what is today modern Turkey), who overran the Babylonian Empire, began inscribing hieroglyphic writings on clay and stone around 1400 BC. Some were written in Akkadian cuneiform, the rest in Hittite hieroglyphics. In 1906 German archaeologists discovered thousands of Hittite clay tablets from the ruins of the ancient Hittite capital Hattusa, (near the modern Turkish town of Boghazkšy, east of Ankara).

Notes. There also exist stone fragments of archaic pre-cuneiform inscriptions, (known as the early Uruk period inscriptions of Sumer) that are older than the Lagash tablets. Three such examples are the Hoffman Tablet, preserved at the General Theological Seminary in New York and another stone tablet at the Pennsylvania University Museum of Archaeology and Anthropology in Philadelphia, both date from 5100 BC. The other pre-cuneiform relic is known as the monuments Blau (or monuments blue), and are pieces of greenish stone housed at the Ashmolean Museum and the British Museum in the U.K. and dated at 4800 BC. All 7000-year-old fragments were retrieved from the royal tombs in the city of Ur (the biblical birthplace of Abraham)

in the 1920s. Even though these are not regarded as full-length examples of human writing, as they are merely short inscriptions and often numerical, nevertheless they are the oldest surviving samples of any form of primitive human writing today. Another empire close to Babylonia worth mentioning, the Persian Empire (occupying parts of modern-day Iran) also produced many ancient texts. At the city of Persepolis founded by Darius I, near today's Shiraz, several cuneiform inscriptions on clay tablets in Old Persian have been found dating back to 560 BC. These tablets were related to the administration of Darius I. But they were not in significant numbers as they were eclipsed by the number inscriptions in Elamite and Aramaic languages also found in Persepolis, one reasons being that not much of the population in Persia were fluent in Old Persian. Later on around 100 BC, Persian was written in

Babylonian clay tablets.

an indigenous alphabet called Pahlavi. When the Arabs conquered Persia in AD 651, Persian was written in a modified version of the Arabic script. Modern Persian is called Farsi.

2. Egypt. Before the ancient Egyptians began using papyrus to write on, inscriptions were made on stone (clay was not available in the Nile Valley). The earliest simple hieroglyphics were in use around 5000 BC (predynastic Egypt, or before Menes, the founding king of the 1st Egyptian Dynasty). The oldest known hieroglyphic inscriptions today are those of the Naqada culture, dating back to 4000 BC and preserved at the Ashmolean Museum in Oxford, U.K. Some of the inscriptions depict the work of Shera, the priest of Send, and hence the stone is known as the *Send Inscription*. The ancient Egyptians first used papyrus reeds, from the plant *Cyperus papyrus* (which gave rise to the word paper), for writing around 3400 BC. The *Prisse Papyrus* made

in ancient Egypt around 2300 BC is the oldest existing written work on papyrus. It was named after Prisse d'Avennes, the French Egyptologist, and the contents of the papyrus, written in hieratic script, are based on the teachings of Ptah-Hotep, Grand Vizier under the 5th Egyptian Dynasty Pharaoh Isesi (Izezi). The National Library of France now houses the 4000 year old papyrus. The *Book of the Dead*, another ancient Egyptian papyrus scroll, dates from 1800 BC. Discovered in Egypt in 1799 by a French archaeologist, the *Rosetta Stone*, dating from 195 BC, was used as a dictionary to translate the first Egyptian hieroglyphics.

Notes. Today the ancient Egyptian language has evolved into the Coptic language, which is still used by minority Christians in Egypt who belong to the Coptic Church, founded when St. Mark introduced Christianity to Egypt during the reign of Emperor Nero in AD 37-68. The Coptic Church is thus much older than the Roman Catholic Church, as

Sample of ancient Egyptian papyri.

The Ashmolean Musuem in Oxford is home to many ancient inscriptions on clay tablets from Sumer, Assyria and Babylonia.

Christianity became the state religion of the Roman Empire only in the 4th century AD. The Coptic language is written in the Coptic script, an adaptation of the Greek alphabet. In ancient Egypt, hieroglyphics took a long time to read and were thus used mostly on buildings and tombs.

For other uses, a hieratic script was developed around 2000 BC for writing on papyrus, and was later replaced by the more simplified demotic script. The Coptic script is believed to have evolved from the demotic script, before being improved with the Greek alphabet.

3. China. Several Chinese poetic inscriptions, written in ancient Chinese ideographs and dating from 2000 BC, were discovered on ox bones such as the scapulae and on tortoise shells. They are known today as the "oracle bones." Some of the largest surviving samples can be seen at the Taiwan National Palace Museum near Taipei. The oldest complete surviving example of ancient Chinese literature is the *I Ching*, also known in the West as the *Book of Change*, written on bones probably around 1800 BC (just after the start of the first Chinese Dynasty know as Xia or Hsia circa 2000 BC). The original work was first written by Fu Xi (also spelled as Fu Hsi, inventor of the calendar and credited with inventing the Chinese script). But the *I Ching* has been enlarged by other writers such as King Wen and his son Tan in 1150 BC during the Shang Dynasty. Centuries later, commentaries from Confucius were added around 510 BC. Scholars believe that the *Book of Change* is the basis for three Asian religions: Confucianism, Taoism, and Zen Buddhism. Today you can buy several versions of the *I Ching* in bookstores around the world.

> *Notes. The Chinese script is the oldest existing script in the world, and after more than 4000 years it has not changed much in structure, apart from a reduction in the number of characters.*

4. India and Pakistan. The ancient Indus Valley civilization, occupying parts of the Indian subcontinent such as Harappa and Mohenjo-daro in present-day Pakistan,

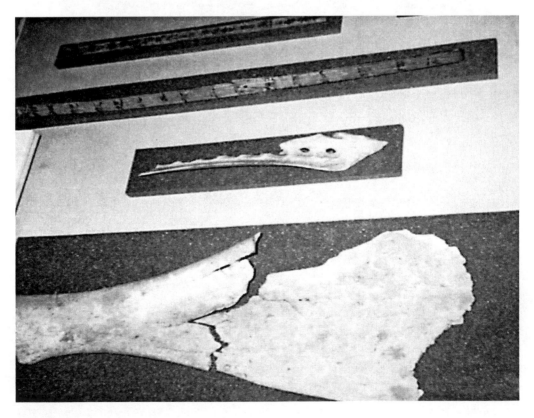

Oracle bones.

The Chinese script used today goes back thousands of years. These stone inscriptions date back to 200 B.C.

produced ideograhic inscriptions (in a partially deciphered Indus Valley script adopted from Sumerian pictograms) on faience and ivory which have been dated to around 2100 BC. The most significant ancient language used on the subcontinent was Sanskrit, from which such languages as Hindi and Bengali were derived. Some of the oldest Sanskrit texts (written originally on palm leaves) from the region are the *Vedas*, epic religious poems that form the basis of Hinduism, the oldest religion in the world. The *Rig Veda* or *Rg Veda,* the oldest of the *Vedas,* dates from 1710 BC. Those that are extant are but not in their original form, having been expanded by generations of several authors. Written works in Brahmi script (from which all scripts used on the Indian subcontinent developed), were in existence from 650 BC. Fragments of Tamil texts from southern

India are among the oldest of the Brahmi-derived texts, the earliest dating from 500 BC. The oldest existing complete Sanskrit manuscripts written in Brahmi script are the work of the Indian grammarian Panini in circa 400 BC. The laws of King Asoka (who once ruled a large portion of modern day India), written in Brahmi and inscribed on monumental columns and pillars, notably at Buddhist Sarnath Shrine, east of Varanasi, mostly date from 290 BC. The oldest extant Buddhist texts from the Indian subcontinent not inscribed on stone are the Gandhran Buddhist Scrolls, which date from about AD 1 and were written in Kharosthi script. Today Hindi, the most widely used language on the Indian subcontinent, is written in the Brahmi script known as Devanagari.

Notes. Buddhism (the second oldest religion in the world) originally began in

India from the 6th century BC, and several of the oldest Buddhists texts came from India. However over the centuries starting from about the 4th century AD, during the Gupta dynasty, Hinduism began to overshadow Buddhism, of which there are today only about 6 million followers. Hinduism is the major religion in India, with over 800 million adherents.

5. Crete. Clay tablets discovered in Knossos in Crete by British archaeologist Arthur Evans date from the Minoan civilization of 1500 BC. They were written in what is called Linear A script and later in Linear B script, and are the earliest texts found in Europe. Unlike Linear B, which is more widely understood by scholars and is an early form of Greek, Linear A is currently not completely deciphered.

6. Syria and Palestine. The Semites who lived in parts of Syria (Aram) and Palestine (Canaan) created the first known crude alphabetic system around 1800 BC or about 3800 years ago. It was an improvement on the ancient Egyptian hieroglyphics and hieratic script, but was not a picture-based writing. The oldest known Semitic alphabetic inscriptions were found on clay tablets in Syria in 1929 at Ras Shamra (near the ancient city of Ugarit), and also close to the Sinai Peninsula in 1904 by British Egyptologist Flinders Petrie, both dating from 1600 BC. Scholars agree that the Semitic alphabet is the origin of all other alphabets, as the three main branches (North Semitic, South Semitic and Greek) are the ancestors of today's modern alphabets. The letter "O" is said by some to be the oldest letter of the alphabet, as it has remained virtually unchanged since the Semites first used it. The Semitic language spoken in ancient Syria, known as Aramaic, became the lingua franca of the ancient Middle East for many centuries.

7. Phoenicia. The Phoenicians living along the coast of the Mediterranean Sea corresponding to modern day Lebanon and Syria, especially at Byblos (near present day Beirut) as well as in parts of Tunisia, developed an alphabetic system related to the Semitic alphabet for their language, called Punic. Phoenician clay tablets such as the one discovered by a French archaeological team in 1923 belonging to a Phoenician King of Byblos called Ahiram, known as the *Ahiram Inscriptions*, have been dated to about 1260 BC, but the alphabet was created much earlier. The Greek script, (ancestor to all European scripts), the Brahmi script (ancestor to most Asian scripts), as well as the Arabic and Hebrew alphabets were all influenced by the Phoenician alphabet. The most famous of all Phoenician inscriptions is King Mesha's *Moabite stone*, parts of it written in Aramaic, and dating from 880 BC. Discovered at Dibon, Jordan, it is preserved at the Louvre Museum in Paris.

8. Israel. The oldest surviving example of Old Hebrew writing (which developed directly from Aramaic) were discovered in the 1930s at the Lachish Palace, southeast of Jerusalem in Israel, dating from 700 BC. But the oldest Hebrew documents are believed to date from 1400 BC. The Dead Sea Scrolls discovered in 1947 are among the oldest existing extensive papyrus manuscripts in Hebrew. The oldest of the scrolls, know as the *Isaiah* scroll, contains parts of the Jewish Old Testament and date from 300 BC. Fragments of the Dead Sea Scrolls are now housed in a building called The Shrine of the Book, in the Israel Museum in Jerusalem. The

Nash Papyrus preserved at the Cambridge University Library in the U.K. dates from 100 BC and is written in ancient Hebrew. It contains the biblical text of the 10 Commandments. The first five, and oldest books of the Jewish Old Testament (*Genesis, Exodus, Leviticus, Numbers* and *Deuteronomy*) are known as the *Torah* or *Pentateuch* and are traditionally said to have been written by Moses. The following are a selection of the oldest books of the Hebrew Old Testament and the approximate first year of events mentioned in the books: *Book of Exodus*, 1300 BC; *Samuel*, 1020 BC; *David*, 980 BC; *Solomon*, 960 BC; *Elijah*, 850 BC; *Psalms*, 700 BC; *Ezekiel*, 597 BC. Some scholars say that the oldest book in the Bible is *Job* because the script, in which some sections of the book was written on clay tablets, is an archaic form of early Aramaic script dating before 1000 BC and *Job* also makes references to the great flood. But parts of *Genesis,* the first book of the Jewish Old Testament, which includes the stories taken from the Sumerian *Epic of Gilgamesh*, about Noah and the great flood, are believed to have been originally recorded on clay tablets around 2900 BC. Despite these few ancient clay texts, biblical stories were not recorded in detail in the early days of Judaism but passed from generation to generation orally. Some early stories managed to be inscribed in detail on stone or clay tablets such as the Sumerian clay tablets described above and the *Moabite stone* (880 BC). The date at which the biblical stories of the Jewish Old Testament were probably first written extensively on papyrus (and then later on parchment), by Jewish scribes in Babylon, was circa 586 BC. Around this time armies of Nebuchadnezzar had destroyed Jerusalem and took the people of Judah

(the Israelites) into captivity. Eventually over the centuries, before the birth of Jesus, other stories of the Jewish Old Testament were written and added to existing texts (the various books of the Bible existed separately for a while, before they were put together to become the complete Bible as we know it today). Most of the older texts of the Bible were written in Aramaic (almost extinct today), then translated into Old Hebrew, which is now extinct. Others parts were written in Greek and Modern Hebrew. Most books in the Christian New Testament from the gospels to the *Book of Revelation* were mostly written in Greek, with some in Latin, even though Jesus spoke Aramaic; they were completed between AD 45 and 110. To some extent, a great deal of the books in the New Testament was believed to have been written by the Apostle Paul. The Bible (written over a period of 2500 years), is thus one the oldest existing compiled works in the world. Today the Bible contains 24 books (Jewish Bible) or 66 to 73 books (Christian Bible).

Notes. *The Bible is the best-selling book of all time and the most translated book. In the whole of the 20th century, over 4 billion copies were printed around the world in over 1000 languages. Mao Zedong's* Little Red Book *(containing quotations and summaries of his work with the Chinese Communist Party) is the second best-selling book of all time, with over 500 million copies published to meet the demands of China's huge population. Today just three books have broken the 100 million barrier, one of them being* The Guinness Book of World Records. *The Bible is not only an interesting book to read it has also been used for other purposes. For instance the founder of modern Ethiopia,*

The Bible is the best-selling book in the world and is also the most translated book in the world.

Emperor Menelik II, a deeply religious leader, is said to have eaten some pages of the Bible each time he felt ill, because somehow he felt better the next day. He once ate all of the pages of the Book of Kings, as part of a massive cure for flu. The Bible was also subjected to severe translation restrictions during the time of the Vatican Inquisition. In 1536 in Belgium, William Tyndale, who had earlier painstakingly translated the Latin Bible into English, was strangled and burnt at the stake for his efforts. "All" copies of his translation had been burnt in 1530 in London.

9. Greece. The Greeks created the first true alphabetic system, by using symbols not just for consonants but also for vowels. The first two letters of the Greek alphabet, alpha and beta, was adopted to form the word "alphabet." The earliest Greek text, in the form of Mycenean Lin-

ear B tablets, dates from 1100 BC. The oldest works of classical Greek literature are those of Homer, who completed his epic poems *The Odyssey* and *The Iliad* around 810 BC, and Hesiod, in 700 BC. Laws written by the statesman Dracon in Athens (the very first in Greece) date from 620 BC. The oldest extant papyrus fragments written in Greek make up the *Persae of Timotheus*, written in about 320 BC. *Papyrus 53*, or *P53*, is the oldest existing biblical text written in Greek on papyrus, as it dates from the middle 2nd century AD. It is part of the collection of ancient biblical papyri fragments at the John Rylands University Library in Manchester, U.K. The oldest extant and complete parchment manuscript from Europe is the *Codex Vaticanus*, a Greek bible dating from AD 300 which is now housed in the Vatican Library; it is also the oldest complete Bible in existence in the world. The

Codex Sinaiticus (preserved in the British Library), dating from AD 350, is the oldest known parchment manuscript of the New Testament in Greek.

Notes. The Codex Vaticanus *was so tightly guarded by the Vatican Library that it was not available to scholars until 1889, after more than 400 years of secrecy.*

10. Roman Empire. Written texts in Latin (Roman script) first began to appear around 600 BC, the earliest known surviving example being a golden fibula, or cloak pin, with Latin inscriptions discovered in the ancient Roman city of Praeneste (today the city of Palestrina, not far from Rome, in the Italian region of Latium or Lazio). The cloak pin is now preserved in a museum in Rome. However the first major authors in Latin were Livius Andronicus around 300 BC and Ennius circa 210 BC. The Latin alphabet was developed from the alphabet of early settlers in what is now Tuscany, Italy, called the Etruscans, who in turn had copied their own Etruscan alphabet from the Greek alphabet (around 800 BC). The word "Latin" is the equivalent of the word "south" because it was the people living south of the Etruscans who began writing in a modified form of the Etruscan alphabet (a precursor to the Latin script). The best known inscription in the Etruscan alphabet is the *Marsiliana Tablet,* discovered in the valley of the Albegna River and dating from 700 BC. The oldest extant manuscript of the

The Codex Sinaiticus **(by permission of the British Library, ADD 43725 f244V-245).**

New Testament in Latin is probably the *Harley Latin Gospels,* which dates from the 4th century AD. It can be seen in the British Library. Although Latin is now used officially only in the Vatican City, the Roman script (with modifications) is used in most European languages, as well as widely outside Europe. The other main scripts used today in Europe are the Cyrillic and Greek alphabets.

Notes. One living organism has existed for thousands of years around the time most of these 10 categories of ancient texts was written. It is however a plant called Bristlecone pine tree (Pinus langueva), which first appeared around 6200 BC. One specimen still alive today, and identified in 1957, is called Methuselah (named in the Bible as the oldest man who ever lived). Methuselah seeded around 2766 BC and is thus more than 4700 years old. Methuselah, which botanists believe will live for another 400

The Harley Latin Gospels (by permission of the British Library, Harl 1775 f390-391).

years, exists among the White Mountains of California in the U.S. From AD 3, parchment and later vellum was preferred over papyrus by Roman scholars for writing manuscripts. By AD 400 parchment had displayed papyrus as the chief material for manuscript production in Europe, until the introduction of paper in the 12th century. The basic structure of a modern book today with pages bound on the left side, to allow pages to be opened easily, was developed from the Roman parchment codex. This was a deviation from the papyrus or parchment scroll, which had to be wound and rewound after use. However both forms of manuscripts, i.e. roll or codex form, were used simultaneously until the introduction of printing with moveable type in the 15th century, which saw the ascendance of the codex form over the roll form. Christian libraries in Medieval Europe after the fall of the Western Roman Empire were the first to employ the codex form extensively for manuscripts. Some of these early collections survive today in libraries such as Dublin's Chester Beatty Library in the Irish Republic. The Latin script in many codices tended to be mostly in capital letters, or majuscule (and had various forms such as uncials and square and rustic capitals). But from the 8th century, during the time of Charlemagne, manuscripts with a combination of capitals and small letters (or minuscule) were used.

126.
Earliest written works in German

The German monk Ulfilas (a bishop of the West Goths and the religious leader of the Visigoths) produced several works including translations of the Bible from Latin and Greek to German in AD 320. Parchment fragments from his works appear in religious manuscripts, which date from the 5th and 6th centuries. One of the oldest extant non-religious texts in German is *Hildebrandslied*, written in the middle 9th century. Apart from ancient Runic inscriptions dating from AD 200 and carved on wood and stone, Ulfilas' work is the oldest surviving German literary text, although it was written in old German, or Gothic.

127.
Earliest written works in Mayan

Popol Vuh, is a Mayan hieroglyphic inscription on stone stelae, describing the creation of the world. It dates from AD 200. Today the ancient Mayan language is still spoken in parts of southern Mexico, such as Yucatan State, and Central America, such as Guatemala.

Notes. The Olmec civilization, the first developed civilization in the Americas (and located in the states of Veracruz and Tabasco) invented a hieroglyphic writing system around 1200 BC, and influenced the later development of the Mayan hieroglyphic system.

128.
Earliest written works in Arabic

The earliest important texts in Arabic (which developed from the ancient Nabatean script of northern Arabia) date from about AD 400. Islam dates from the time Muhammed fled to Medina from Mecca, circa 622. The standard text of the original Koran, or *Quran* (which has 114 chapters or *Suras),* was completed between 650 and 651. It was written for Othman, the 3rd caliph, who was the first to order that the various separate writings of Muhammed be combined together into a single book. This Koran, called the *Mushaf of Othman,* is preserved and on display today in a library in Tashkent, Uzbekistan. The second oldest existing version of the Koran (attributed to Imam Al-Hasan al-Basri), dates back to AD 697. The oldest existing non–Islamic Arabic manuscript is the *Mount Sinai Arabic Codex 151* (an Arabic translation of the Bible), written in 867.

A handwritten Koran dating from AD 1280.

129.
Earliest written works in Japanese

Two of the oldest existing manuscripts written in Japanese are *Kojiki* (AD 681) and *Nihon Shoki* (AD 720). Both of them detail the ancient history of Japan. Although Japan is situated close to China (which has written works over 4000 years old), Japan had no written language until Korean scholars in AD 405 introduced Chinese (*Kanji*) script for writing documents in Japanese. Later on in the 9th century AD, the phonetic syllabary *Kana* (invented by Kukai, a Japanese Shingon Buddhist priest) helped to simplify writing in Japanese. The Chinese script was also used in Korea, until King Sejong of the Chosun (Chos?n) Dynasty invented the current Korean alphabet called *Hangul* (*Hankul*) in AD 1446.

> **Notes.** *The diary belonging to Kino Tsurayuki, a prominent Japanese poet and governor of Tosa Province, known as Tosa Nikki or The Tosa Diary, is the oldest existing one in the world. It records his travels in Kyoto, Japan and was written in Kana in AD 935. Japan is probably the only country that uses three different scripts concurrently. While Chinese ideographic scripts or Kanji represents ideas, and objects, the phonetic Kana scripts Hiragana and Katakana represent sounds only.*

130.
Earliest written works in French

One of the earliest written major texts in French is the *Strasbourg Oath (Serments de Strasbourg)* written on parchment in AD 842. It is an Old French version (Western Franks) of an oath sworn by two of Charlemagne's sons. The oldest extant epic is *La Chanson de Roland*, an Anglo-Norman poem which dates from the early 11th century.

Notes. *During the French Revolution of* *the 18th century, the skins of some of the aristocrats executed with the guillotine, were used by a bookbinder in Meudon, France, to produce a copy of the new Constitution of 1791 drafted by the Constituent Assembly.*

131.
Earliest written works in Spanish

Two versions of Spanish exist today in Spain, Catalan and Castilian Spanish. The former is spoken in areas of Spain known as Catalonia, the Balearic Islands and in Andorra, while the latter is the official language of Spain. Manuscripts found near the Liga region in Spain, and written in Castilian Spanish, date from the 10th century AD. The best known earliest epic is probably the 11th century *Poema del Cid* (Poem of Cid), about a military commander Rodrigo Diáz de Vivar who fought against the Arab occupation of Valencia.

Notes. *The Basque language (known locally as Euskara), spoken in the Basque Provinces of Spain, is more than 2000 years old (much older than Spanish), as it is one of the few surviving languages in Europe that existed before Latin became the dominant language. The oldest existing documents in Basque date from the 8th century AD. Basque has contributed just a handful of words to European languages; one such is "bizarre." Poems written by King Sancho I of Portugal in the 11th century are among the oldest existing Portuguese texts today. The oldest extant text in Catalan Spanish (found in Barcelona) date from the 12th century. On April 23 of each year, which is St. George's Day in Spain (known as Festa de Sant Jordi in Catalan Spanish, after the patron saint of Catalonia who famously killed a dragon), people present each other with books and red roses, in a massive celebration of reading. While the celebrations, dubbed as "a gigantic literary orgy" by the Spanish press, are going on, Gambetta Square in Barcelona is the big meeting place for authors and publishers. Armies of booksellers also take possession of roads such as the famous Las Ramblas, for the whole day. On April 23, 1996, UNESCO launched the United Nations World International Book Day based on St. George's Day in Spain. Hence April 23 is a big day for books in Spain and the international community.*

132.
Earliest written works in English and Irish

The oldest comprehensive Old English (or Anglo-Saxon) texts date from about AD 680. *Beowulf,* a fascinating poem of a Danish warrior, was written around AD 885, at a time when armed Danish (Viking) raids into what is now

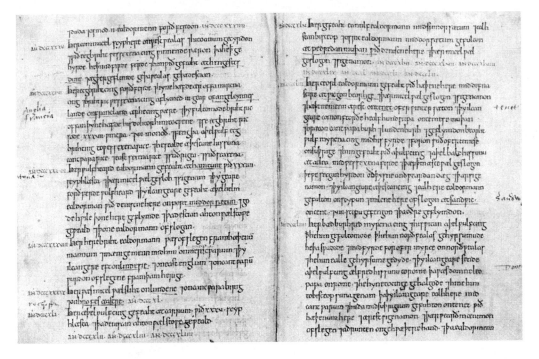

Anglo-Saxon Chronicles. **This 9th century book provides a year by year history of England from the Roman Conquest, and was updated until the 12th century (by permission of the British Library, (Cott. Tib.C.ii F93-94V).**

the U.K. were common. It is the oldest surviving Old English manuscript and is now housed in the British Library. The 9th century *Anglo-Saxon Chronicle*, written around the time of King Alfred, is the oldest extant historical document in Old English. The oldest comprehensive legal document in English (Middle English) is the *Magna Carta,* which dates from 1215, during the time of King John I, and describes terms of agreement between the king and the barons on issues such as taxes. Another significant existing manuscript written in Middle English is the *Provisions of Oxford* of King Henry III, written in 1258. This was a governmental reform document (written on parchment) forced upon the king by the leader of the barons, Simon de Montfort, limiting the power of the king. Although papermills were not set up in the U.K. until 1494,

paper made outside the U.K. was imported. The oldest extant major document written in Middle English on paper was a letter written to King Henry III by the son of the duke of Navarre, Spain in 1275.

Notes. Most of the earliest surviving religious manuscripts written before the 10th century in the U.K. are not in Old English but in Latin, because most of the earliest religious documents in Europe were written either in Greek or Latin. The most ancient religious documents were written in Hebrew and Aramaic. Christianity itself reached England in AD 596 with the arrival of St. Augustine of Canterbury, who was sent by the Pope. There are three important Latin texts written in the U.K. The Lindisfarne Gospels were written and illustrated in AD 698 by the monk Eadfrith on the En-

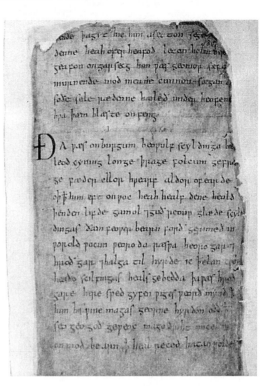

Beowulf, the first great literary masterpiece in English (by permission of the British Library, (CotT. Vit. A.XV f133V-134).

glish Island of Lindisfarne. The Historia Ecclesiastica Gentis Anglorum (Ecclesiastical History of the English People), finished in 731 by the Venerable Bede, a monk in Jarrow, is the earliest text on the early days of Christianity in the U.K. and is preserved at the British Library. Incidentally King Alfred and his staff did manage to translate Bede's work from Latin into Old English about 150 years later. The Domesday Book is not a religious book but a sort of official record of landholdings in the U.K. Its compilation began in 1085 during the reign of William the Conqueror

The oldest texts in Irish (Gaelic) existing today in Roman script date from AD 650. But Irish as a spoken language dates much further back, having been introduced into Ireland by the Celts around 500 BC. This makes Irish Gaelic, alongside Latin and Greek, one of the three oldest vernacular languages today in Europe. The Irish alphabet was first written in the ancient Celtic Ogham alphabet and the oldest extant texts today are inscriptions that date back to the 4th century AD. After St. Patrick arrived in Ireland (to help in the spread of Christianity) in 432, the Roman script was used to write Irish texts. A form of Celtic Gaelic was introduced in Scotland (Scottish Gaelic) in the 5th century AD.

Notes. The Celts also inhabited the British Isles from around 2000 BC, before the Romans led by Julius Caesar invaded in 55 BC. But the lands ruled by the Romans did not include Ireland and much of Scotland (divided from England by Hadrian's Wall). This meant the influence of Latin on the development of

Gaelic happened much later, compared to English, the reason why Irish and Scot- *tish Gaelic have fewer words originating from Latin.*

133.
Earliest written works in Dutch

The manuscript called *Wachtendonk Psalm*, fragments of which survive today, were written around AD 910, and are the oldest of several religious manuscript fragments from 10th century Netherlands.

Notes. Most written work in European languages not mentioned above, such as early Slavic Cyrillic texts in Russian and Serbo-Croat as well as manuscripts in early Scandinavian languages (such as Old Norse, with the exception of Finnish), all date from the 10th to 12th century AD. The oldest extant Scandinavian manuscript is the Necrologium Lunense, *written in AD 1123. The oldest East Asian text (excluding Chinese, Korean and Japanese texts) are Tibetan (7th century); Javanese (used in Indonesia, 8th century); Burmese (11th century); Khmer (12th century) and Thai (13th century). Vietnamese, Malaysian and In-* *donesian texts are all written today in the Roman script, although the last two (technically the same Malay language) were once written in the Arabic script, before European colonialism. The oldest Malay texts date from the 9th century. Vietnamese texts were previously written in the Chinese script until the 17th century. Out of the 53 alphabets in use today for over 6000 language, both the Roman and the Arabic scripts are the most commonly used international alphabets, as they are used officially by several countries. For most languages around the world today, writing is horizontally from left to right. There are however some exceptions. Arabic and Hebrew documents are both written horizontally from right to left, while Chinese and Japanese can typically be written in vertical columns from right to left or horizontally from left to right, or from right to left.*

134.
Earliest written works from Africa

Outside of Egypt, the African languages (totaling more than 2000 at the last count) with the oldest ingenious alphabet are Ge'ez, Amharic, Old Nubian and Berber. The earliest inscriptions on granite steles in ancient Ge'ez script used in ancient Ethiopia (the kingdom of Aksum) date from AD 190. Ge'ez as a lan- guage dates back to the 1st century BC when the language and its script was first used in the Sebaean Kingdom in southern parts of the Arabian Peninsula (modern-day Yemen and southern Saudi Arabia). Today Ge'ez is not an official language in Ethiopia anymore, having been superseded by a later version of the language called Amharic, but Ge'ez is still used as a liturgical language in the Ethiopian Coptic Church. The oldest extant Ge'ez text in parchment are 4th century AD religious texts, most notably the Coptic Christian works of St. Frumentius (Abba Salama), the first bishop of Ethiopia. Christianity first reached Ethiopia (the second country to adopt the religion in Africa after Egypt) in AD 350; the nation managed to hang onto this religious faith while most of its neighbors adopted Islam. Old Nubian was spoken in parts of northern Sudan (known also as Kush or Nubia in ancient times, with its capital at Meroe near modern-day Khartoum) before Arabic was introduced. It has written text, based on both Egyptian hieroglyphics and the Coptic script. But today modern Nubian (Nile Nubian) is hardly in written form, although some modern texts have been written in Arabic script. The Berbers were the original inhabitants of north-western Africa (Morocco, Algeria, Tunisia and western Libya), before the Arabs invaded North Africa from the 7th century AD. One group of Berbers, called the Tuareg, speak a dialect called Tamashek which had been in a written form long before the introduction of Arabic. The ingenious alphabet of Tamashek is related to the Phoenician script (see entry **125**). The Ethiopian Amharic language adopted its ingenious script from the one used in the Sebaean Kingdom, but Ge'ez today is still written in the original Sebaean script. Old Nubian, in its earliest form, was first written in what was called the Meroitic script, (based on Egyptian hieroglyphics, due to its proximity with ancient Egypt), which dates from about 400 BC. Later, around the 8th century AD, Old Nubian adopted the Coptic script (based on a pre–Islamic script used in Christian parts of Egypt be-

fore it was Arabized). One of the oldest written works in Coptic Old Nubian script is *The Old Nubian Miracle of Saint Menas*, written on parchment circa AD 900, and now housed in the British Museum. A Coptic Psalter found in 1984 in Beni Suef, south of Cairo, Egypt, and dating from AD 300, is the oldest existing complete handwritten book (in an alphabetical script) in Africa. This Coptic book of Psalms is on display at the Coptic Museum in Cairo, Egypt.

Notes. Even though the Ethiopians had written versions of their Amharic language since the 3rd century AD, neighboring Somalia had no written version of the Somali language until 1972. Not counting Arabic, used officially in many parts of Africa where Islam is the official or majority religion, most of sub–Saharan Africa today did not have any indigenous texts until the arrival of the Arabs in the 9th century, mostly in the areas south of the Sahara and the northeastern coast of Africa). Two reasons for this were the presence of a strong oral tradition going back for centuries, and the crucial fact that only northern and north-eastern portion of Africa was directly exposed to the civilizations of ancient Egypt, the Roman Empire and the Fertile Crescent, the cradle of early civilizations. The huge Sahara desert and the tropical rainforests formed some natural barriers preventing direct exposure of the early civilizations to other parts of Africa. In the Middle Ages, when Islam managed to penetrate the Sahara Desert, reliable early texts about African arts, customs and culture were written mainly by Arabic writers, such as Ibn Battutah in AD 1352, who lived and travelled extensively in parts of central, western and eastern Africa. These manuscripts, although not indigenous, and written in

Arabic, were the only comprehensive texts about Africa until the arrival of the European explorers, in the 15th century. One of the earliest such Europeans was Alvise da Cadamosto, an Italian explorer from Venice, in the service of Portugal, who wrote one of the most authentic firsthand written accounts about the African way of life, during his voyages there in 1450s. The first African language to be translated into an Indo-European language, to enable written texts (in Roman script) of the African language to be produced, *was the translation of Kongo, the language spoken in the ancient kingdom of Kongo (now in modern day Angola), into Portuguese in 1624. Later on a Franciscan friar Giacinto Bruciotto produced a Kongo dictionary with Portuguese, Latin and Italian translations in 1650. The first major sub–Saharan African language to adopt the Arabic script was Hausa (spoken in the northern parts of Nigeria), in the 16th century. But the Roman script was taken up in the 19th century.*

135.
Oldest written medical works

The following are the oldest and most comprehensive medical texts surviving today:

1. Ancient Egyptian papyri. About 9 important ancient Egyptian medical papyri exits today, preserved in Europe. They all date from 1900 to 1600 BC, and include the *Ebers Papyrus, Ramesseum Papyrus,* *Berlin Papyrus, Leiden Papyrus* and *Kahoun Papyrus.*

2. *Atreya Sumhita.* India. Written on leaves around 800 BC, it is part of the ancient Sanskrit *Veda* texts called *Atharva.*

3. *Neijing* or *Yellow Emperor's Classic of Internal Medicine.* Written on bones in China, circa 770 BC.

136.
2 oldest existing books made from paper

Two documents are the oldest existing paper manuscripts in the world. The first is the *Dharani Sutra*, made in South Korea in AD 704. It is about 21 feet long and is stored at the Seoul National Museum. The second is the *Diamond Sutra* (*Chin-kang Ching* or *Jin gang Jing*) which was made in China circa AD 868 by Wang Chieh (Jie). A seven-page scroll printed with wood blocks on paper and measuring 1 foot wide by 17 feet long, it is one of the discourses of the Buddha (first of a series of books on Buddhist incantations ordered by Japanese Empress Shotoku). Discovered in the early 20th century by Aurel Stein, a British archaeologist, the document is now housed in the British Library.

Notes. *The earliest use of paper in Europe dates back to AD 950 in southern Spain, notably Islamic Murcia, Granada and Córdoba, where the large Arab com-*

munities (Moors) used it for administrative purposes. The art itself of making paper from wood fiber first reached Spain around AD 1098 when Arab traders from Fez, in Morocco, took paper making techniques with them to the Spanish towns of Játiva (formerly called Xativa) and Capellades, both of which had the earliest papermills in Europe. Not surprisingly, the second oldest extant manuscript made from paper in Europe is the Spanish Silos Missal, a prayer book used by Spanish Catholic priests in Burgos, which dates back to AD 1110. After Spain, paper was later introduced into central Europe through the Italian ports at Genoa, Venice and Palermo from 1258 (the oldest document on paper being a deed of King Roger I of Palermo, Sicily, written in Greek and Arabic in AD 1102). In these Italian ports commerce had long existed between the Italians and Arabs from faraway Baghdad, Damascus, and Cairo. In these Arabic cities, paper was already in use and manufactured in papermills in the 8th and 9th century. But paper had remained unknown outside China for over 600 years, having been invented by Ts'ai Lun (Ts'ai Louen) in Lei-yang earlier in AD 105, when he used vegetable fibres to make the very first paper from pulp and officially told Emperor Ho Ti, who decided to keep it officially secret. From China, the first countries to learn about paper production were Korea in AD 602 and Japan in AD 610. The Arabs were said to have discovered how to manufacture paper soon after the AD 751 Battle of Talas River, near the city of Samarkand (the famous center of the Chinese silk trade route now in modern-day Uzbekistan). This battle between Arab Muslim forces led by Ziyad bin Salih and a Chinese army led by Kao-Hsien-Chih, during the Chinese Tang Dynasty (618–907), was the only

major conflict between Arabs and the army of the Chinese Empire. After Samarkand was captured by the Arabs, the few papermakers among the Chinese prisoners taken in the battle passed on the secret of making paper to the victorious Arabs. The technique of making paper then reached Mecca, then Baghdad in 793 and other Arabic cities such as Damascus, which became a major supplier of paper for many centuries. Chinese religious libraries were the first libraries in the world to stock manuscripts made from paper, and the earliest such libraries included those of the Han Dynasty, which ruled China when paper was invented. Islamic libraries were the next libraries to have book collections made from paper. After the introduction of books made with paper at the Spanish university libraries of Palencia and Salamanca, the first European academic libraries to stock books made with paper were such Italian university libraries as those at Bologna and Padua. The Italian papermills at Fabriano and Amalfi were set up around 1276. From Italy and Spain, the art of paper making and the setting up of papermills spread to other European countries such as France (1348, in the Saint-Julien region near Troyes); Germany (1390, in Nuremberg); Poland (1491 in Kraków); the U.K. (1494, in Hertfordshire); and Sweden (in 1690). It is worth mentioning that paper imported from Arab papermills was used in significant quantities in some parts of Europe well before papermills were set up. Outside Europe, and the Middle East, in places such as the Americas, papermills were set up, first in Mexico by Spanish colonists in 1575, and then in 1690 in the American English colonies and a few years later in the French colony of Quebec. Elsewhere in central Asia, friendship between Arab merchants from Samarkand and Asian

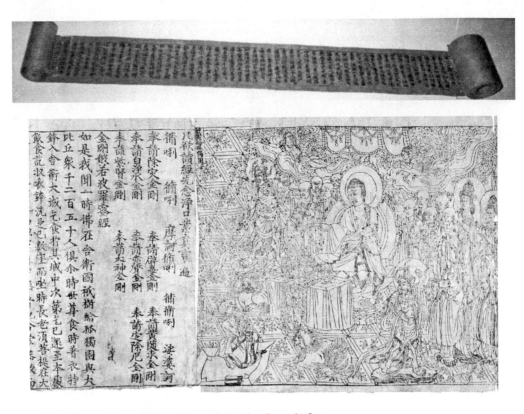

Top: The *Dharani Sutra* is the oldest existing book made from paper.
Bottom: The *Diamond Sutra* is the second oldest existing book made from paper (by permission of the British Library, Or8210f2).

leaders such as King Zanulabin Budshah of Kashmir bought paper production knowledge to the Indian subcontinent from 1420. Until the onset of the industrial revolution in the 19th century, most paper production was a manual process done by hand. The use of machines in paper production was not widespread in India during the colonial times and today India has the largest population of hand papermakers in the world. Paper production itself around the world has been so similar that a problem of paper decay was not treated seriously until the middle of the 20th century. In research carried out in 1980, the New York Public Library in the U.S. estimated that over 98% of books published between 1900 and 1937 would disintegrate completely in 30 to 50 years' time because of the amount of acid in the paper on which the book is printed. The only way to ensure that the books' contents survive is to microfilm them or digitize them. Some libraries decided on mass deacidification projects in which they deacidify old books with a chemical treatment such as magnesium oxide (MgO) to neutralize acid in the paper. Today alkaline-based paper is used in book production, as the paper lasts longer. International Paper, based in Stamford, Connecticut, in the U.S., is the largest manufacturer of paper in the world, with sales of over $25 billion in 2000.

137.
First book printed with movable type

Johann Gutenberg, in Mainz, Germany, printed the 42-line *Gutenberg Bible* in 1455. This was the first successful attempt to make multiple copies of any manuscript very quickly, without the need to reproduce them by handwriting, which was slow and frequently inaccurate. In many parts of Europe there was some form of block-printing activity before Gutenberg's invention. An original *Gutenberg Bible* is today housed in a museum of printing in Mainz.

Notes. Before the advent of printing in the 15th century, production and copying of text around the world was done manually. The Chinese and Koreans were the first to break this tradition by experimenting with movable type (typographic printing), using clay, wood, bronze and iron in the 9th and 10th centuries, after successfully using block-printing for centuries. The complexity of the Chinese ideographic scripts discouraged further development, but a book was successfully printed in AD 1050 by Pi Sheng (Bi Sheng) with a crude form of movable type. Meanwhile UNESCO actually recognizes a Korean book as the oldest evidence of movable metal type. The book titled Jikji Simgyeong, *printed in 1377 in Chongju, is a collection of texts of Zen Buddhism compiled by a Korean priest named Baegun, and is today preserved at the National Library of France.* Jikji *has been included in the UNESCO' Memory of the World Register, which was set up to preserve valuable library collections around the world and ensure their dissemination. The Arabs (who themselves had passed on the secrets of making paper to the Europeans), were interested only in the hand-copying of books, as they felt nothing else could replace the fine handwritings of Arabic calligraphers. This dislike of movable type printing explains why throughout the Arab world the Koran was only hand-copied until 1825, when the first official copies of the Koran were printed with movable type. The Gutenberg Bible was printed in Latin, not German. About 46 paper and vellum copies are still in existence in places such as the Mazarin Library in France, the British Library, the U.S. Library of Congress, the National Library of France, the New York Public Library, and the libraries at Harvard and Yale universities in the United States. While paper found its way from China to Europe, it was Gutenberg's method of movable type that was finally adopted in China as the de facto method of printing books, when Jesuit priests introduced it there in 1589. From Mainz, printing presses were established in Basel, Switzerland (1466); Subiaco, Italy (1465); Utrecht, the Netherlands (1470); London, U.K. (1473); Valencia, Spain (1473); Paris, France (1480); Lisbon, Portugal (1487); St. Petersburg, Russia (1562); Mexico City, Mexico (1533); and Cambridge, Massachusetts (U.S.) (1638). Color printing arrived in 1456 with the production of the Mainz Psalter by Fust and Schoffer. The use of paper in medieval Europe did run into early problems. There was a very lucrative market for parchment and vellum in the 13th century. And the fact that paper was introduced into Europe by Arabs was enough for the Holy Roman Emperor Frederick II (who led the 6th Crusade), to issue an edict in 1221 that any official or legal document written on paper was*

The 42-line *Gutenberg Bible.* 1455. For centuries it has been accepted as the first book printed with movable type; UNESCO, however, also honors the Korean book *Jikji Simgyeong* as the oldest printed book because it was printed in 1377 (by permission of the British Library, C.9.d.3 f4V-5).

invalid. However when Gutenberg printed the first book and printing presses began to appear all over Europe in the 15th century, the dislike for paper in Europe was soon forgotten. Following the invention of printing with movable type, the first attempt to speed up printing, i.e. mechanically with a machine, was the invention of the linotype machine by Otto Mergenthaler in Germany in 1884, which worked on the principles of the modern typewriter. Full integration of computers with printing began with the invention of Desk Top Publishing or DTP in 1985 with the introduction of Aldus PageMaker version 1 for the Apple Macintosh, by Paul Brainerd, founder of Aldus (now part of Adobe). Later on, the Quark Xpress version 1 was introduction in 1987. The latest revolution in print-

ing and publishing books was the introduction of CD-ROM based-books in the middle 1980s, and the advent of the Internet and publishing on the web, which became feasible when Netscape Navigator version 1 (based on the 1993 Mosaic web browser) was released in October 1994. The latest innovation in the production of books is the electronic book or e-book, which can either be available on a CD-ROM or can be downloaded from the Internet onto laptops or hand-held PDAs (Personal Digital Assistants). These devices, such as the Palm, Handspring, and Psion, use the Pocket Windows or EPOC operating systems. Software for reading e-books includes Microsoft Reader, Glassbook and Softbook Gemstar. E-books began to make a major impact from early 1999 with publishers such

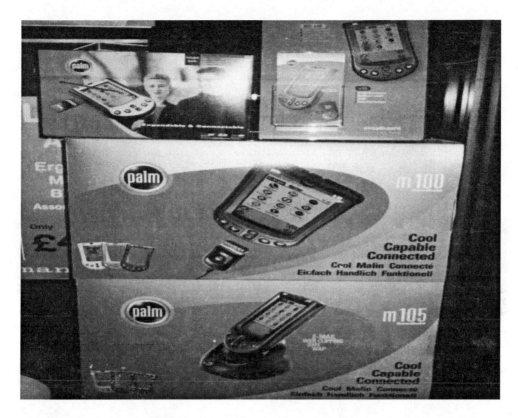

PDAs like this one, called Palm, have software for reading electronic books, or e-books.

as Oxford University Press releasing e-book simultaneously with printed books. In 2000 horror fiction writer Stephen King invited his readers to pay $2.50 to download from the Internet an e-book version of his novella Riding the Bullet. In this way his readers bypassed his publishers, who were shocked at the development. Since then more than 600,000 downloads have been made.

138.
First book printed in English

Recuyell of the Histories of Troye was printed by William Caxton on 1474 in Belgium. It was written by Raoul Lefevre.

139.
First book printed in English in the U.K.

William Caxton printed *Dictes and Sayings of the Philosophres* in 1475 at his printing press in Westminster, London, when he returned there from Belgium. This printed Caxton work and others are preserved at the British Library.

Geoffrey Chaucer's *Canterbury Tales*, printed by William Caxton in 1476, was the second book printed in English in the U.K. (by permission of the British Library).

140.
First book printed in English in the U.S.

Stephen Day printed the *Bay Psalm Book* in 1640 in Cambridge Massachusetts. In January 1947, Yale University Library bought the last copy up for sale.

Notes. *Before New Mexico became a state in the U.S. following the 1846 Mexican-American War, it was part of independent Mexico from 1821. Going back further in time, New Mexico was part of the Spanish colony of Neuva España or New Spain. During this time the Spanish Governor Gasparde Villagra had a book he wrote on the history of Mexico,* *printed in 1610 in Santa Fe, thus this book (although written in Spanish) was the first to be printed in the U.S. In 1765,*

Joseph Briand's book Catechism, *printed Quebec, was the first in Canada*

141.
First book printed in French

Éditions de Luxe, was printed by Jean Dupré in Paris in 1481.

142.
First book printed in Italian

Arnold Pannartz and Konrad Swein-heim printed *De Oratore*, in Subiaco (east of Rome) in 1465.

143.
First book printed in Spanish

Verge Maria and Lambert Palmart printed *Obres Otrobes la Hors dela*, in Valencia in 1475.

Notes. *The first book in the Basque language (used officially alongside Spanish in the Basque Provinces of northern Spain), was printed in 1545. Samuel Gacon printed the first book in Portuguese in 1487 in Faro, Portugal.*

144.
First book printed in Russian

Ivan Fedorov printed the first book, a Russian translation of a Latin Bible, *Apostol,* in 1564 in Lyov in Ukraine, where he was in exile. But copies of his book found their way to Russia. He also produced the first book in Ukrainian. Early in 1520 Fedorov published the first hand-written book in Russia, on the Bible's New Testament. It is known as the Russian Gutenberg.

Notes. *The years in which the first books were printed in other East European languages are as follow: Ukrainian, 1494; Romanian, 1510; Polish, 1513; Lithuanian, 1521; Hungarian, 1533; Latvian, 1585.*

145.
First books printed in Scandinavia

Johan Snell printed *Dialogus Creatururum Moralizatus* in Stockholm, Sweden, in 1483. Gotfried van Os (Gotfred of Ghemen) printed several books in Copen-hagen, Denmark, in 1489. Bartholemeus Ghota's *Missale Aboense* was printed in Turku, Finland, in 1488.

146.
First book printed in Irish

In 1571, John Ussher's *An Irish Alphabet and Catechism* was the first book printed in Irish, while Humphrey Powell's *Book of Common Prayer*, printed in 1551 in English, was the first book printed in Ireland.

Notes. *Although made before printing was invented, the 7th century* Book of Kells, *has been described as the most beautiful book in the world. It is an ancient manuscript from medieval Celtic Ireland and is preserved at Trinity College, Dublin University Library. The book, produced in St. Columba's monastery of Iona, contains the four gospels of the Bible in Latin. Some parts of the book at the beginning and at the end have been lost in time.*

147.
First book printed in Farsi

Iran (formerly called Persia), like most other Islamic countries, did not adopt printing with movable type till the early 19th century, hence the first book printed in Iran was an Armenian translation of the Bible, printed in 1638 in New Julfa by Armenian Primate Khach'atur. Located near the border with Azerbaijan, New Julfa, at that time, was part of the Persian Safavid Dynasty of Shah Abas I.

Notes. *The Armenians, who were Christians, had adopted movable type printing way back in 1512 when the first Armenian book was printed in Italy.*

148.
First book printed in Hebrew

Arba'ah Turim (*The Four Rows*) by Jacob Ben Asher was printed in Sefed in 1475. Sefed, also known as Safed, was part of the Turkish Ottoman Empire. It is now the Jewish holy city Tzfat. However the first book printed anywhere in Hebrew was a work by Rashi on the *Torah* that was printed in Rome in 1470.

149.
First book printed in Hindi

The first major book printed in India was *Coloquios dos Simples e drogas he da India,* by Garcia D'Orta in 1563 in Goa, then a Portuguese colony. The first book written in Hindi was printed in 1670 by Bhimjee Parikh in Bombay (Mumbai), who had a book printing business. The first book to be printed in an Indian language was *Thambiran va Nakkam,* which was printed in Tamil in 1578 by Portuguese Jesuit missionary Henrique Henriques in Goa.

150.
First book printed in Turkish

David and Samuel Ibn Nahmias printed *Arbaah Turim* (*Four Orders of the Code of Law*) in 1493 in Istanbul.

Notes. *The book was printed in Arabic script because Turkish was not written in Roman script until 1928. During the time the Turkish Ottoman Empire ruled Greece following the capture of Athens in 1456, there was a total ban on the printing of books. As such, Greece had no printing press until 1921, when by that time it was already independent. Books in Greek before then had to be imported from Venice, Italy, and from other European countries.*

151.
First book printed in Latin America

Bishop Juan de Zumarraga printed, in Mexico City in 1536, the first book that is still extant. But Juan Pablos in Mexico City had printed a much earlier book in 1534, but no copies exist today.

152.
First book printed in Africa

Samuel Nedivot's *Abudarham* was printed in Arabic in Fez, Morocco, in 1516.
Notes. *In 1513, a book of Psalms was printed in the ancient Ethiopian language of Ge'ez, by a German printer with the help of Ethiopian monk Abba Tesfatsion, but it was printed in Rome. However, after Dutch settlers set up a printing press in South Africa in the late 18th century, Ethiopia set up the second oldest printing press in non–Muslim Africa in the 1863 in Massawa. Ethiopia*

adopted Christianity in the 4th century AD, making it the earliest African country after Egypt to do so. It also has the second oldest civilization in Africa after that of Egypt; it is more than 2000 years old. These two facts give some credence to the mysterious link between the Ark of the Covenant, as described in the Bible, and Ethiopia. According to ancient Ethiopian tradition and backed up by stone inscriptions in Ge'ez, going back to the time Ethiopia was part of the kingdom of Aksum, Menelik I, the first emperor of Ethiopia, was a son of the biblical King Solomon and the Queen of Sheba. The young Menelik I grew up in Ethiopia and at some point in his adult life was able to travel to Jerusalem around the 7th century BC during the reign of reign of King Manasseh. When he was about to return home, Menelik I and his entourage removed the original Ark of the Covenant from King Solomon's temple and took it back with him

to Ethiopia. It was then stored in the Church of St. Mary Zion. Inside this religious artifact is believed to be Tablets of the Law that were given to Moses on Mount Sinai circa 1400 BC. This stone tablet, written in ancient Hebrew, contained inscriptions found today in the five oldest books of the Jewish Old Testament or the Torah, most notably the 10 Commandments. The location of the Ark of the Covenant today is unknown. It may still be in Ethiopia, but the 1981 film Raiders of the Lost Ark *depicts the Ark of the Covenant as being in Egypt. Some say it rests beneath the Temple Mount in Israel. Western journalists have spent years researching in libraries trying to find the location of the original Ark of the Covenant. If it is ever found again, the Tablets of the Law will probably be the most important religious text ever discovered since the Dead Sea Scrolls in 1947.*

153.
First book printed in Southeast Asia

Spanish colonialist in Manila in the Philippines printed *Doctrina Christiana* in 1593.

Notes. *The first book printed with movable type in Japan was in 1596, while the Chinese produced their first printed book (based on Gutenberg's model) in 1589. The first book printed in Australia was Raffaello Carbini's* New South Wales General Standing Orders, *in 1802.*

154.
Largest collection of books printed before 1501

The Bavarian State Library located in the German city of Munich, has the most extensive collection of incunabula, or books printed before 1501, in the world. The library, founded in 1558, has been actively collecting 15th and 16th century books dating from the time of Gutenberg.

Notes. The Library of Congress in Washington, D.C., also has a very large collection of books dating from the 15th century.

155.
5 earliest dates in copyright

Once paper production was common in Europe and movable type printing invented, it began to occur to many that there was a need to protect books from piracy, since mass production of them was now possible. Following are five significant dates that played a major role in the development of copyright as we know it today.

1. 15th century. Venetian government in Venice, Italy, introduces the *Privilegii,* a series of privileges pertaining to the protection of printed works in the republic. These were the forerunners to modern copyright.

2. The first copyrights under the *Privilegii* rules are granted to John de Speyer (1469), Marc Antonio Sabellico (1486), Bernadinus de Choris (1491), and the famous Aldus Manutius (1496), who gave us *italic* type.

> *Notes. In comparison, the first recorded patent for an industrial invention was granted to Italian Filippo Brunelleschi in 1421.*

3. Thomas Godfry is granted the first British copyright in 1510 for his book *The History of King Boccus.* This is the first English book to be given a copyright. The second was granted to Henry VIII's printer Richard Pynson in 1518.

> *Notes. The copyrights were issued before the 1710 Statue of Anne, which is the basis for modern copyright in the U.K.*

4. In 1514, Thomas Murner, who wrote *Geuchmatt,* was the first author to be paid royalties for a published work.

5. The world's first copyright law was legalized in the Venetian Republic in 1533, replacing the *Privilegii.* The first comprehensive statutory copyright law was the British Copyright Act of 1710 also known as the Statute of Anne. After this, several other nations introduced similar statutory copyright laws, such as the U.S. in 1790, France in 1793 and Germany in 1839.

> *Notes. Denmark was the first to introduce international copyright in 1828. This was a reciprocal agreement in which foreign authors in Denmark would receive the same protection of their work as Danish authors. The Bern Convention of 1886 legalized the standard for international copyright. With the explosion of electronic versions of books, such as encyclopedias on the web or on CD-ROM, copyright laws have been drafted to protect such new digital formats. An international digital copyright treaty put forward in December 1996 by the Geneva-based World Intellectual Property Organization (the Internet Treaties) covers international protection of copyright on the Internet and other digital media such as CD-ROM books and DVDs. A number of countries around the world have already ratified the treaty. The 1998 Digital Millennium Copyright Act, passed by the U.S. Congress, is concerned with, among other things, the application of copyright law to digital formats such as e-books and websites.*

156.
First regular newspapers

Nieuwe Tijdingen, produced in Antwerp, Belgium, in 1605, was the first printed modern newspaper in the world. The first English newspaper was the *Corante,* a translation of a Dutch newspaper which was published in London in 1621. Austria's *Wiener Zeitung* is the oldest continuously published newspaper, having begun in 1703 in Vienna. Here are the years in which the first modern newspapers were printed in other continents: North America (the U.S. in 1689); South America (Peru in 1744); Africa (South Africa in 1800); Caribbean Islands (Dominican Republic in 1804); Asia-Pacific region (the Philippines in 1811); the Middle East (Turkey in 1831).

*Notes. The largest daily circulation of newspapers in the world by continent are: Europe (*Bild-Zeitung, *Germany); North America (*Wall Street Journal, *U.S.), South America (*O Estado de São Paulo, *Brazil); Asia-Pacific region (*Yomiuri Shimbun, *Japan); and Africa (*The Star, *South Africa).*

157.
First printed magazines

Erbauliche Monaths-Unterredungen (Edifying Monthly Discussions) was published in Berlin, Germany, in 1664. *Mercure Galant* was published in Paris, France, in 1672. The first English language magazine was *The Gentleman's Magazine,* published in London in 1708.

158.
First scholarly or academic journal published in the U.K.

Philosophical Transactions was first published in 1665 by the Royal Society in London. It is also the oldest continuously published periodical in the world.

159.
First law journal

Journal du Palais was published in Paris, France in 1673.

160.
First medical journal

Miscellanea Curiosa Medico-Physico Academiae Naturae Curiosorum Sive Ephemerides Germanicae was published in Leipzig, Germany in 1670. The oldest continuously published medical journal is the *New England Journal of Medicine*, first published in Massachusetts, U.S., in 1812.

161.
First paperbacks

Crude versions of what we call paperbacks (pocketbooks), first appeared in Florence, Italy, in the 16th century. In 1932 Albatross Books appeared in Paris and Milan bookstores. The first mass-produced paperbacks were Penguin Books founded in 1935 by Allen Lane in Bristol, U.K. His revolutionary paperback allowing the mass production of copies of cheaper smaller book versions of original expensive hardback titles. The first three Penguin titles were *Ariel* by André Maurois, *A Farewell to Arms* by Ernest Hemingway and *Poet's Pub* by Eric Linklater. The first mass-produced paperbacks in the Americas were issued by Pocket Books, founded in 1939.

162.
Earliest professional handbooks for librarians

1. Gabriel Naudé's *Advis pour dresser une bibliothèque* published in 1627.

2. John Durie's *The Reformed Librarie-Keeper* published in 1650.

   Notes. Frenchman Gabriel Naudé was the first librarian for the famous Mazarin Library, in Paris, France (which owns the first copy of the original Gutenberg Bible). John Durie was a Scottish cleric and librarian who later became a librarian for the British royal family.

163.
Most popular handbook
for librarians in the U.S.

George Eberhart's *Whole Library Handbook*, published by the American Library Association, is read by more librarians than any other handbook.

164.
Oldest existing library periodical

Library Journal, published in the U.S., is the oldest independent national library publication. Begun in 1876, it is the "Bible" of the library world and each issue is read by probably over 100,000 people.

165.
First library serial in the U.S.

Benjamin Franklin and friends began the first library serial in the U.S. in the middle 1700s.

166.
Oldest and largest general reference book in the English language

The first printed edition of *Encyclopædia Britannica* (originally a 3-volume book, and today in 32 volumes), was released in 1768 in Edinburgh, Scotland. Today the CD-ROM version first released in early 1994 sells more than the printed version. In 1997 the Internet version was released.

Notes. *Greek scholar Speusippus wrote the first known encyclopedia around 350 BC. The first modern encyclopedia was written in Arabic by Ibn Qutayba in AD 800. The first publication to use the title "encyclopaedia" was Johann Alsted's book published in Switzerland in 1631. The oldest extant encyclopaedia is the one written by Pilny the Elder called Historia Naturulis in AD 77.*

167.
Largest general reference book in the French language

Encyclopédie Français published in Paris in 1971.

168.
Biggest and smallest books

For those used to metric units, 12 inches (i.e. 1 foot) are equal to 304 millimetres or 30.4 centimetres.

The Super Book, a huge visitor's book, produced in Denver, Colorado, U.S., is the largest existing book today. It measures 9 feet by 10 feet, and contains 300 pages and weighs just over 252 kg.

Because it is not very easy to rate and accurately measure contenders for the title of the world's smallest book, a shortlist of four contenders are given below and the claimed dimensions. All of them however need both a needle to turn the pages and a powerful magnifying glass to read it properly.

1. *Old King Cole* measures approximately 0.04 inches by 0.04 inches. It is part of the U.S. Library of Congress book collections.

2. *Kobzar of Taras Shevchenko* is about 0.11 inches by 0.11 inches. It was published in Ukraine in 1840.

3. A book appropriately titled *The World's Smallest Book* measures 0.12 inches by 0.13 inches. It was produced in Germany in 2001.

4. Published in Germany in 1958, *The Lord's Prayers* or *Het Onze Vader* is 0.22 inches by 0.22 inches.

To understand what these measurements mean, half an inch or 0.5 inches is 12.7 millimetres, 0.25 inches is equal to 6.3 millimetres, and 0.12 inches is approximately 3.1 millimetres. A comparative object is the size of a match head, which is roughly 0.23 inches in diameter.

Any one of these four books would comfortably sit on a match head — while opened!

Notes. The biggest book in the U.S. Library of Congress in Washington, D.C., is John James Audubon's Birds of America, *measuring 3 feet high because it contains life-size pictures of birds. In 1660, Dutch merchants from Amsterdam presented to the English King Charles II a 6 feet by 3 feet high world atlas. The atlas, which is now housed in the British Library, is the biggest book in existence in Europe. The second largest book published in Europe is probably* Carte Topographique de l'Egypte. *It was printed in France in 1809 for Napoleon Bonaparte and is was almost 4 feet high and 2.5 feet wide. Before the invention of printing several gigantic manuscripts over 2 feet in height were produced, notably* Gigas Librorum, *a huge bible made from parchment and preserved in a Swedish library in Stockholm. The ancient Egyptian* Harris Papyrus *(dating from 1200 BC and now in the British Library in London) is the longest existing papyrus. It is over 140 feet long and has to be kept in dozens of separate frames. In the port of Mandalay, Burma, the Kuthodaw Pagodas, built in 1868 by King Mindon, contains over 700 marble slabs joined together and inscribed with the* Tripitaka Canon *(the holy book of Theravada Buddhism). Written in Pali, it was a massive feat that took more than 2,500 Buddhist monks years to build and is often symbolically called the "biggest book in the world." The* Tripitaka Canon *in Chinese script was completed on paper in China in AD 972, and is composed of over 120,000 printed pages. This makes it the book with the largest number of pages in the world. The English language book with the largest number of pages was the 1988 edition of Victor Hugo's* Les Misérables, *which has over 1,400 pages. The heaviest book published in existence today is the* Arabic Legislation Encyclopedia, *written by Mohammed Younis and weighing over 400 kg. The heaviest book published in Europe to date is Helmut Newton's* Sumo, *which weighs 30 kg. See entry number* **172** *("12 most expensive books") for more details.*

169.
Most overdue library book

In 1667 Robert Walpole borrowed a book from the library of Sidney Sussex College (one of the 31 colleges of Cambridge University). The book, titled *Scriptores Rerum Germanicarum Septentrionalium*, was published in Germany in 1609. A direct descendant of Robert Walpole returned the book 289 years later in 1956. (However no fine was charged ...)

Notes. *In 2002, a student from the University of Iowa in the U.S. was jailed for not returning books he had borrowed from the Iowa City Public Library. His charge was fourth-degree theft. His overdue fines for the books from the library were almost $450, which he had not yet paid before he was jailed.*

170.
Most popular author among library users in the U.K.

According to figures published by the U.K. Public Lending Right in 2001, for the 15th year books by Catherine Cookson were the most popular. Between July 1999 and June 2000 she came in at the top of a list of 12 authors who saw their books borrowed on more than a million occasions, beating the likes of William Shakespeare and Jane Austen. Danielle Steel's novels are the next most borrowed books in public library. But the two most published authors in the U.K. are William Shakespeare and Charles Dickens.

Notes. *Some British authors earn an extra income from the U.K. Public Lending Right, on top of their royalties, whenever their books are lent out in libraries, hence the more books borrowed, the more they earn.*

171.
First major book-burning ritual

Right up to the 20th century, major book-burning ceremonies have been carried out in various countries by their governments or rulers. These rituals were mostly for religious, political, or ideological reasons. Medieval Europe witnessed several huge religious book-burning ceremonies, such as the famous "Bonfire of the Vanities" in Florence, Italy, in the 15th century, when books by authors such as Dante, Plato, Boccaccio and Ovid were destroyed in public for being "anti–Christian." The first major book-burning event on a very large scale probably occurred with the complete destruction, which took 7 months to complete, of the huge collections of the Alexandria library in Egypt in the 7th century AD, by Arab invaders. The reason given then was *to destroy the books of the infidels.* With Egypt about to be completely Islamized, the Arabs felt the contents of the papyrus and parchment books in the library went against the principles and teachings of Islam.

Notes. The largest recorded mass burning of books in the 20th century occurred in Germany and parts of occupied Europe during the Nazi regime in the 1930s and 1940s, such as the May 1933 burning of over 30,000 books at Berlin University. This was part of the policy of Gleichschaltung *(synchronization) to control library collections. Joseph Goebbels, Hitler's propaganda minister, conducted many of the public book-burning ceremonies. During the Qing Dynasty (1644–1911) in China, for almost 10 years there were big book-burning ceremonies, due to the Qing rulers' concerns about the activities of intellectual Chinese scholars, which it felt could destabilize the government. Going back earlier in time, the first Chinese Emperor Qin Shih Huang (Ch'in Shih Huang) of the Qin Dynasty was known to have carried out a massive book-burning exercise around 213 BC. To suppress the spread of classical Chinese literature, he issued an edict for the destruction of books, especially those of Lao-Tzu, Confucius and Mencius. The emperor also went a step further by carrying out executions of several scholars alongside the book-burning rituals. Scholars believe that in ancient Greece and the Roman Empires, in an effort to prevent unexpected destruction by fire, several important books were written deliberately on vellum and not on parchment or papyrus. This was because vellum does not burn as easily as the other two. An alternative to book-burning is banning books from reaching the public. (This is the more civilized method used today by governments.) In an early instance, Roman Emperor Caligula simply banned Homer's* Odyssey *from libraries in the entire Roman Empire, rather than destroy them with fire. Some famous government sanctioned book bans include that of Russian dictator Josef Stalin who banned both the Bible and the Koran in the former USSR. Iran's Ayatollah Khomeini banned Salman Rushdie's* The Satanic Verses *and issued a* fatwa *(or death sentence) against him, and Augusto Pinochet disallowed the sale of* Don Quixote *in Chile in the 1970s. The longest list of major government sanctioned banned books started around the time of the infamous 16th century era of the Inquisition. In 1559 the Vatican pub-*

lished the first edition of a book listing over 4,000 published works that were censored and banned in Roman Catholic countries, because they contained opinions that were considered to be heretical or anti–Christian. During the time this ban was in force, there were of course several book-burning events. Over the years, among the famous books on the Vatican's banned list, known as the Index Libroram Prohibitorum *(Index of Prohibited Books),* have been those written by such novelists, scientists, philosophers and astronomers as Victor Hugo, Francis Bacon, René Descartes, Emmanuel Swedenborg, Blaise Pascal, Nicolaus Copernicus, Giovanni Casanova, Galileo Galilei and Jean-Paul Sartre. During periods of book banning, there have been efforts on the other side to protect books,

especially those in university libraries. In the mid–1700s, Pope Benedict XIV issued a papal bull which in effect punished anyone caught stealing or destroying books in universities or public libraries. The banned list was discontinued in 1966, after more than 400 years, although the Inquisition officially ended much earlier, in 1820. Turkey once banned the sale of the complete set of Encyclopaedia Britannica in the 1980s because they felt it was "too politically incorrect" and thus a bad influence on its younger generation. Not only was the book forbidden in Turkey, all existing copies were destroyed and recycled to make more acceptable Turkish publications. In Israel, it was a custom not to throw away or burn religious texts but to store or bury them in a synagogue's Genizah.

172.
12 most expensive books

There are two kinds of expensive books, those bought from auction houses such as Sotheby's and those bought from bookstores or from the publisher. Naturally books sold by the former are several times more expensive than the latter, because they are often rare, very old and collector's items. The following are the most expensive books and manuscripts auctioned by the time this book went to print.

1. The Estelle Doheny Collection (rare book collections of U.S. millionaire Estelle Doheny). Six-part book sale bonanza, sold in total for $38 million at Christie's, New York, in 1987. The collection included 12th century manuscripts to 19th and 20th century American literature.

2. Leonardo da Vinci's notebook *The Codex Hammer* (16th century manuscript). Sold for $29 million at Christie's, New York, in 1994. Microsoft's Bill Gates was the proud buyer of the manuscript.

3. The *Rothschild Prayer Book* (16th century manuscript). Sold for £8.5 million (about $12.5 million) at Christie's, London, in 1999. The book was sold by the famous German Rothschild banking dynasty.

4. The Duke of Saxony's manuscript *The Gospels of Henry the Lion* (12th century German manuscript). Sold for £8 million (about $11.8 million) at Sotheby's, London, in 1983.

5. John James Audubon's book *The Birds of America* (1827). Sold for $8 million at Christie's New York in 2000.

6. Geoffrey Chaucer's *The Canterbury Tales* (15th century). It was printed by the famous London-based William Caxton and sold for £4.5 million (about $6.7 million) at Christie's, London, in 1998 to Paul Getty.

7. *The Gutenberg Bible* (1445). Sold for $5.3 million at Christie's, New York, in 1987.

8. *The Northumberland Bestiary* (13th century English illuminated manuscript). Sold for £2.8 million (about $4.1 million) at Sotheby's, London, in 1990.

9. *The Cornaro Missal* (16th century Italian manuscript). Sold for £2.5 million (about $3.7 million) at Christie's, London, in 1999. The famous German Rothschild banking dynasty sold the book.

10. Hebrew Bible (6th century AD). Sold for £1.7 million (about $2.5 million) at Sotheby's, London, in 1989.

11. *Biblia Pauperum* (14th century German block-printed Bible). Sold for $2.2 million at Christie's, New York, in 1987. It is older than *The Gutenberg Bible* by almost 100 years.

12. *The Hours and Psalter of Elizabeth de Bohun* (14th century English manuscript). Sold for £1.4 million (about $2.1 million) at Sotheby's, London, in 1988.

Many books and manuscripts in this list are record holders in their own right; e.g., John James Audubon's book *The Birds of America* is the most valuable, or at least the most expensive modern book ever sold. Leonardo da Vinci's notebook *The Codex Hammer* is the most valuable manuscript in the world. Meanwhile Geoffrey Chaucer's *Canterbury Tales,* the

Biblia Pauperum and the Gutenberg Bible (one of Johannes Gutenberg's original copies) are the three most valuable incunabula in the world. The Duke of Saxony's manuscript, the 12th century *Gospels of Henry the Lion,* is the oldest expensive item in the list.

The most expensive book that could be purchased from a bookstore or the publisher was Helmut Newton's *Sumo.* Published in January 2000 by Taschen it had a price tag of $2,400. The book was about the controversial career of German erotic photographer Helmut Newton and has over 450 photographs in over 500 pages. It weighs about 30 kg, making it the heaviest book to be published in English. The mammoth book project that produced *Sumo* took more than three years with more than 50 people working with the author. The final cost of the book production was estimated at $5 million. *Sumo* is available in English, German and French. It also comes complete with it own coffee table. Anyone wanting to buy a copy of the book may be out of luck, as only a limited edition of 10,000 hand-bound copies was printed. Some libraries (with big budgets, of course!), in particular those with large collections of books on photography, may have bought a copy. In 2001 a film about the book was made in Germany.

Notes. Sotheby's was founded in 1774 and is the largest auction house in the world. It auctioned only books from the start, until 1780 when it began to auction other items such as paintings and sculptures. The second of the famous two auction houses, Christie's, is slightly older, having been founded in 1766. The first recorded major public auction of rare books and manuscripts occurred in 1599 (about 145 years after Gutenberg printed the first book), with the sale of the contents of Philip Van Marnix's library in Amsterdam, the Netherlands. The Sherborne Missal, a 15th century English illuminated manuscript bought by the British Library and valued at $21 million, is better seen as a fine example of medieval art than an illuminated manuscript and so does not make the most expensive list. The Estelle Doheny Collection is still a lot cheaper than the world's most expensive painting, Vincent Van Gogh's Portrait of Doctor Gachet,

which was sold at Christie's, New York, in 1990 for approximately $81 million. When Microsoft's Bill Gates purchased the Codex Hammer in 1994 he displayed a rare modesty. Bill Gates chose not to name the manuscript after himself, i.e. call it Codex Gates, as previous owners of the Leonardo da Vinci's notebook had done in the past, when they named the manuscript after themselves. The Codex Hammer, also known as Codex Leicester, is named after its previous owners.

173.
5 earliest writers of dictionaries in English

1. Robert Cawdrey. Published in 1604.

2. Henry Cockeram. 1626.

3. John Kersey. 1700.

4. Nathaniel Bailey. 1721.

5. Samuel Johnson. 1755 (first comprehensive and authoritative dictionary). All were published in London.

> **Notes.** The earliest U.S. English dictionaries were those written by Samuel

Johnson junior, published in 1798, and Noah Webster, published in 1828, both in New York. The first dictionary in the world is believed to be a Chinese work written in 1150 BC. The first edition of the famous Oxford English Dictionary was completed in 1860. The largest dictionary is the 33 volume German dictionary Deutsches Wörterbuch that was started by Wilhelm Grimm in 1854 and finished in 1971.

174.
Oldest book museum

For almost 100 years, the German Book and Writing Museum (*Deutsches Buch- und Schriftmuseum*) in Leipzig has been collecting, preserving and indexing documents about the history and development of books from 5000 year old ancient clay tablets to the electronic book (e-book) of the third millennium. The

museum also holds the world's largest collection of watermarks.

> **Notes.** The largest museum library in Europe is the German Museum of Science and Technology Library, based in Munich and Bonn. Its library has over 850,000 books and 20,000 journals relating to the history of science and technology.

175.
Oldest continuously trading bookstore in Europe

John Smith & Sons Bookshop in Glasgow, Scotland, had been booksellers since 1751. Sadly in November 2000 it closed for the last time, a victim of the phenomenal growth of the online bookstore revolution. Popular poet Robert Burns was a regular customer of the bookstore.

176.
Oldest existing bookstore

The Moravian Bookstore has been in existence in the quiet town of Bethlehem, Pennsylvania, U.S., since 1745.

Notes. The origin of the Monrovian bookstore dates back to 17th of November 1745 when Bishop Augustus Spangenberg, the leader of the Bethlehem Moravian Congregation in the U.S., suggested to Samuel Powell, keeper of the Bethlehem Inn, the possibility of importing and distributing books in Bethlehem. Aware of the importance of a well-organized commerce in books for Bethlehem (then a new settlement), with its missionary and educational activities, Powell began to buy and sell books, initially religious book, but later books on other subjects as well. The store will be 260 years old in November 2005.

177.
First book club

Swiss Co-operative Movement of Switzerland was founded in 1900.

Notes. The largest book club in Europe is probably Book Club Associates or BCA.

It is jointly owned by Germany's Bertelsmann and the Anglo-Dutch Group Reed Elsevier and is based in London, U.K.

178.
Largest bookstore

Barnes & Noble Bookstore, with its headquarters in New York City, is the largest in the world in volume and total floor space. Currently the bookstore has a stock of over 4.5 million titles. The largest bookstores in the U.S. are in Manhattan and Queens. Barnes & Noble operates over 800 bookstores in the U.S.

Barnes & Noble Bookstore, New York City. This branch at 33 East 17th Street is some 60,000 square feet in area (courtesy of Barnes & Noble Bookstore, New York).

179.
Largest online bookstore

Amazon was founded in 1995 by Jeff Bezos and based in Seattle in the U.S. In 2001 it had over 9 million titles. Its annual sales average $2 billion. Online advertising is very important to online bookstores. According to Thomson Intermedia, a leading advertising monitor, Amazon is also the largest online advertising spender in the U.K., with more than 90% of its total advertising budget of $22 million going towards web and WAP advertising. Although Amazon started the online bookstore revolution a decade ago, today all major bookstores and book publishers also have websites to enable readers to browse and purchase books. Bookfinder.com is the largest book search engine, searching over 30,000 bookstores and online bookstores including Amazon. It currently has over 40 million new, used, rare, and out of print titles.

Notes. The largest online bookseller of used, rare, second hand, out-of-print and antiquarian books is 21 North Main. The company has more than 11 million books available from more than 2,800 rare book dealers.

180.
Largest online bookstore in Europe

The Internet Bookshop, which is a division of the book and magazine retailer WHSmith (Swindon, U.K.), currently has a stock of over 4 million titles. It was set up in 1994, and is probably the oldest online bookstore, as it was set up before Amazon.

181.
Largest online bookstore in Asia

Xinhua, with offices located in Beijing, China, has a collection of over 6 million titles on the web.

182.
Largest online bookstore in Latin America

Brazil's Livraria Cultura has over 2 million titles. The online bookstore is based in São Paulo.

183.
Largest online bookstore in Africa

Exclusive Books, located in Johannesburg, South Africa, has over 100, 000 titles.

184.
Largest online bookstore in the Middle East

Based in Beirut (Lebanon), Nile & Euphrates offers more than 50,000 Arabic books on the Internet. The second largest online bookstore in the Middle East, Almaktabah, is also located in Beirut.

185.
Largest bookstores around the world

I found it hard to compile an accurate list of the largest bookstores in the world, because bookstores acquire new books faster than libraries. So I have decided instead to provide a list of the largest bookstores from a selection of countries. Most of these bookstores now have online versions similar to Amazon, but as always Amazon is "unique" in that it has no physical branch you can visit, you can only browse or buy books online. Some bookstores aided me by sending in current total number of books, but this may not represent the actual total by the time this book went into print. Unless otherwise noted, each bookstore listed here represents all the branches of that particular bookstore in the same city.

ARGENTINA

Librería ABC, Buenos Aires

Note. The Spanish word for bookstore is *Librería.*

AUSTRALIA

1. Angus & Robertson Bookshop, Sydney.

2. Australian National University, Co-op, Canberra.

3. Dymocks, Sydney.

4. Birchalls Bookshop, Launceston, Tasmania. Founded in 1844, it is the oldest bookstore in Australia.

AUSTRIA

Lektüre Buchhandlung, Vienna

BELGIUM

1. Standard Boekhandel, Brussels.

2. Belgique Loisirs, Brussels.

3. Club, Brussels.

   Notes. Belgium is bilingual, so names of bookstores are in French (Librairie) and Flemish (Boekhandel), depending on location. The largest online bookstore in Belgium is Brussels-based Proxis.

BRAZIL

1. Livraria Siciliano, São Paulo.

2. Livraria Nobel, São Paulo.

3. Livraria La Selva, São Paulo.

4. Livraria Lojas Saraiva, Rio de Janeiro.

5. Livraria Vozes, Belo Horizonte.

   Note. The Portuguese (and Brazilian) word for bookstore is Livraria.

CANADA

1. Chapters Bookstore, Toronto.

2. WBB or World's Biggest Bookstore, Toronto. Stocking over 1 million titles.

3. McNally Robinson Bookstore, Toronto.

4. Librairie Gallimard, Montreal.

   Note. The French word for bookstore is Librairie.

CHINA

1. Xinhua, Beijing.

2. Shanghai Book City, Shanghai. The building is massive: 26 floors. Possibly the largest bookstore in China, with over 500,000 books.

3. Wang Fu Jing, Beijing.

   Note. The Chinese word for bookstore is Shu-Dian.

DENMARK

1. Arnold Busck, Copenhagen

2. Politikens Boghallen, Copenhagen.

3. GEC GAD, Copenhagen. The bookstore was founded in 1855 and is the oldest in Denmark.

   Note. The Danish word for bookstore is Boghandel.

DOMINICAN REPUBLIC

Cuesta, Santo Domingo

EGYPT

Madbouli's Bookstore, Cairo
Note. The Arabic word for bookstore is Maktaba.

FINLAND

1. Akateeminen Kirjakauppa, Helsinki. Founded in 1893, oldest in Finland.

2. Suomalainen Kirjakauppa, Helsinki.

   Note. The Finnish word for bookstore is Kirjakauppa.

FRANCE

1. Librairie FNAC, Paris.

1. Librairie Le Furet du Nord, Lillie. Its 10 floors of books make it a leading contender for the largest bookstore in Europe.

2. Librairie Mollat, Bordeaux. Oldest bookstore in France, as it was founded in 1896.

3. Librairie Decitre, Paris.

4. Librairie La Procure, Paris.

   Note. The French word for bookstore is

Librairie, which is also used in the French speaking parts of Belgium, Switzerland and Canada.

GERMANY

1. Thalia, Hamburg.

2. Kiepert Buchhandlung, Berlin.

3. Kulturkaufhaus Dussmann Buch-handlung, Berlin.

4. J.F. Lehmanns Fachbuchhandlung, Berlin.

5. Hugendubel Buchhandlung, Munich.

6. Phönix-Montanus Buchhandlung, Berlin.

> *Note. The German word for bookstore is Buchhandlung, used also in Austria and Switzerland.*

GREECE

1. Eleftheroudakis, Athens.

2. Mihalopoulos, Thessaloniki.

IRELAND

1. Eason and Sons Bookshop, Dublin.

2. Hodges Figgis Bookshop, Dublin.

INDIA

1. Metropolitan Bookshop, New Delhi.

2. Higginbothams' Bookshop, Madras. It claims to be the largest in India.

3. Flora Fountain Bookshop, Mumbai (Bombay). Over two kilometers of books in open space, meaning that you can "window shop" for hours. Over 500,000 books available to buy on a single day.

Note. New Delhi–based Firstandsec-ond.com, with over 1 million titles, is the largest online bookstore in India.

INDONESIA

Gramedia, Jakarta

ISRAEL

1. Steimatzky's Bookstore. Tel Aviv. It is also the oldest in Israel, having been established in 1925.

ITALY

1. Libreria Marzocco, Florence.

2. Libreria Feltrinelli, Milan.

3. Libreria Rizzoli, Rome.

4. Libreria Flaccovio, Palermo.

> *Note. The Italian word for bookstore is Libreria.*

JAPAN

1. Kinokuniya, Tokyo. 3 million titles.

2. Maruzen, Tokyo. 2.5 million tiles. It is the oldest existing bookstore in Japan, originally founded in 1869.

3. Kanda Book Town, Tokyo. 2 million titles.

4. Junkudo, Tokyo. 1.5 million titles.

5. Sandeido, Tokyo.

> *Notes. The Japanese word for bookstore is Hon-ya. The largest bookstore district in Japan is Tokyo's Kanda-Jimbocho in the Chiyoda-Ku section of the city.*

KOREA

1. Kyobo, Seoul. 1.4 million titles.

2. Yeongpung, Seoul.
   Note. *The Korean word for bookstore is Seo-Jeom.*

LATVIA

Jāna Rozes, Riga. It is the largest bookstore in the Baltic States.
Note. *The Latvian word for bookstore is Libro.*

MALAYSIA

1. Kinokuniya, Kuala Lumpur.

2. MPH, Kuala Lumpur.

3. Reader's World (Plaza Kotaraya), Kuala Lumpur.

MEXICO

1. Librería de Cristal. Mexico City.

2. Librería Gandhi, Mexico City.

3. Librería Porrúa, Mexico City.
   Notes. *The Spanish word for bookstore is Librería. The largest online bookstore in Mexico is Librería Jovellanos.*

THE NETHERLANDS

1. Scheltema Holkema Vermeulen Boekhandel, Amsterdam.

2. Donner Boekhandel, Rotterdam. Probably the tallest bookstore building in Europe, with 11 floors. May have more books than Waterstone's Bookshop in London.

3. Athenaeum Boekhandel, Amsterdam.

4. De Slegte Boekhandel, Amsterdam.

5. Bruna Boekhandel, Rotterdam.
   Note. *The Dutch word for bookstore is Boekhandel, which is also used in the Flemish speaking parts of Belgium.*

NEW ZEALAND

Whitcoullis and Bennetts, Auckland

NORWAY

1. Tanum Bokhandel, Oslo.

2. Bokkilden Bokhandel, Oslo

3. Norli Bokhandel, Oslo.
   Note. *The Norwegian word for bookstore is Bokhandel.*

THE PHILIPPINES

Goodwill Bookstore, Manilla

PORTUGAL

1. Livraria Bertrand, Lisbon.

2. Livraria Barata, Lisbon.

RUSSIA

1. Biblio-Globus, Moscow.

2. Book House (Moskovsky Dom Knigi), Moscow.

3. Molodaya Gvardia, Moscow.

4. Moskva, Moscow.

5. Presstorg, Moscow.
   Note. *The Russian word for book store is Knizhniy Magazine.*

SAUDI ARABIA

1. Jareer. Riyadh.

2. Obeikan. Riyadh.
   Note. The Arabic word for bookstore is Maktaba.

SLOVENIA

Mladinska Knjiga. Ljubljana

SINGAPORE

1. Kinokuniya. Claims to be the largest bookstore in southeast Asia.

2. Popular Bookshop.

SOUTH AFRICA

1. Juta Bookshop, Cape Town.

2. Juta Bookhop, Johannesburg.

SPAIN

1. Diaz de Santos, Madrid.

2. Casa de Libro, Barcelona.
   Note. The Spanish word for bookstore is Librería.

SWEDEN

1. Akademibokhandeln, Stockholm.

2. Nyströms Bokhandeln, Stockholm.

3. Bokia Bokhandeln, Stockholm.
   Notes. The Swedish word for bookstore is Bokhandeln. Bokus.com is the largest online bookstore in Scandinavia, and the third largest in Europe; over 1.5 million titles are available.

SWITZERLAND

1. Orelli Fuessli Buchhandlung, Zürich.

2. Stauffacher Buchhandlung, Zürich.

3. Luthy Buchhandlung, Zürich.

TAIWAN

Eslite, Taipei

THAILAND

1. Asia Books, Bangkok.

2. DK Books, Bangkok.
   Note. The Thai word for bookstore is Rarn-Khai-Nang-Seur.

TURKEY

1. Enderun Kitabevi, Istanbul.

2. Dünya Kitabevi, Istanbul.
   Note. The Turkish word for bookstore is Kitabevi.

U.K.

1. Waterstone's Bookshop. London. Many branches were formerly known under the name Dillons. The Piccadilly Circus branch of Waterstone's is the largest single bookstore in Europe, with a stock of 3 million titles, covering 7 floors. The Glasgow branch of Waterstone's is the third largest bookstore in the U.K.

2. Foyles Bookshop, London. Most probably the second largest single bookstore in Europe, with a stock of about 2 million titles.

3. Blackwell's Bookshop. London.

4. Books etc, London.

5. Borders Bookshop, London.

6. WHSmith, London. It is also the largest seller of magazines and newspapers in the U.K.

Top: Waterstone's Bookshop near Piccadilly Circus in London is the largest in Europe. *Bottom:* Foyles Bookshop in London. Is it the second largest in Europe?

7. Grant & Cutter, London. Largest foreign bookseller in the U.K.

UNITED STATES

1. Barnes & Noble Bookstore New York City. Largest bookstore in the world. Over 4.5 million titles to choose from. There are over 800 bookstores.

2. Borders Bookstore, New York City. 2 million titles.

3. Powell's Bookstore, Portland, Oregon. More than 1.5 million books.

4. Waldenbooks Bookstore, headquartered in Ann Arbor, Michigan. It runs the largest mall-based bookseller in the U.S. with over 900 bookstores.

5. Lectorum Bookstore (Librería Lectorum), New York City. It is the largest bookstore in the U.S. stocking books in Spanish for the Hispanic community.

Notes. The U.S. Government Printing Office, better known as the GPO, is the largest publisher of government documents, reports and books in the world, with over 30,000 publications issued each day. The GPO, which began printing in 1861, also operates about 25 bookstores around the U.S. that sell its publications.

VATICAN CITY

Libreria Editrice Vaticana. Rome.
***Note.** The Latin word for bookstore is Libreria.*

VENEZUELA

Librería Lectura, Caracas.

VIETNAM

1. Fahasa. Ho Chi Minh City.

2. Xuan Thu. Hanoi.

YUGOSLAVIA (SERBIA).

1. Nolit, Belgrade.

2. Prosveta. Belgrade.

3. Narodna Knjiga. Belgrade.

186.
Largest publishers of books

Here are lists of some of the largest publishers around the world, publishing in the official language. Some are government owned, others are private.
Australia: Collins.
Banglaesh: UPL.
Canada: Harlequin.
China: China Publishing Group.
Denmark: Gyldendal.
Egypt: Dar Al Ma'aref.

Finland: Werner Soderstrom Oyi (WSOY); Otava
France: Havas; Lagardère.
Germany: Bertelsmann. Largest book publisher in the world. Revenues in 2000 were over $16 billion; Axel Springer (Ullstein Heynelist); Holtzbrinck; Weltbild.
Indonesia: Gramedia
Israel: Stemzky.

Italy: Arnoldo Mondadori.

Feltrineli: De Agostini; Garzanti.

Japan: Kodansha.

Malaysia: Dewan Bahasa dan Pustaka (DBP).

Norway: Cappelen.

Poland: Wsip (Wydawnictwa Szkolne Pedagogiczne).

Russia: Adolf Marx.

South Africa: Nasional Pers.

Spain: Planeta Actimedia.

Sweden: Bonnier Group (Arnold Bonnier, AB).

Switzerland: Edipresse.

Sri Lanka: M.D. Gunasena.

Taiwan: Cite.

U.K.: Oxford University Press; Hodder Headline. Pearson; Cambridge University Press.

Notes. Cambridge University Press is also the oldest publisher in the world, having been continuously-publishing books since 1584.

U.S.: Time Warner Books. Second largest book publisher in the world, with revenues of $300 million in 2001.

Random House.

Penguin Putnam.

IDG.

Scholastic. Largest publisher of children's books in the U.S.

Macmillan Computer Publishing. World's largest computer book publisher.

HarperCollins. Third largest publisher in the world.

Yugoslavia (Serbia): Narodna Knjiga, Belgrade.

187.
Countries with the largest number of books published in more than 10 major local languages

Among the 20 major languages in the world with the largest number of native speakers, India is home to 11 major languages with more than 30 million speakers each. These are *Hindi, Bengali, Guajarati, Telugu, Bihari, Maharati, Tamil, Malayalam, Kannada, Punjabi* and *Oriya*. Annual production of books, magazines and newspapers and other publications in all 11 of these languages in India for the masses is thus staggering. China has 8 major languages with more than 30 million speakers each. These are *Mandarin (Han),* by far the largest, *Cantonese (Yue), Min, Jinya, Min Nan, Xiang, Hakka* and *Wu.* Because of the size of its population, China produces the largest number of books in the world, while UNESCO has calculated that Iceland publishes the most books per capita in the world.

Notes. Chinese languages, with millions of speakers each, vary greatly in their spoken versions. But the Chinese script (which thankfully is not alphabetic) makes it possible for a speaker of Mandarin Chinese living in Beijing to visit a bookstore in Hong Kong or Macao and read books written by an author fluent in Cantonese Chinese. The same situation does not exist in India, where several separate scripts exist—e.g., for Hindi, Bengali, Guajarati and Tamil, even though they all descend from the same ancient Brahmi script. However it should be noted that the different Chinese languages are in fact different dialects, which adopted a single Chinese script. For instance Mandarin is a dialect that *originated in Beijing, Cantonese originated from Canton (Guangzou), and Wu originated from Shanghai.*

188.
Largest annual book fair

The Frankfurt International Book Fair, in Germany, typically has over 6,000 exhibitors from over 100 countries each year. It was first held in 1534. The London Book Fair with over 1000 exhibitors is the second largest book fair in Europe.

189.
Largest annual book fair in the U.S.

About 2500 exhibitors came to the Miami Book Fair International in Florida in 2000.

The same year, the Book Expo of America, held in Chicago and San Francisco, had more than 2000 exhibitors at each.

190.
Largest annual book fair in Asia

Three countries vie for the largest annual fairs in Asia. The 2000 Hong Kong Book Fair had more than 900 exhibitors from over 30 countries. The Taipei International Book Exhibition in Taiwan sometimes attracts more exhibitors. The New Delhi World Book Fair and the Calcutta (Kolkata) Book Fair in India both averaged about 1,000 exhibitors over the last few years.

191.
Largest annual book fair in Latin America

The *Feria International de Libros*, or Mexican International Book Fair, had more than 700 participants in 2000.

192.
Largest annual book fair in the Middle East

The annual Tehran International Book Fair in Iran and the Turkish Book Fair in Istanbul are both the largest in the Middle East.

193.
Largest annual book fair in Africa

The Zimbabwe International Book Fair, held each year in the capital, Harare, attracts over 200 exhibitors.

WORLD RECORDS FOR
LIBRARY BUILDINGS

194.
Oldest existing library buildings

The famous Indian librarian Shiyali Ramamrita Ranganathan once remarked in his equally famous *five laws of library science* that "A library is a growing organism." Very true, as today's libraries see their book collections grow in size at a faster rate than decades before. The U.S. Library of Congress in 1979 had about 16 million books, but today that figure is over 25 million. While Harvard University had 901,000 books in 1900, today that figure is over 13 million. As libraries acquire more books, naturally more space is needed, meaning expanding an existing library building or constructing a new library building with bigger space from scratch. Listing the oldest library building proved a bit difficult to research. Should the list include library buildings renovated but with several parts of the original buildings intact?

The earliest library buildings were those built by the Sumerians (part clay and part stone) to store collections of their written documents in the form of clay tablets, around 2700 BC. These libraries do not exist intact anymore. The ancient

Egyptians were the first to build library buildings made entirely of stone. But the oldest existing stone building in ancient Egypt and indeed the world is not a library building but the Step Pyramid of Djoser, in what is now Saqqara. It was completed in Third Egyptian Dynasty (circa 2800 BC).

Library buildings built with concrete (pozzolana) first appeared in the Roman Empire about 180 BC. Many of the libraries in the oldest universities in the world, (see lists **66** and **68**), were actually part of the university buildings themselves and so cannot count as separate buildings. But it is worth mentioning that universities in existence before the first half of the 13th century — i.e., before AD 1250 (see entry **315**) — and still existing today have some surviving buildings with some parts devoted to a library, some of which have now been replaced with modern buildings. These libraries include the universities of Bologna, Padua, Modena, Parma, Piacenza, Vicenza, Perugia and Sienna in Italy; Salamanca University in Spain; Paris and Montpellier universities in France;

Oxford and Cambridge universities in the U.K.; Hacetteppe University in Ankara, Turkey; Al-Azhar University in Cairo, Egypt, and Al-Qarawiyin University in Fez, Morocco. Padua University in Italy possibly has the oldest existing university library building in Europe.

The following are some of the oldest library buildings in the world, (with the exception of national and university library buildings).

Asia-Pacific region (excluding the Middle East): The Tianyi Library building in the Chinese coastal city of Ningbo was built in 1562, during the Ming Dynasty. It also houses some of the oldest

Chinese manuscripts to be found outside the national library in Beijing.

Notes. The four major religions of Asia, Hinduism, Buddhism, Islam and Christianity, all had some of the earliest buildings for storing sacred manuscripts and books. The oldest religion, Hinduism, had temple buildings housing libraries that date back to the first millennium BC, but few exist today. Some of the few library buildings of Buddhist monasteries (or Vihar) date from the 7th century BC. The Huaisheng Mosque in Canton (Guangzhou), China, built in the 7th century AD, also included an Islamic library.

Pope Sixtus V, shown on the left, as he commissions work for the new Vatican Library building in 1588 (© Biblioteca Apostolica Vaticana).

Europe: The monastic Malatesta Library building (*Biblioteca Comunale Malatestiana*) was constructed in 1452 in Cesena, northern Italy, and is probably the oldest surviving original library building in the world today. Prince Novello Malatesta founded the library and the architect was Matteo Nutti. Today most of the books of the library are in the Laurentian Library in Florence. The present Vatican Library building dates back to 1588, when Pope Sixtus V asked Domenico Fontana to design a new library building. The oldest monasteries that still exist today had some form of library, and they included the 4th century AD St. Maurice Monastery of Switzerland, the 5th century St. Honorat island monastery of France, and the 12th century Poblet Monastery in Spain. There are many existing cathedral buildings with libraries in Europe, some dating back to the Middle Ages such as the Canterbury Cathedral in U.K., Notre Dame Cathedral in France, and the Toledo Cathedral in Spain.

Latin America: The oldest existing non-academic library building in Latin America is the Palafox Library (*Biblioteca Palafoxiana*), in Puebla, Mexico. It dates back to 1645. The oldest book in its collection was printed in 1493, a year after Christopher Columbus discovered the Americas. The library was founded by Bishop Juan de Palafox y Mendoza, and is housed in the Archdiocese Palace, south of the baroque cathedral.

*Notes. The Palafox Library is not older than the oldest university in the Ameri-*cas, Santo Domingo University Library, in the Dominican Republic, which dates back to 1538.

Middle East: The mosque libraries are undoubtedly the oldest kinds of libraries in the Middle East. It was common in the early days of Islam, for libraries to be built in the same compound as mosques. Some mosque libraries were later part of a university library, such as Morocco's 9th century Al-Qarawiyin University library in Fez. Most mosque libraries were used for storing and consulting sacred Islamic manuscripts and books such as the Koran. Among the oldest existing mosque buildings dating from the 7th century AD (when the first mosques in the world were built), are the Umayyad Mosque in Damascus, Syria, the Al-Aqsa Mosque in Jerusalem, Israel (then under Arab rule), and the Amr Mosque in Cairo, Egypt.

United States: In the U.S., the oldest existing library building is the Sturgis Library in Barnstable, Massachusetts, built in 1644. It is listed in the U.S. National Register of Historic Places. The building is also one of the oldest houses remaining on Cape Cod. And the oldest structure still standing in America where religious services were regularly held.

Notes. The oldest continuously-operated university library building in the U.S. is the South Carolina University Library in Columbia. It dates back to 1840 and is also called the South Carolinian Library.

195.
First library building to use
extensive electrical lighting

The most important invention used in library buildings in the 19th century, with the industrial revolution in full swing, was that of harnessing electric power to illuminate the library. One can imagine how hazardous it was in those days to have lamps in big libraries, with the possibility of books catching fire or arson being encouraged. The British Library in 1879 (then part of the British Museum Library), was the first major library in the world to have permanent electric light bulbs in its reading rooms. At first electric Jablochtoff arc lamps were used, then carbon lights. In the 1890s

electricity was fully installed in the Reading Room. The electric power was achieved with two pairs of dynamos driven by two steam engines. For more details on other great inventions used in libraries see entry **297.**

Notes. British public libraries were the first public libraries to use electricity. Thomas Edison's Electric Light Company opened the first public power station in London on January 12, 1882, based on direct current technology. It was later replaced with technology based on George Westinghouse's use of alternating current. The provision of general public electricity was a first in the

The British Museum Library had permanent electric lights from 1879.

196.
8 tallest library buildings

1. Shanghai Library, China. Architect(s): Zhang Jie Zheng et al. The new public library building has two towers: the tallest is 348 feet tall with 24 floors, while the other tower has 190 feet tall with 11 floors. It employs an elaborate retrieval system of "little trains" to transport books throughout the tall building. It is still quite shorter than Malaysia's Petronas Twin Towers in Kuala Lumpur, which is over 1,400 feet tall.

2. University of Massachusetts, W.E.B. Du Bois Library, Amherst, U.S., opened in 1973 and has 28 floors, scaling over 295 feet from the base. Architect(s): C.E. Macguire.

3. Notre Dame University, Hesburgh Library. Notre Dame, Indiana, U.S., is 215 feet tall with 13 floors. Completed in 1963. Architect(s): Doug Marsh et al.

4. Toronto University, Robarts Library, Canada. It is the largest university library in Canada, and is 182 feet tall with 13 floors. Built in 1964 and opened in 1973. Architect(s): Mathers and Haldenby et al.

The University of Massachusetts W.E.B. Du Bois Library is the tallest academic library building in the world (courtesy of University of Massachusetts Amherst Photographic Services).

5. Calgary University, MacKimmie Library Tower, Canada. It has 12 floors, and is 167 feet tall. Constructed in 1975. It is also the home of the Canadian Architectural Archives. The library is the sixth largest university library in Canada.

6. Los Angeles (California) Central Public Library, U.S., measures about 160 feet. It is made up of 12 floors. Architect(s): Bertram Goodhue.

7. New York University, Bobst Library, in New York City, scales 151 feet and has 12 floors. Architect(s): Johnson and Foster.

8. University of Memphis Library, John Wilder Tower, U.S, is about 120 feet in height, with 12 floors.

Notes. Lomonosov State University, in Moscow, Russia, is the tallest and largest university building in world. The building, opened in 1953, has 32 floors and over 40,000 rooms and is 787 feet tall. The University of Pittsburgh's Cathedral of Learning building, completed in 1956, in the U.S., is a 42-story building. At 535 feet, it is the second tallest university building in the world. Germany's Leipzig University building built in 1971 is 502 feet in height, making it the second largest university building in Europe. "Library Tower," opened in 1990 and located in Los Angeles, California, has 75 floors and is 1018 feet tall. But its name is misleading; it is actually an office building not a library building. São Paulo Municipal Library (Mario de An-

The Albertina Library, completed in 1891, is part of the Leipzig University campus, which has Europe's second largest university building (courtesy of Sylvia Dorn, Universitaet Leipzig, PR).

drade Library), Brazil, is the tallest library building in Latin America. The li-

brary, which was opened in 1938, has 7 floors and is 106 feet tall.

197.
5 largest library buildings

For those used to metric units, one square meter is about 10.76 square feet and 43,560 square feet roughly equals about 1 acre.

1. The U.S. Library of Congress in Washington, D.C., has three buildings. The main building, or Jefferson Building, was completed in 1897; the adjacent Adams Building was completed in 1939; and the Madison Building was completed in 1981. All three of the library buildings are close together and are the world's largest group of library buildings occupying an overall space of 2.5 million square feet. The largest of the three buildings is the Madison Building.

2. While the British and French national libraries relocated to new sites in the city to build a brand new library building, the Russian State Library in Moscow, like the U.S. Library of Congress, decided to remain on the original site, and expand the building. The total area of the library building is now 2.2 million square feet. The original building, built in the 1930s, was immense, with 18 floors.

Thomas Jefferson Building of the U.S. Library of Congress, Washington, D.C. (courtesy of Stephan Erfurt).

3. The National Library of Japan, Tokyo. The two buildings that make up the National Diet Library measure 1.8 million square feet in total area.

4. The National Library of China, Beijing. The main building, which opened in 1987 is the largest single library building in the world, giving about 1.5 million square feet of floor space. It occupies 22 floors, allowing for 33-odd reading rooms with more than 3,000 seats.

5. The British Library, London. The new building, which opened to the public in 1998, is about 1.2 million square feet in area. In addition there are four levels of storage basements for books, which go down as deep as the London Underground tunnels.

The National Library of China, in night-time and daytime views (courtesy of Ben Gu, National Library of China).

Exterior and interior view of the National Library in Japan (© National Library of Japan, Tokyo).

The British Library building inside.

Notes. *The largest national library building in the Middle East is the National Library of Turkey building in* *Ankara, which occupies 419,640 square feet.*

198.
3 largest university library buildings

1. Toronto University, Robarts Library, Canada, roughly measures about 1 million square feet. Architect(s): Mathers and Haldenby et al.

2. University of Chicago, Regenstein Library, U.S., has 577, 085 square feet. Architect(s): Skidmore, Owings and Merrill. Completed in 1970.

3. Indiana University, Central Library, Bloomington, U.S., has just over 378,420 square feet, and was opened in 1969. Architect(s): David Meeker (James Associates).

199.
4 largest public library buildings

1. Shanghai Library, China. Architect(s): Zhang Jie Zheng et al. The two present buildings that make up the library occupy 902,300 square feet.

2. Harold Washington Library Center, Chicago, U.S., has 756,640 square feet. It is Chicago's central public library and opened in 1991.

> **Notes.** *Architects Hammond Beeby & Babka won an international competition to design the building, and spent $195 million to carry out the massive project.*

3. Cincinnati & Hamilton County (Ohio) Public Library, U.S. The new building, completed in 1997 occupies 542,527 square feet. Architect(s): Abott Design and Shepley Richarson.

4. San Antonio (Texas) Central Public Library, U.S., measures 240,000 square feet, which includes a 1,300-seat auditorium. It opened in 1995 at a cost of $28 million.

200.
Largest scientific and technical library building

Grainger Engineering Library Information Center, University of Illinois, Urbana-Champaign, U.S. The library building which opened in 1994 is about 130,000 square feet. Architect(s): Evans Woollen.

201.
Most fascinating library buildings

As we may appreciate, library buildings are nowadays as fascinating as their book collections. Often the appearance of a building outside gives us some insight of what to expect inside. What really makes a library building fascinating? The size of the building, the shape of the building, the age of the building? Perhaps the architecture of the building is groundbreaking, or perhaps it is simply a very expensive building!

During the months of March and April 2001, the author sent out e-mails to several Internet based bulletin boards for librarians around the world, asking for a vote on the most fascinating library buildings in the world they had visited or seen. The categories voted for were:

1. 10 most fascinating national library buildings.

2. 10 most fascinating university library buildings.

3. 10 most fascinating public library buildings.

Each respondent voted for one or more of the four categories. The response was staggering. Here are the results of all the votes.

202.
10 most fascinating national library buildings

1. **U.S. Library of Congress**. Washington D.C. Architect(s): John L. Smithmeyer, Paul J. Pelz, Pierson &Wilson, DeWitt, Poor and Shelton et al. This library was the overall winner of the votes for this category. We already know, from this book, a lot about the largest library in the world and most librarians who voted for the library in particularly mentioned the magnificent Thomas Jefferson Building which looks so endearing outside and so slick inside, especially the decorations and artifacts. The author adds that when he first visited the library, on his first trip to the U.S. in the early 1990s, he felt like he was entering a huge palace.

2. **National Library of Austria**. Vienna. Architect(s): Johann Fischer. Several voters noted that it has more space for decorations and artifacts than books itself, including a big baroque state hall (*Prunksaal*) with statues of King Charles IV and several princes of the Habsburg Dynasty.

3. **National Library of Japan**. Tokyo. Three buildings comprise the National Library of Japan, or National Diet Library. The *Nagata-cho* main building, adjacent to the National Diet (Japan's parliament), opened in 1968, and an Annex was added in 1986 to keep up with the expanding book collection. The *Nagata-cho* main building is based on a stack system, with the stack space unit measuring 45m by 45m with 17 vertical levels. The Annex has four floors above the ground, and 8 floors below ground level. Both buildings are in Tokyo, while a third building, *Kansai-kan,* in the Kansai Science City, outside Kyoto was due to be opened in 2002. The winners of an open international architecture competition held in 1996 designed the new building. The main architects are T. McQuillan and L. Funck. A notable feature of the new library will be its "light and chameleon effects" in which abundant greenery and the transparency of the glass exterior blend well with the surroundings. The illumination of the building is governed by the time of the day and the season.

4 **National Library of France.** Paris. Architect(s): Dominique Perrault. Cost between $750 million and $970 million. The new building, opened officially to the public in December 1996, in southern Paris, is composed of 4 glass towers (housing the books and the offices), each facing the other in a square arrangement, and a lovely big garden in the center. A new metro station and a new metro line were constructed in 1998 specifically for the national library, allowing reduced travel time as an alternative to using a car to get there through the Paris traffic in rush hour. There was controversy over Perrault's design because books were to be stored on the upper floors and offices

National Library of France, old building.

located on the lower floors, an arrangement which ran against the traditional arrangement of books in a tall library building.

5. **National Library of the Czech Republic**. Prague. Architect(s): Marek Fontana, Lurago brothers et al. The most fascinating sight is the baroque architecture of the Klementium Complex in which the library is situated.

6. **The British Library**. London. Architect: Colin St. John Wilson. The project for the new library building began way back in 1975, and only opened its doors to the public in December 1997. There is one nostalgic part of the British Library that is absent to anyone who has used the British Museum Library before it became separate from the British Museum in

1973: the famous Round Reading Room. This spectacular domed reading room has been used by the likes of Vladimir Lenin, Charles Dickens and Karl Marx. But the new British library does have its own spectacular features, most notably the King's Library tower inside.

Notes. British King George III loved books so much he had his own bindery and a lot of books produced in his bindery had beautiful binding designs. In 1823 King George IV presented the library collected by his father, King George III, to the British public. The collection of some 65,000 books and 20,000 pamphlets as well as more than 400 manuscripts is today known as "The King's Library" and can be seen in the British Library. The King's Library is actually housed in a glass-walled tower and a spectacular sight is watching the way staff

National Library of the Czech Republic and the Klementium Complex (courtesy of the National Library of the Czech Republic, Prague).

at the British Library gently retrieve and replace books.

Here is a 18th century poem written by one of the binders, Peter Pindar to celebrate book bindings at King George III's bindery.

And yet our monarch has a world of
  books,
And daily on their backs so gorgeous looks,
So neatly bound, so richly gilt, so fine,
He fears to open them to read a line!
But here's the dev'l — I fear many know
  it —
Some Kings prefer the Binder to the
  Poet!

7. **National Library of Taiwan.** Taipei. The new building won the 1986 Taipei Outstanding Architecture and Construction Award. The architects have combined dramatic open spaces, courtyard gardens, and sky lit atria.

8. **National Library of Malaysia.** Kuala Lumpur. Architect(s): Kumpulan Akitek. Located in the same city, which is home to the Petronas Twin Towers, the world's tallest building, the National Library of Malaysia architectural design mirrors Malaysian culture. For instance the design of the shape of the roof of the building resembles the traditional Malay headgear called *tengkolok*, a symbol of pride and esteem in Malaysia. And the blue tiles of the roof itself remind visitors of the *songket*, a hand-woven luxurious ceremonial fabric. The staircase leading to the

Berlin State Library building.

various floors of the library is itself beautifully structured.

9. **Berlin State Library**. Germany. Architect(s): Scharoun and Wisniewski.

The large library building, which opened in 1978, is part of the *Kulturforum*, a complex of buildings including the *Philharmonie,* the *Kammermusiksaal* and the *Neue Nationalgalerie*. The library was featured in Wender's classic film *Wings of Desire*. The first impression of the library on the outside is that it resembles an airport hanger. The reading spaces are very spacious, and coupled with the numerous stairways and splendid arrangements of the lights on the ceiling, it is an intriguing sight to a first time visitor. Generously financed by successive Ger-

man governments, the building housed the largest library in post-war Germany, until the former East and West German national libraries merged in 1990. Today it is the second largest library in Germany.

10. **National Library of Denmark**. Copenhagen. Architect(s): H.J. Holm

Known locally as *Det Kongelige Bibliotek,* the new library building was opened in 1999, and is on the Isle of Slotsholmen. There are two other locations of the Royal library at Amager and Fiolstræde, but these are part of the Copenhagen University library, as the university library and national library are one institution. The new building, called the Black Diamond (because it is a huge black glass building), is very compact, making it stand out more like a massive sculpture.

203.
10 most fascinating university library buildings

1. **University of Massachusetts, W.E.B. Du Bois Library**. Amherst, U.S. Architect(s): C.E. Macguire. Naturally Robert Wadlow, at almost 9 feet tall the tallest known man in the world according to the *Guinness Book of World Records*, standing alongside men of average height, would immediately attract curious attention and create a scene. The University of Massachusetts W.E.B. Du Bois Library is 295 feet tall and certainly caught the attention of the majority of voting respondents (see entry 201) for this category. You only have to look at a photo of the library building (see page 154).

2. **Toronto University, Robarts Library**. Canada. Architect(s): Mathers and Haldenby et al. The tall concrete building has been described as "so imposing." It is somewhat triangular in shape, due to the hundreds of study carrels in the library, each of which has its own window. The carrels were an important priority in the design of the building. It costs a reported $50 million to build, making it the most expensive academic library building in Canada.

3. **Beinecke Rare Book and Manuscript Library, Yale University.** New Haven, Connecticut. U.S. Architect(s): Skidmore, Owings & Merrill. The building protects its rare books by keeping them in air-conditioned glass cages within a large and windowless rectangular void in white marble. Although the walls are windowless, the marble panels in the walls (held within a concrete and steel grid) are cut sufficiently thin that they are translucent.

During the day, the building is lit by an eerie but pleasing yellowish light glimmering through the whole walls of marble, supplemented by lights around the book cages. At night the effect is reversed, and the interior lights cause the whole building to glow gently when seen from the outside. The mystique of this structure is further emphasized by its being raised off the ground by concrete piers, with a glass shell around the space beneath the building providing the entrance. The purity of the walls is therefore uninterrupted by either doors or windows.

4. **Mexico National Autonomous University Library**. Mexico City. Architect(s): Juan O'Gorman et al. The building, of Mexico's number one library, is based on tiled mosaic facades, with Aztec culture themes. The mosaic-decorated stackroom tower by Diego Rivera is fantastic. O'Gorman who was inspired by the works of U.S. architect Frank Lloyd Wright, is one of Mexico's famous architects. The 10 story and almost windowless building opened in December 1979, is located along the famous Insurgentes Avenue (Avenida Insurgentes), and rubs shoulders with the also famous Olympic Stadium.

5. **Lancaster University, Ruskin Library**. U.K. Architect(s): MacCormac.

The simple, clean, white geometry of the outside contrasts with the warm materials and colors used within — deep red and black paints, waxed and polished Venetian plaster. The contrast is the more striking because the curved walls stop short at both front and back, allowing the warmth of the building to be felt from outside. Within, there is plenty to appreciate in the materials and the detailing: the wooden furniture designed by the architect, the extraordinarily tall and extraordinarily narrow shutters that allow library-friendly levels of natural light in through the slits that punctuate the curved walls on the outside.

6. **Waseda University Library**. Tokyo, Japan. What makes it fascinating is the central library's triangular top of the building (opened in 1991), a large circular clock making it resemble a church. It is the third largest university library in Japan.

7. **Trinity College Library, Dublin University**. Dublin, Ireland. Architect(s): Thomas Burgh. Built between 1712 and 1724. Voting respondents in particular

mentioned the Long Room, which has arched ceilings, with books the entire length of the room, as well as to the ceiling.

> ***Notes***. *The library houses the famous Book of Kells. The most recognized and most remarkable artifact of medieval Celtic art.*

8. **Bodleian Library, Oxford University**. Oxford, U.K. Architect(s): Giles Scott. The new building of the U.K.'s most famous university library, opened in 1946. It consists of 11 floors with external walls of Bladon stone and Clipsham dressings.

> ***Notes***. *Sir Christopher Wren, who designed St. Paul's Cathedral, helped in the construction of Cambridge University in 1678 (Trinity College Library).*

9. **Tamkang University Library**. Taipei, Taiwan. The new 9-story library building

Waseda University Library (courtesy of Waseda University).

Top: The new Bodleian Library building. *Bottom:* The old Bodleian Library.

opened in 1996. The building follows the trend found in many modern building in big cities around the world, where a lot of emphasis is given to ensuring that during the daytime maximum sunlight can illuminate the interior of the building, with the use of large windows. Once in the building, on the upper floors you can get carried away by the bird's-eye view of the Taiwan Straits and the Tamsui River, as well as the Kuan Yin and Ta Tun mountains.

10. **University of Michigan Library**. Detroit, U.S. The new central library will probably have become the first new library building to open to students in the U.S. in 2002. The architecture is unique: a half circular shape attached to half of a rectangular building. A voting respondent noted that students were eager to sign up for tours for the building. The architects were URS, and Woollen Molzan and Partners.

204.
10 most fascinating public library buildings

1. **Harold Washington Library Center**. Chicago, Illinois, U.S. Architect(s): Hammond Beeby & Babka. It is the largest public library building in the U.S. Its size alone accounted for almost all the votes among the respondents (see entry 201). It is made up of 9 floors and is neo-classical in design with stunning red brick walls forming columns and arches.

2. **Shanghai Library**. China. Architect(s): Zhang Jie Zheng et al. Its massive size and height (it is the largest and tallest public library in the world) alone makes it stand out along the busiest shopping street in downtown Shanghai, the fifth largest city in the world. Known locally as *Shanghai Tushugan,* its merging with the Shanghai Institute of Scientific and Technical Information has meant it has international connections and foreign librarians and information professionals visiting China almost certainly pencil-in a visit to the library in their diary if possible. Construction of the new building of Shanghai Library started in early 1993 and it was officially opened

in 1997. Among decorations inside the library building is the statue of Chinese philosopher Confucius, and multilingual versions of the slogan *Knowledge Is Power.* Once again here its size alone accounted for almost all the votes.

3. **Malmö City Library**. Sweden. (*Malmö Stadsbibliotek*). The massive building housing the library is the largest public library building in Europe. In terms of numbers of books, it is the second largest public library in Scandinavia and among the top six largest in Europe. Branches of the Malmö City Library include a hospital library and a mobile library.

Joint 4th.
   Rotterdam Municipal Library. the Netherlands. (*Gemeentebibliotheek Rotterdam*) Architect: Bakema and Weeber.
   Phoenix (Arizona) Central Public Library. U.S. Architect(s): Will Bruder and DWL. The new precast concrete building opened in June 1995. The library building was specifically designed to be

One of the two tall towers of the Shanghai Library (courtesy of Ben Gu, National Library of China).

energy efficient. It has five floors and is 93 feet tall, complete with a majestic staircase. The $28 million cost of building the library is said to be one of the lowest costs for a new building of its size (280,000 square feet) in the U.S. The top-floor reading room gives breathtaking views of the city of Phoenix on both sides.

5. Newark Public Library. Nottinghamshire. U.K. It is fascinating because it is made almost entirely of glass. It sits at the back of a municipal garden in front of a large old Victorian town house (now council offices), and is supposed to represent the "conservatory" (or greenhouse as the locals call it) to the house and garden, complete with well established shrubs and bushes around the outside. All walls and the sloping roof are glass. It provides a great deal of natural light and good views everywhere on a sunny day. The downside is that it has no walls to put bookshelves against (all shelving is free-standing) and air conditioning costs are high.

Joint 6th.

Pasadena (California) Public Library. U.S. Renovation of the library building was completed in 1990. Original architects of the 1920s building were Myron Hunt and H.C. Chambers, who were chosen from an architectural competition.

Vancouver Public Library. British Columbia, Canada. Architect(s): Moshe Safdie. The exterior of the library build-

Shanghai Library main entrance (courtesy of Ben Gu, National Library of China).

ing resembles the remnants of the ancient Roman Coliseum in Italy and is 7 floors tall. So stunning is the design of the building that it was difficult to choose two photographs of it for this book from the seven provided.

7. **Helsingborgs City Library**. (*Helsingborgs Stadsbibliotek*), Sweden. Architect(s): Arton et al. The original library building dates back to 1965. A high-tech feature used inside the library is an automatic return system called TOR-*IN*, which accepts and sorts returned library books. This is the first such system of its kind to be used in Europe.

Joint 8th.
 Derby Central Library. U.K.
 San Francisco Public Library. U.S. Architect(s): Peicobb Freed.

Joint 9th.
 Peckham Public Library and Media Center. London. U.K. Architect(s): Alsop & Stormer. In 2000 it won the Stirling Prize for Building of the Year (U.K.'s richest and most prestigious architectural prize awarded annually to architects of European buildings). The building cost $25 million.
 The Hague Public Library. (*Openbare Bibliotheek Den Haag*). the Netherlands. Architect(s): Richard Meier.

10. **Handley Public Library**. Winchester, Virginia. U.S. The darkened passageways, wrought iron spiral staircases, and stained glass dome are just some of the things that make this library fascinating.

Top: Pasadena (California) Central Public Library (courtesy of Tavo Olmos). *Bottom:* Vancouver (British Columbia) Public Library (courtesy of Diana Thompson and Oi-Lun Kwan).

Peckham Public Library and Media Center, London

205.
10 other fascinating library buildings

Here are 10 other libraries taken from the library "votes" submitted by the respondents (see entry 201). They did not make the top 10 list, but there is something about them that makes them tick!

1. **Alexandria Library**. Cairo, Egypt. This new library, which opened in 2002, is probably the most innovative library building ever built in the Middle East. The roof of the building is shaped like a disk partly plunging into the ground, and this also resembles a rising sun. The new building cost some $230 million, making it the most expensive library building ever built in Africa. The Norwegian architectural firm Snohetta, which was involved in designing the library, was the winner of the first prize of the 1989 international architectural competition. The chief sponsors of the library were the Egyptian government and UNESCO, with donations from the Gulf states and Iraq. Admirers of the building call it the fourth pyramid. The building is 11 floors high and occupies an area of 31,000 square feet. Also included are a planetarium, a large conference center and a space museum.

2. **Laurentian Library** (*Biblioteca Medicea Laurenziana*). Florence, Italy. The most famous library in Italy, based on stone masonry. Michelangelo was involved in designing the building. The most notable feature is the bizarre staircases designed by Amanati in 1559.

Joint 3.
    Silesian University Library. Katowice, Poland. The building is very large and has a state-of-the-art book storage room. The outside view of the building is absolutely stunning. The new building was completed in 1997.
    The Hague Public Library. Architect(s): Marek Gierlotka et al.

4. **Dong-Eui University Library**. Pusan, South Korea. The Central Library is the largest university library building in South Korea, about nine stories high and one story under the ground.

5. **National Security Agency Library**. Fort George Meade, Maryland, U.S. The main library is located inside the massive rectangular building, one of the most closely guarded and secretive buildings in the world, with 24 hour video surveillance cameras in every single nook and corner. If that is not enough, the library has the latest high-tech James Bond gizmos to ensure restricted access to the library at all times. Its massive library budget is the biggest in the world.

6. **Vatican Library**. Rome. Pope Sixtus V initiated the construction of the present building in 1588. What is really fascinat-

Inside the Vatican Library (© Biblioteca Apostolica Vaticana).

The Vatican Library's incunabula collections (© Biblioteca Apostolica Vaticana).

ing about the building are the interior decorations, such as the beautiful paintings on the ceilings and walls.

7. **Temasek Polytechnic Library**. Singapore. Once again size *does* matter. Voting respondents noted that the library building is the tallest library in Singapore, scaling 10 floors.

8. **National Library of Egypt**. Cairo. (*Dâr el-Kutub Al-Misrîyya*). The Italian architect Alfonso Manescalo and others employing a neo–Mamluk style designed the library building in 1904. Manescalo was also involved in designing other magnificent buildings in Egypt with the neo–Mamluk style, such as the Rifai Mosque in Cairo.

9. **King's College London, Central Library**. London University, U.K. Architects(s): Pennerhorne and Taylor. In 2001 its new central library building (called the Maughan Library) was opened. This magnificent grade II listed building was, however, not built from scratch but was renovated. The original building used to be the home of the Public Records Office. Hence while the outside of the building does not look very modern, resembling the same Gothic architectural design as, say, the Houses of Parliament, the inside looks very much the 21st century.

10. **Chester Beatty Library**. Dublin, Ireland. Founded in 1954, the library building is located in the gardens of magnificent Dublin Castle. It houses over 9000

View of the King's College new library building in central London.

ancient clay tablets and manuscripts, many of them early Christian codex manuscripts of the 2nd century AD, and is used by scholars from around the world.

Notes. A number of library buildings that could have made it into the top 10 lists were being expanded or renovated while this book was being written, and some may have been completed by the time this book went into print. Two notable U.S. libraries that could have made the list are: California's Berkeley Public Library, which is undergoing a $35 mil- *lion renovation to include earthquake retrofitting and an auditorium which can seat 125 people for events such as concerts and lectures. The Owasso Public library (Tulsa, Oklahoma), is undergoing a $22 million renovation with a 25-foot tower jungle theme mural painted by local high school art students. In the U.K., the Norfolk and Norwich Millennium Library building caused a sensation when it was opened in 2001, because of the many high-tech designs of the interior of the library. New stunning library buildings were also completed in 2001 at Oxford University (Sackler Library) and the*

Chester Beatty Library in Dublin, Ireland (courtesy of the Trustees of the Chester Beatty Library, Dublin).

Stratford Public Library in London. Librarians are increasingly at the forefront when it comes to helping architects come up with new designs for library buildings. In fact every second year since 1988, the International Federation of Library Associations or the IFLA holds the International Seminar on Library Buildings.

WORLD RECORDS FOR LIBRARY CATALOGS, DATABASES AND TECHNOLOGY

206.
Oldest library classification scheme

A good classification scheme makes it easy for library users to quickly locate a book in a library; this is particularly useful when locating books in large libraries with thousands or millions of books. Each book has a unique classification mark or class number for identification, which is typically a combination of numbers and letters. In 1876 U.S. librarian Melvil Dewey put forward the Dewey Decimal Classification or DDC, the first successful attempt by a librarian to classify books by subject. A few years later Dewey went on to set up the first university course in the world for training librarians. DDC has been revised several times the last major one being the 22nd edition in 2003. The DDC is also the most widely used classification scheme in the world, at least in the English speaking world, but it has been published in over 35 languages. An international version of the DDC known as the Universal Decimal Classification

also exists. Today other classification schemes are available alongside DDC, such as BLISS Classification and Colon Classification. In the U.S., a different system, called the Library of Congress Classification, has been in use since 1898.

Notes. Before DDC or the Library of Congress Classification was translated into major languages, it presented a dilemma to libraries wanting to adopt the system but whose official language was not English. For example, the National Library of France abandoned the use of the Library of Congress Classification because no French version was available. And with only an abridged version of the DDC translated into French, the national library, when it was based at the old building, continued to use an indigenous Clement Classification originally developed by Nicolas Clément in 1670.

207.
Most popular library cataloging principles

While a classification scheme identifies a single item in a library such as a book, a cataloging rule standardizes the way entire collections in a library such as books, maps and periodicals are indexed. Hence a catalog is the list of the entire collection in a library. If the catalog includes the combined collections of several libraries, then it is called a union catalog. For centuries, catalogs were typically filed on paper index cards but from the 1970s they have increasingly been filed on computers as Online Public Access Catalogs or OPACs. Given the international use of English, the Anglo-American Cataloging Rules 2 or AACR2, first set up in 1966, is the most popular in the world. Well more than half of the libraries in the world use the AACR2 or versions of it.

Notes. Although AACR2 unifies cataloging principles throughout the English-speaking world, it is based on the 1961 Paris Principles introduced at the International Conference on Cataloging Principles where discussions focused on creating a single standard for cataloging. It is the Paris Principles that several non–English speaking countries used to set up their own cataloging rules. Such as the RAK (Regeln für die Alphabetische Katalogisierung) cataloging rules in Germany, the AFNOR (Normes de Catalogage Publiées par l'Association Française de Normalisation) cataloging rules in France, and the Nippon Cataloging Rules or NCRT in Japan. The very first catalog of a major library is attributed to the one called Pinakes, and compiled by a librarian of the ancient Alexandria Library in Egypt in the 4th century BC.

208.
Largest national library catalog

The computerized National Union Catalog of the U.S., which includes the collections of the Library of Congress, currently has over 20 million books, 2.5 million recordings, 12 million photographs, 4.5 million maps, and 54 million manuscripts.

Notes. Among the treasured maps at the Library of Congress is the only remaining copy of German geographer Martin Waldsemüller's original map of 1507, which was the first to show the American continent and the first to use the word "America" in honor of Italian explorer Amerigo Vespucci. In the summer of 2001 the German government gave permission for the former owners of the map (Prince Johannes Waldberg-Wolfegg-Waldsee library in Wolfegg, Baden-Württemberg) to sell it to the U.S. Library of Congress for $10 million. The map had been rediscovered in 1901 by Joseph Fisher, a Jesuit historian, after nearly 400 years during which it was listed as "missing."

209.
Largest national union library catalog in Europe

The British Library's computerized catalog is by far the largest in Europe, a factor in this being the international use of English. Every new book received by the British Library is published regularly in the *British National Bibliography* or *BNB*. In 1987 an Internet version called OPAC 97 was introduced.

Notes. A search of the British Library's computerized catalog will come up with the oldest known Valentine's Day message in the English Language. It was written in 1477 by Margery Brews to her fiancé.

210.
Largest unified university library catalog in the U.S.

The MELVYL computerized union catalog (the name given to the combined catalog of the University of California libraries and the California State University libraries) currently includes over 20 million books, making it is larger than the Harvard University Library catalog (the largest individual university library catalog in the world).

211.
Largest unified university
library catalog in the U.K.

Since 1987 the Consortium of University Research Libraries, or CURL, provides a unified access to the catalogs of more than 20 of the largest university research libraries in the U.K. and Ireland. Over 10 million books are included in the catalog along with thousands of periodicals. The computerized catalog of CURL is better known as COPAC, and the main computer system hosting the catalog is based at the John Rylands University Library in Manchester.

212.
Largest unified library catalog in France

The computerized French Union Catalog or CCFR (*Catalogue Collectif de France*), has a combined total of over 12 million books, encompassing collections from the National Library of France as well as those held by the major university and public municipal libraries. Included in the catalogue are 15 million engravings and photographs, 800,000 maps and 350,000 periodicals.

Notes. Among the millions of photographs at the French National Library is the world's oldest photograph, taken by Joseph Niepce in 1825.

213.
Largest unified international library catalog

WorldCat, a union catalog maintained and updated daily by OCLC (Dublin, Ohio, U.S), covers library items held by 40,000 libraries in 76 countries and territories on the OCLC network. Over 50 million records of books, periodicals, newspapers, maps, music, audio-visual materials, manuscripts, are included in the catalog, and in 400 languages. The database continues to grow at a rate of more than 2 million records per year or a new record added every 15 seconds, making it the world's largest bibliographic database.

214.
First computerized catalog or OPAC

Today to find a book in a library we consult a computer or technically a computerized catalog or an OPAC. The first libraries to set up OPACs were Canada's Guelph University Library and Waterloo University Library in 1976 and 1977 respectively. They both used OPACs designed by Geac.

Notes. Prior to the introduction of computerized catalog in libraries, paper cards were used to index library items. For large libraries this meant thousands if not millions of cards. For instance, the New York Public Library once employed the use of some 10 million cards in over 10,000 drawers for its catalog. The first step towards computerizing catalogs was the introduction of MARC. First developed in the U.S. in 1965, MARC or Machine Readable Cataloging, is a standard for cataloging library materials in com-puterized format, for easy access with a computer. In short MARC is a sort of standard for creating database records on library items. A MARC record is typically arranged according to the cataloging principles of such as AACR2, and each field in a MARC record lists variables such as title or author and a class mark such as a DDC number. Such computerized catalogs or OPACs are now very widespread in libraries around the world. But in many developing countries OPACs are still gradually replacing the older tradition of card-based cataloging, while in industrialized counties, very few libraries are without an OPAC. Today different versions of MARC are used around the world, such as CANMARC in Canada, IBERMARC in Spain, JPNMARC in Japan and RUSMARC in Russia. Harmonization between the different MARC versions are ongoing pro-

jects in major libraries. With the intro-
duction of the Internet, many OPACs can
now be accessed with a web browser, and
this means one does not necessarily have
to be in a library to access its OPAC.

215.
First library OPAC in the U.S.

The Ohio State University Library installed a Geac OPAC in 1979.

216.
First library OPAC in Europe

Hull University Library in the U.K. began using the Geac in 1980.

217.
First library OPAC in Australia

Deakin University Library, Victoria, began using Dataphase OPAC, and the Tasmania University Library, Hobart, began using URICA OPAC, both in 1982.

218.
First public library OPAC in the U.K.

Librarians at Somerset County Public Library were the first to use the Geac OPAC in 1982.

219.
First companies to develop library OPACs

Geac Library Automation Systems was established in 1976. A Canadian company based in Markham, it originally developed the Geac OPAC for libraries from computer systems sold to financial institutions, such as banks.

Three other strong candidates that began similar library automation products in the late 1970s were CLSI (Computer Library Systems Inc.) in 1977, Dataphase in 1976 and Gaylord in 1978.

Notes. In 1966 the National Library of Germany in Frankfurt was the first library to compile a national bibliography with the aid of computers. Going back in 1941, an experimental electromechanical library automation system was installed at the Newark (New Jersey) Public library, in the U.S. And in the 1930s, the University of Texas Library and the Boston Public Library both introduced library circulation and acquisition systems using punched cards. For many years Libertas was the favorite OPAC for university libraries in the U.K., but today both Geac and Talis are the leading OPACs.

220.
First library to make use of microfilm

The National Library of France began providing microfilm copies of some of its collections in 1884. René Dagron in France had improved the technique of creating microfilms following its invention by British optician John Dancer in 1852. Libraries eventually began using microfilms (to preserve items such as newspapers), made with the technology developed by Eastman-Kodak, in 1935, with the *New York Times* the first ever newspaper on microfilm. Since 1938 Harvard University Library in the U.S. has had the oldest and largest microfilm collections in the world. Today, thanks to computer technology and the Internet, libraries can now digitize their collections, relying much less on microfilm except where absolutely necessary.

Notes. The microfiche was invented in 1939 by C.H. Kleukens, and for a while it was used principally in European libraries, as the technology did not gain much acceptance in the U.S. and elsewhere.

221.
First major computer database

The very first crude databases were developed during the 1950s. The first and most important database developed was the U.S. Census Bureau's office database, released in 1951. The custom designed database software was run on a UNIVAC mainframe computer supplied by Remington-Rand (now part of Unisys Corporation). This database was thus used 5 years after ENIAC, the world's first general-purpose electronic digital computer was released.

Notes. The relational database theory was developed by E. Codd in 1972 at IBM laboratories. The first commercial relational database package was Aston Tate's (now Borland) dBASE version 1 (for MS-DOS) in 1983. The first commercial SQL database package was de-

veloped by Oracle in 1980. Databases with Graphical User Interface or GUI, such as buttons to press and input boxes for entering data, became feasible when the Palo Alto Research Center, PARC, in the U.S., released the first computers to use GUI as a means of input. The first two from PARC were the Dyna Book computer in 1973 and the Xerox Star

computer in 1979. Both these computers influenced the later development of the first successful commercial computer to use GUI, the Apple Macintosh, launched in January 1984, and the development of the first successful GUI operating system for PCs, Windows 3 in 1990. CD-ROM databases where among the first GUI databases.

222.
First and largest database host

Apart from books and periodicals, libraries are increasingly offering access to several CD-ROM, Internet or online databases covering a wide variety of subjects. Most public libraries tend to offer CD-ROM and Internet access to databases, while academic and special libraries, such as business and law libraries, in addition to CD-ROM and Internet access, also offer online access to databases via commercial Wide Area Networks or WANs such as X.25 networks. Some databases are used for finding articles in periodicals such as newspapers and magazines. Other databases contain specific data and information such as in the business, biomedical, or legal fields. Big libraries such as university and national libraries often subscribe to one or more database hosts. Database hosts are online services proving access to dozens or hundreds of databases, allowing a single access point and thus a single subscription to

several databases, the bulk of these databases being produced by different companies and not the database host itself. The first commercial online database host was DIALOG database host, introduced in 1972. Lockheed Missile and Space Corporation originally developed it for a NASA database project in 1965. In 1988 DIALOG (based in Cary, North Carolina, U.S.) was sold to Knight-Ridder Information and in 2000 it became a subsidiary of Thomson (Toronto, Canada). DIALOG, used in over 120 countries, offers over 600 huge international databases to access from.

Notes. SDC's Orbit database host (now part of Questel-Orbit) is also a strong candidate for the first commercial online database host, as it began developing online information retrieval systems as far back as late 1960 and began a commercial service in the early 1970s.

223.
First database host in France

Telesystemes-Questel database host was introduced in 1979. It merged with Orbit in 1994 to become Questel-Orbit and is based in Paris, France. Over 160 databases can be accessed with Questel Orbit. It coverage is mostly on intellectual property information such as scientific and technical patents and trademarks.

> ***Notes.*** *The largest French language scientific and technical database is PASCAL, produced by the National Center for Scientific Research in Paris.*

224.
First database host in the U.K.

BLAISE database host was introduced by the British Library bibliographic services in London back in 1978. It provides access to several bibliographic databases such as the British National Bibliography (which is also available in print form) the U.S. National Library of Medicine MEDLARS databases, such as MEDLINE and U.S. Library of Congress MARC records.

225.
First database host in Germany

The German Institute for Medical Documentation and Information in Cologne established the DIMDI database host in 1975. It currently offers access to over 100 databases mostly in the biomedical field.

226.
Largest database host in Russia

Russia's Integrum-Techno database host in Moscow offers over 400 databases covering legislation of Russia and the Commonwealth of Independent States as well as political, business, commercial, investment, legal, scientific databases, most of which are available in Russian and English. It is the largest bibliographic database host after DIALOG.

227.
First database host to introduce networked CD-ROM access

Bibliographic Retrieval Services (BRS online), a database host, introduced networked CD-ROM access to its databases in 1986. Established in 1976 at the State University of New York in the U.S., it became part of Ovid Technologies (a pioneer in CD-ROM information retrieval) in 1994. Ovid Technologies (New York, U.S.), offers over 100 databases.

228.
Largest database host in Europe

Radio Suisse, Bern, Switzerland, introduced the DataStar database host in 1980 in Switzerland. It offers access to over 350 databases. In 2000 it became a subsidiary of Thomson (Toronto, Canada). It is the second largest database host in the West after DIALOG.

229.
Oldest database host in Europe

In 1969 the European Space Agency's Information Retrieval Service or ESA-IRS database host, located in Frascati, near Rome in Italy, became Europe's first on-line database host. In 1988 ESA-IRS became part of the British Library initiative called European Information Network Services or EINS. It offers access to over 60 scientific, technical and medical databases, some provided by other European database hosts.

Notes. The oldest and largest African database host is South Africa's SABINET service.

230.
Largest database host in Japan

Based in Tokyo, NIFTY–Serve with over 300 databases and PC-Van offering over 200 databases are the largest database hosts in Japan.

231.
Largest database host in Scandinavia

With over 70 databases, Sweden's InfoTorg (operated by Sema InfoData, Stockholm) is the largest database host in Scandinavia.

232.
First indexing service

With the proliferation in the publication of periodicals in the Victorian age, William Poole, a U.S. librarian, indexed by subject over 100 Victorian periodicals from 1802 to 1881, and published the results as *An Index to Periodical Literature*. This was the first attempt to provide an indexing service for scholars. Poole's brilliant work is the forerunner of *Reader's Guide to Periodical Literature*, a popular index, first published in 1901, to the periodicals found in the English language. Today automated or manual indexing services are an essential part of the production of bibliographic databases.

233.
First citation indexes

Shepard's Citations, covering cited works in legal information and first published in 1873, was the first major citation index. It is now part of the huge legal databases of Lexis-Nexis. Twelfth century Hebrew citations called *Analysis of Judaica* are the earliest authentic citation index.

234.
Largest citation index database service

Citations Indexes for science, arts, humanities and social science literature developed from 1958 by Professor Eugene Garfield of the Institute for Scientific Information or ISI (Philadelphia, Pennsylvania, U.S.), are the largest in the world. Citations from over 8,000 journals published in 35 languages are indexed. ISI is now part of Thomson Corporation (Toronto, Canada).

235.
First major KWIC indexing service

KWIC, or Key Word in Context, indexing was an efficient method of indexing words developed by Hans Peter Luhn, a German inventor. In 1960 the American Chemical Society adopted Luhn's method to index the journal *Chemical Titles*. Today, there are KWIC indexes in almost every branch of knowledge.

236.
First table-of-contents database

The Institute for Scientific Information (Philadelphia, Pennsylvania, U.S.) Current Contents database was released in 1984. It is also the largest table-of-contents database.

237.
First and largest full-text databases

Lexis-Nexis began full-text databases in the 1970s with Lexis in 1973 to provide legal databases, and Nexis in 1979 for news and business databases. It was originally introduced in 1966 by Data Corporation, becoming Mead Data Central in 1968. The Anglo-Dutch giant Reed Elsevier bought the company in 1994.

238.
Largest commercially available
microform collection

UMI, or University Microfilms Inc., one of the ProQuest Information and Learning services, and a Bell & Howell company (Ann Arbor, Michigan, U.S), contains over 5.5 billion page images (microfilm and microfiche) drawn from thousands of literary, journalistic, and scholarly works such as dissertations. About 37 million images are added each year. Eugene Power founded UMI in 1938, after successfully microfilming rare and foreign books in the British Museum. Bell & Howell acquired UMI in 1985.

239.
Largest electronic information services

Thomson (Toronto, Canada), which owns some of the leading electronic database producers, database hosts and information providers such as DIALOG, DataStar, Information Access Company, Micromedex, Sweet & Maxwell, Gale and the Institute for Scientific Information, had global sales approaching $10 billion in 2001. Its business is very diverse, covering a wide variety of subjects such as scientific, financial and legal information. Thomson itself is a pioneer in the old print economy, and helped create the electronic age with early proprietary online systems and CD-ROM products.

240.
Largest periodicals database

Ulrich's International Periodicals Directory (R.R. Bowker, New Providence, New Jersey, U.S), indexes information and contact details for over 200,000 periodicals and serials from 80,000 publishers in 200 countries. It also lists over 14, 000 newspapers.

241.
Largest collection of electronic journals

EBSCO*host* (Ipswich, Massachusetts, U.S.), provides access to over 7,600 electronic journals and over 100 databases. OCLC's FirstSearch database service (Dublin, Ohio, U.S.) has a collection of over 7,500 electronic journals. Ingenta (Bath, U.K.) offers more than 5,400 academic and professional electronic journals. ScienceDirect (part of the Amsterdam-based Elsevier Science in the Netherlands), gives its users access to more than 1000 scientific, technical and medical electronic journals. In addition it also links up to external databases giving a grand total of over 10,000 electronic journals. Ovid Technologies (New York, U.S.) Journals@Ovid service is the largest scientific and medical full-text electronic journal service. Over 800 journals from over 60 different publishers are currently available for searching in the journal database.

Notes. Project Gutenberg started by Michael Hart at the University of Illinois, in the U.S., in 1991 is the world's largest free electronic library. It contains over 10,000 public domain texts of non-copyrighted books (e.g. pre–1923), such as novels and reference texts, among which are books written by William Shakespeare and Lewis Carol. Dictionaries, maps and encyclopedias are also available in the electronic library. In March

2002, the 5,000th e-book was added: The Notes of Leonardo da Vinci. An average of about 200 books is added per month to Project Gutenberg.

242.
First major reference book on CD-ROM

First encyclopedias were all in print format, then Sony and Phillips introduced the compact disk and suddenly large amounts of information could fit in a disk, which you could grasp in your hand. *Grolier Electronic Encyclopedia* on CD-ROM was first released in 1986.

Notes. *The next 5 digitized encyclopedias available on CD-ROM were* Compton's Interactive Encyclopedia *(1989),* Hutchinson Electronic Encyclopaedia *(1991),* World Book Encyclopedia *(1992),* Microsoft Encarta Encyclopedia *(1993), and* Encyclopaedia Britannica *in 1994. Most now have Internet versions as well, and some such as* Microsoft Encarta Encyclopedia *have a DVD-ROM version to cater for huge audio and video multimedia files.*

243.
Oldest electronic newspaper coverage

Gale Group (a subsidiary of Thomson, Toronto, Canada), which provides access to a number of U.K. electronic newspapers, reached an agreement with *The Times* newspaper of London (the oldest U.K. broadsheet) to provide access to digitized back issues of the newspaper from 1785. The database will be ready by 2004. Prior to this you had to use a microfilm reader to look at 18th century copies of the newspaper.

244.
Largest producers of newspapers on CD-ROM

CD-ROM databases produced by NewsBank (Naples, Florida, U.S.), offer access to over 200 U.S. newspapers. Its databases can also be accessed via the Internet. EBSCO, Lexis-Nexis, InfoTrac (Gale Group), DIALOG and Datastar are some information services that also provide abstracts or full text of major world newspapers online or on CD-ROM.

245.
Largest database on the latest books published in English

BookBank (Whitaker Information Services, Farnham, U.K.) provides monthly updates and prices on CD-ROM of over 2 million forthcoming English language publications as well as current titles from several of the largest English speaking countries including the U.K., the U.S., South Africa, Nigeria, India, Australia and New Zealand. It also holds out-of-print titles since 1970. Books in Print or BIP database from Bowker-Saur (East Grinstead, U.K.) has over 1.5 million titles. The database is available on CD-ROM and in other formats such as microfiche, hardback and tape.

246.
Largest company information databases

Kompass database (Saint Laurent, France) and Dun & Bradstreet database (Parsippany, New Jersey, U.S) both list over 50 million businesses in over 70 countries around the world. Printed versions of both databases are also available. They provide detailed company information such as company addresses, company products and services, number of employees, key staff members, financial figures such as company sales (turnover or revenue), and profit/loss for the financial year. Hoover's (Austin, Texas, U.S.) is the second largest provider of company information in the U.S. The largest provider of daily company news and newswires is Dow Jones Interactive (which is now merged with Reuters to form Factiva).

Notes. *In the financial world the three largest providers of financial data such as share prices to investors and stockbrokers are Reuters, based in London, U.K.; Bloomberg (New York, U.S.) and Thomson Financial Services (Toronto, Canada). All major stock exchanges around the world employ the services of at least one of these big three, which supply thousands of specialized computer terminals giving real-time financial data. The four largest databases on company credit ratings are those compiled by Moody's (New York, U.S.); Standard & Poor's (New York, U.S); Experian (Costa Mesa, California, U.S.) and Equifax (Atlanta, Georgia, U.S.).*

247.
Largest database on businesses in the U.S.

Reference USA database (Omaha, Nebraska) contains contact information such as addresses and telephone numbers on more than 12 million U.S. businesses and 102 million U.S. residents.

248.
Largest database on companies in the U.K.

ICC British Company Directory database produced by ICC Information (Hampton, U.K.) indexes over 3 million U.K. registered companies. Thomson Directories Database lists over 2.5 million U.K. businesses.

249.
Largest database on companies in Germany

Genios (a division of Handelsblatt Publishing Group, Düsseldorf, Germany) has the largest source of business databases in Germany.

250.
Largest English language database on companies in Japan

Teikoku Databank provides the latest information for approximately 240,000 Japanese companies. The database is in the English language and produced by Teikoku Databank America in New York City, U.S.

251.
Largest economics and financial database in Japanese

Nikkei Economic Electronic Database, or NEEDS, has over 5 million records in Japanese on financial and economics data.

252.
Largest business and economics periodicals databases

ABI / Inform database produced by ProQuest Information and Learning (Ann Arbor, Michigan, U.S.), indexes over 1200 journals in over 2 million records, in the fields of business and economics. EBSCO*host*, (Ipswich, Massachusetts, U.S.), provides access to 2300 business and management journals.

Notes. Based in London, the Economist Intelligence Unit, or EIU, produces the largest and most comprehensive international databases on economics covering areas such as country economic forecasts, economic indicators and market analysis. The largest economics database in the U.S. is EconLit, from the American Economic Association in Pittsburgh.

253.
Largest collection of U.S. legal databases

Westlaw databases totalling over 9000 are the largest databases on law in the U.S. and they include legal electronic journals. West Publishing Company developed the databases back in 1976 with help from the Ohio Bar Association.

254.
Second largest U.S. legal databases and largest European legal databases

Lexis databases (part of Lexis-Nexis), released in 1973, are the second largest source of legal databases in the U.S. and by far the largest in Europe.

255.
3 largest U.K. legal databases

Butterworths, Lawtel, and Sweet & Maxwell databases are the largest U.K. produced databases for professional lawyers, as well as law school students in the U.K.

256.
Largest Canadian legal databases

QuickLaw database host, developed in 1975 by QuickLaw (Kingston, Ontario), provides over 2500 databases covering recent civil and criminal Canadian law cases from all jurisdictions in Canada, as well as some Australian and British legal materials.

257.
First and largest biomedical database

MEDLINE database was released in October 1971 by the U.S. National Library of Medicine, following an experimental project, which began in 1966 with help from New York University's SDC database host. It has over 11 million records and abstracts from over 4000 biomedical journals from 75 countries. It also employs the largest database thesaurus in use, called MeSH from the words: Medical Subject Headings. Today over 500 million searchers are done on the database each year.

Notes. MEDLINE is just one of several large medical databases hosted by the U.S. National Library of Medicine MEDLARS database host. Other major medical databases that can be accessed include CancerLit, PopLine, SDLine, SpaceLine, ToxLine, HistLine and ChemID.

258.
First and largest printed
medical indexing service

U.S. Surgeon John Billings developed *Index Medicus* in 1879. It is the printed version of the MEDLINE database.

259.
Largest biomedical and pharmaceutical
database in Europe

EMBASE database produced by Elsevier Science in Amsterdam, the Netherlands, contains over 8 million records, with 400,000 records added annually. It is the electronic version of the printed book known as *Excerpta Medica*.

Notes. The largest pharmaceutical database covering drug research and development is the Ensemble database, produced by Prous Science (Barcelona, Spain). It covers over 100,000 bioactive chemical compounds being developed into potential drugs. Updated daily the IDdb³ or

Investigational Drug Database, developed by Current Drugs (Philadelphia, U.S.), is the largest pharmaceutical database covering the development of drugs from development, right up to eventual launch and marketing.

260.
Largest DNA database

GenBank DNA database maintained by the U.S. National Center for Biotechnology Information (a division of the U.S. National Library of Medicine and the U.S. National Institutes of Health) currently contains more than 13 billion nucleotide base pairs (individual units in a strand of DNA) from over 100,000 species including humans. Because of the rate at which scientists from around the world submit new DNA sequences to be added to the database, GenBank grows at an exponential rate, with the number of nucleotide bases doubling approximately every 14 months. There are other major DNA sequences databases around the world, though smaller in size, notably the DNA DataBank of Japan or DDBJ and the database of the European Molecular Biology Laboratory or EMBL.

Notes. In early 2001 GenBank DNA database received data from the multimillion dollar global Human Genome

Project, which had released a draft DNA sequence of the human genome. The draft covered all 3 billion nucleotide base pairs of the human genome, representing 50,000 to 100,000 genes. The international collaboration was carried out in labs primarily in the U.S., the U.K., Italy, Russia, Japan, France, and the Netherlands. The largest protein sequence databases are the SWISS PROT, produced and maintained by the European Bioinformatics Institute and Geneva University in Switzerland and the PIR database. DNA and protein are not the only materials of human origin that have been extensively recorded; in the field of forensic science several countries have huge national fingerprint databases with hundreds of thousands of records. The FBI fingerprint database based in Clarksburg, West Virginia, and known as Automated Fingerprint Identification System or AFIS, is the largest in the world, containing over 40 million records.

261.
Largest agricultural databases

The U.S. National Agricultural Library's Agricola database, available since 1970, has over 3.5 million records. The United Nations Food and Agricultural

Organization (FAO) Agris database, introduced in 1975, contains roughly 2 million records.

Notes. The largest databases on food sci-

ence and nutrition are those produced by Leatherhead Information Services (Foodline database), and the International

Food Information Service (Food Science and Technology Abstracts database).

262.
Largest biological abstracting and indexing service

Biosciences Information Service or BIOSIS (Philadelphia, Pennsylvania, U.S.), produces the BIOSIS Previews database which indexes over 6,000 biological journals and has over 13 million records going back to 1969.

Notes. The largest biotechnology database is Biotechnobase, from Elsevier Science (Amsterdam, the Netherlands). There are over 1.5 million records, dating back to the early days of commercial biotechnology in 1980.

263.
Largest zoological databases

Zoological Record database (produced by BIOSIS, Philadelphia, Pennsylvania, U.S.) contains over 2 million records dating from 1864, making it also the oldest-continuing database in animal sciences. The U.K. Zoological Society of London Library helps to produce the database.

Notes. The largest international microbiological databases are those produced by the World Data Center for Microorganisms in Japan, the American Type Culture Collection and the United Nations Microbial Strain Data Network.

264.
Largest science and technology database in Asia

The Tokyo-based Japan Information Center for Science and Technology, JICST database has over 9 million

records, covering, among others, scientific and technical research in Asia.

265.
Largest chemical abstracting and indexing service

Chemical Abstracts Service or CAS, of Columbus, Ohio, U.S., was founded in

1907. Its CAS databases now number over 15 million records, extracted from over

2000 periodicals in chemistry. CAS also introduced (with Germany's FIZ Karlsruhe), the well-known STN database host in 1984, which provides access to CAS databases among others, including the ability to search for matching chemical structures. The CAS Registry System, better know as the CAS number, currently holds information on over 31 million chemical substances, making it the largest chemical register in the world.

Notes. *The Russian Institute of Scientific and Technical Information or VINITI (Vserossiisky Institut Nauchnoi i Tekh-*

nicheskoi Informatsii), also has a very similar large chemical abstracting service, like CAS, and produces the huge chemical database known as RZK or Referativnii Zhurnal Khimiya. But a great proportion of the literature is in Russian, hence it does not have wide international usage outside Eastern Europe. The largest organic chemistry database is the Beilstein database. It currently has extensive details of over 8 million organic compounds. The main source of the database was originally published as a handbook by Russian chemist Friedrich Beilstein in 1881 in Germany.

266.
Largest engineering abstracting and indexing service

Engineering Information (Hoboken, New Jersey, U.S.) produces the major database Ei Compendex (the electronic version of the publication *Engineering Index*), which provides abstracted infor-

mation from the world's significant engineering and technological literature. About 6 million records are available for searching; the sources are more than 2,600 journals.

267.
Largest civil engineering database

International Construction Database, or ICONDA, covers worldwide technical literature on civil engineering, urban and regional planning, architecture,

and construction. Fraunhofer Informationszentrum in Stuttgart, Germany, produces the database.

268.
Largest electrical and electronic engineering database

The Information Services for the Physics and Engineering Communities, or

INSPEC, database has over 6.5 million records, from almost 4000 journals. The database is produced by INSPEC Inc. (Edison, New Jersey, U.S.) and the Institution of Electrical Engineers in London, U.K.

Notes. The largest central resource for government-funded scientific, technical, engineering, and business related information is the National Technical Information Service of NTIS. Based in
Springfield, Virginia, it was established in 1952, but the origins of the NTIS go back further to the days of the OSS, the predecessor of the CIA. Before the CIA was founded in 1947, the NTIS was part of the library acquisition service of the OSS, until it was taken over by the Office of Technical Services. The NTIS has well over 2 million publications covering over 350 subject areas.

269.
Largest technical standards database

IHS Engineering databases (Englewood, Colorado, U.S.) are the largest source of technical standards, specifications, and regulations for the industry and the military, with data obtained from 450 of the world's largest standards-developing organizations.

Notes. Cambridge Scientific Abstracts (Bethesda, Maryland, U.S.) is the largest publisher of scientific research databases. Its Internet Database Service contains over 50 technical and scientific databases used by more than 4,000 research institutions worldwide.

270.
Largest database on pulp and paper industries

Paperbase is world's most comprehensive database for the pulp and paper industries. More than 300 international trade and technical journals as well as conference papers are scanned to provide weekly updates for the database. Paperbase is a joint venture partnership of the Center for Paper Technology in France, Keskuslaboratorio Centrallaboratorium in Finland, Pira International (UK) and the Swedish Pulp and Paper Research Institute. International Paper, based in Stamford, Connecticut, in the U.S., is the largest manufacturer of paper in the world with sales of over $25 billion in 2000.

271.
Largest database in psychology

The PsycINFO database (American Psychological Association, Washington, D.C.) has more than 1.5 million records starting from 1887, providing access to the largest source of international literature related to behavioral and social sciences, including psychiatry, sociology, anthropology, and linguistics.

272.
Largest genealogical database

Ancestry Plus databases, produced by Gale Group (a subsidiary of Thomson, Toronto, Canada), have over one billion names in more than 3,000 databases.

273.
Largest index to journal articles and documents in education

The Washington-based U.S. Department of Education ERIC database (Educational Resources Information Center), contains over 1 million records on education-related documents and journal articles dating from 1966.

274.
Largest bibliographic database on transportation information

With 500,000 records, the Transportation Research Information Services, or TRIS, database is produced by the U.S. Transportation Research Board, in Washington, D.C. The TRIS database contains worldwide abstracts of published articles and reports, or summaries of ongoing or recently completed research projects relevant to the planning, development, operation, and performance of transportation systems and their components.

Notes. In the airline and travel industry the four largest airline reservation databases (known as GDS or global distribution system) are SABRE, Amadeus, Galileo, and Worldspan. Every major travel agency around the world uses at least one of these four databases to book airline seats. The first and largest GDS database was SABRE, introduced in 1964. It materialized when an IBM employee and an employee of American Airlines happened to be sitting next to each other on a flight to Los Angeles and began talking about improving the booking and reservation system on American Airlines. The largest provider of airline and rail transport timetables and schedules is OAG.

275.
Largest library and information science abstracting and indexing service

The librarian's firm favorite since 1969, the Library and Information Science Abstracts database, or LISA, contains over 180,000 records covering library and information science research, information retrieval and information management. Bowker-Saur (East Grinstead, U.K.) produces the LISA database.

Notes. The largest online purchasing directory for library and information professionals in the U.S. is the Librarian's Yellow Pages, which also exists in print with the same name. The database (accessed via the Internet and produced in New York) currently covers over 1000 companies supplying library products and services.

276.
First commercial information brokerage

FIND/SVP, based in New York, U.S., was the first comprehensive information brokerage in the world. It was created in 1937 as SVP and known from 1969 as FIND/SVP. Today over 1100 information consultants worldwide provide specialized business consulting and advice.

277.
Most popular stand-alone bibliographic database software

A study has shown that academic researchers, lecturers and university students writing up projects, theses and dissertations are more likely to use either Reference Manager, Endnote or ProCite database software to organize their journal references and bibliography.

278.
Largest online information event in the U.K.

Every year since December 1977, a major exhibition and conference for information professionals and librarians called Online Information has been held in London. The event held at London's Olympia Exhibition Hall is the world's largest and oldest event for the information industry, with an average 15,600 visitors from 46 countries and over 300 exhibitors. The 27th Online Informa- tion meeting was held in December 2001.

279.
Largest online information event in Germany

Infobase. Held annually at Messe Trade Center in Frankfurt. The 17th In- fobase meeting event was held in May 2001. From 2002 the event will be held during the Frankfurt International Book Fair.

280.
Largest online information event in France

IDT. Held annually in Paris. The 18th IDT event with more than 160 ex- hibitors was held in May 2001.

281.
Largest online information event in the U.S.

National Online Meeting. Held an- nually in different cities in the U.S. The 21st meeting was held in 2000.

282.
Largest digital images database

The Corbis Collection has over 65 million digital images (photographs, art and illustrations). Part of this collection is accessible via the Internet as the Corbis Picture Experience. Microsoft's Bill Gates founded the Corbis Collection in 1989, and its headquarters is in Seattle, Wash- ington, U.S.

283.
Largest patent databases

IBM (New York, U.S.) is part owner of the largest patent database in the world. The latest estimates suggest that the Delphion Patent Database (set up in 1997) has over 45 million patent records and over 40 million records on technical reports and bulletins. Combined, this makes it the largest single database of any kind in the world. MicroPatent (East Haven, Connecticut, U.S.) has built up a collection of over 5,000 CD-ROMs since 1989, on patent and trademark information. Over 33 million patents and 50 million trademarks are covered. Its databases are also accessible via the Internet. Questel-Orbit database host (Paris, France) offers over 160 databases on trademarks and patents, making it the largest online patent database host in the world.

Notes. Trademark Scan, from Thomson & Thompson (North Quincy, Massachusetts, U.S.) is the largest trademarks database in the world. The trademarks database of Questel-Orbit, is the largest in Europe with over 14 million records.

284.
Largest patent database in Europe

Derwent Information (London, U.K.) produces the Derwent World Patent Index database, which indexes over 9 million patent records covering over 13 million patents, sourced from over 40 international patent-issuing authorities, since 1963. It has the largest specialist collection of European patents.

Notes. The British Library in London has the world's largest collection of patent specifications in a public library, while the Swiss Federal Institute of Technology Library in Zürich has the largest patent library in Europe in an academic library.

285.
Largest database of U.S. patents

IFI/Plenum, based in Wilmington, North Carolina, U.S., has the largest specialist collection of U.S. patents, called CLAIMS. IFI began indexing U.S. patents in 1955 and today its databases cover over 4.5 million United States patents. The U.S. Patent and Trademark Office has offered large free databases on patents since 1976, but searching is limited to text terms.

286.
Largest database on chemical
and pharmaceutical patents

Available since 1998, the Merged Markush Services, or MMS (run by both Derwent Information in the U.K., and the French Patent and Trademark Office), has over 300 million chemical substances listed, which can be searched by chemical structure. Since chemical and pharmaceutical patent applications give diagrammatic information on how the substance was synthesized, the MMS database is very popular among scientists especially those working in the pharmaceutical industry. Chemical Abstracts Service (Columbus, Ohio, U.S.) databases contain the second largest number of chemical patents in the world. Incidentally in today's competitive global market, a huge amount of a major pharmaceutical company's annual budget is often allocated for fighting lawsuits on patent infringements and cheap generic copies from rival companies.

287.
Most popular CD-ROM information
retrieval software used in libraries
to access networked CD-ROM databases

SilverPlatter's SPIRS (New York, U.S.) and Ovid Technologies (New York, U.S.), search and retrieval software, are both widely used for accessing CD-ROM networked databases and are available in more libraries worldwide than any other similar product.

288.
First major CD-ROM database used in libraries

The InfoTrac CD-ROM database, released in 1984 by Information Access Company (now part of Gale Group, and a subsidiary of Thomson, Toronto, Canada), was originally a general reference database helping libraries to track down and retrieve periodical documents.

289.
Largest search engine

Founded in 1997 by scientists from Norway's leading technical university in Oslo, FAST or Fast Search and Transfer has the largest search engine today (known as AllTheWeb). As of December 2001 it held over 700 million of the estimated 2 billion web pages on the Internet, much larger than any competing search engine.

290.
Largest archives of web pages

The Internet Archive is a non-profit venture founded in 1996 and based in San Francisco, U.S. Its database, called Way-Back-Machine, archives an estimated 10 billion web pages, dating back to 1996. Over 80% are thus old web pages, some first appearing on the web as far back as 1993 (when Mosaic was the only popular web browser widely available). Standard search engines such as Google, Yahoo and Alta Vista no longer pick up these old web pages, because the web pages have long been deleted or moved from the hosting web server.

Notes. Today the largest Internet cafe is easyInternetCafé in New York City, U.S. Founded in 1999 by Stelios Haji-loannou, the Internet cafe currently offers about 800 Internet terminals. Each month over 2 million people use easyInternetCafé's 22 stores in the U.S. and Western Europe. It is hard to imagine that back in 1993 very few people outside the scientific community had ever heard about the Internet. The very first Internet node (more commonly called Internet host today) goes back much further, when the University of California Library in Los Angeles set up the earliest node in 1969, one of four U.S. academic institu-

tions setting up an Internet node in 1969. Credit for designing the first website (i.e. installing the first web server) goes to Tim Berners-Lee's group at the Swiss-based research institute CERN in December 1990. His group used a NeXT computer as the web server, and their web browser, (called WorldWideWeb), was non-graphical, as navigation was achieved by typing in text commands, very much like as in DOS before Windows was available. info.cern.ch was the domain name address of the CERN web server, and one of the first websites was the address book of CERN employees. In recognition of the pioneering work of Tim Berners-Lee, the name of his web browser, i.e. WorldWideWeb, or just the Web, was adopted as the general name of the graphical Internet system used today with browsers such as Netscape Navigator and Internet Explorer. Several text-based web browsers and crude graphical web browsers appeared between 1991 and 1993 such as libwww, Pello, Erwise, ViolaWWW, Midas, Samba, Lynx, Cello, Arena and Mosaic. But it was the Mosaic browser, developed at the computer department of the University of Illinois, Urbana-Champaign, that proved the most popular, as it later gave rise to both Netscape and Internet Explorer browsers. In early 1994, the University of Illinois library became the first to set up a website. St. Joseph County Public Library, in South Bend, Indiana, U.S., set up the very first public library website in late 1994. Today over 90% of all major public libraries and universities around the world now have a website. The most important part of a library website is access to the library catalog. An alternative to the web is the Wireless Application Protocol or WAP. This is a technology that makes it possible to view a customized website with a WAP-compatible mobile phone or a hand-held computer also known as a

PDA. Vienna Public Library in Austria established its WAP site back in May 2000, becoming the first library in the world to do so. Its WAP site ensures that one does not need a computer to get information on the library. The central library of Hampshire County in the U.K. set up its own WAP site in June 2000. WAP is not the only new technology being harnessed by public libraries; increasingly a number of public libraries in the West now offer e-books or electronic books for members of the public to borrow, which are can be read with laptop computers or PDAs.

291.
Largest document supply service and inter-lending service

The British Library Document Supply Center based at Boston Spa in West Yorkshire handles up to 4 million requests, for inter-library loans or photo-copies of periodical articles or book extracts, a year. In 2001 it delivered its 100 millionth document.

292.
Largest scientific document supply services

ISI Document Solution (formerly The Genuine Article), which is the document delivery service of the Institute for Scientific Information (Philadelphia, Pennsylvania, U.S.), and the document delivery service of the Chemical Abstracts Service (Columbus, Ohio, U.S.) both handle over 2 million requests for scientific literature a year, from around the world. Other large commercial document delivery services include Adonis, CatchWord, Doc Deliver, Faxon, Infotrieve, Swets, and UnCover.

Notes. *Because there are more journals in the various fields of medicine, science and technology, compared to other subjects such as law and business journals, several countries have a central or national medical, scientific and technical document supply center, which is also part of a national institute or a library, such as the U.S. National Library of Medicine, the Canada Institute for Scientific and Technical Information (CISTI); the French National Institute for Scientific and Technical Information (INIST), the*

Japan Information Center for Science and Technology (JICST), and the Indian National Scientific Documentation Center (INSDOC). In Turkey, the Documentation Center of the Turkish Scientific and Technical Research Council *in Ankara, known as TUBITAK-TUR-DOK, has a collection of over 800 periodicals on science and technology, making it the largest periodicals library and document supply service in the Middle East.*

293.
Largest library network or consortium

OCLC founded in 1967 as a nonprofit computer library service and research organization and based in Dublin, Ohio, in the U.S. has a membership of more than 9000 libraries. More than 40,000 libraries in 76 countries and territories use OCLC's products and services.

Notes. *The largest information consortium is the Electronic Information for Libraries Direct. Formed in 1999 by EBSCO and the Open Society Institute (part of the Soros Foundation Network), it encompasses libraries in 39 countries in Europe, Africa, and Latin America. Members have access to all EBSCO's full-text electronic journals.*

294.
Largest providers of subscription services for libraries

EBSCO Subscription Services, based Birmingham, Alabama, U.S., and founded in 1958 by Elton B. Stephens, works with over 50,000 publishers in 21 countries to help libraries buy bulk copies of books and periodicals. Its database covers 282,000 titles. Swets Blackwell (Lisse, the Netherlands) handles more than 2 million subscriptions each year, dealing with about 65,000 publishers from 20 countries. It maintains a database of 250,000 titles.

295.
Oldest providers of subscription services for libraries

The company Everetts in London began offering book and subscription services to libraries in 1793. Baker & Taylor, based in Charlotte, North Carolina, in the U.S., has been providing subscription services to libraries and bookstores since 1828, and is the largest such service in the Americas.

296.
Largest electronic trading services for libraries in the U.K.

Located in Tonbridge, First Edition has provided a large scale EDI trading network, (a standard for transmitting information and commercial messages), for library acquisitions services. The network encompasses publishers, booksellers, library suppliers and the libraries themselves.

297.
10 greatest inventions used in libraries today

1. **Paper.** AD 105. Inventor: Ts'al Lun, China. Main use: manufacture of books and periodicals.

2. **Book Printing**. AD 1450. Inventor: Johannes Gutenberg, Germany. Main use: manufacture of books and periodicals.

3. **The Internet**. Late 1960s. Inventors: various people invented the many components that make up the Internet, as we know it today. It began as ARPANET, and in 1969 the first Internet host was set up at the University of Los Angeles, California, in the U.S. Main use: searching for information, browsing library catalogs and online publishing.

4. **Microfilm**. 1852. Inventor: John Duncan, U.K. Main use: preservation of periodicals, especially newspapers.

5. **Electric bulb**. 1879. Inventor: Thomas Edison. Main use: illuminating the library.

6. **Television**. 1926 and 1927. Inventors: John Logie Baird, U.K., and Philo Farnsworh, U.S. Main use: watching videos in the library.

7. **Photocopying**. 1938. Inventor: Xerox, U.S. The Xerox 914 was the first office photocopier. Main use: duplication of printed works.

8. **Personal Computer**. 1975. Inventors: like the Internet, various people invented the many components that led to the personal computer. All the inventors were American. Ed Roberts built the first personal computer kit in 1975 and called it the Altair. Microsoft's Bill Gates and Paul Allen wrote the first personal computer software for the Altair. Main use: too much to list here.

9. **CD-ROM disk**. 1984. Inventors: Sony in Japan and Philips in the Netherlands. Main use: storage of databases and huge books such as encyclopaedias.

10. **DVD-ROM disk**. 1995. Inventors: Several Japanese companies including Sony and Toshiba. Main use: storage of huge books such as the Microsoft Encarta Encyclopedia Reference Suite, which is rich in huge multimedia files that cannot fit in a CD-ROM disk.

WORLD RECORDS FOR LIBRARY AND INFORMATION SCIENCE ORGANIZATIONS

Prior to the late 16th century, librarians were generally scholars with special interests in book and manuscript collecting. With the organization and opening of larger libraries in late 16th and early 17th centuries, the work of a librarian came to be recognized as requiring special expertise and skills, if not specialized education. Soon librarians became more involved in the organization of library facilities and its services to the user. While the first library school was not introduced until the 19th century, several early important publications on the work of librarians included Gabriel Naudé's *Advis pour dresser une bibliotheque* published in 1627 in France, and John Duries's *The Reformed Librarie-Keeper* published in 1650 in Scotland.

298.
First library school

The Columbia University School of Library Service in New York City was set up in 1887. Its founder, Melvil Dewey, had in 1876 constructed an expandable scheme for classifying books, known today as the Dewey Decimal System. The library school was closed in late 1992, but many of the original librarianship book collections used by Dewey are still in existence and part of the Columbia University Library.

299.
Oldest accredited library school in North America

The American Library Association provides a list of library schools that it finds to meet a high standard. Pratt Institute School of Information and Library Science in New York was the first library school to be accredited, having been established in 1890.

300.
5 oldest university library schools in Europe

George August University library school, Göttingen, Germany. Founded 1888.

Munich University library school, Germany. 1905.

Leipzig University library school, Germany. 1914.

Copenhagen University library school, Denmark. 1918.

University College library school, London University. UK. 1919.

301.
Oldest university library school in Asia

Wuhan University library school in China was founded in 1920.

302.
Oldest university library school in the Middle East

The library school of Hebrew University, Jerusalem, Israel, was founded in 1956.

303.
First university in the U.S. to offer an extensive program in information science

Unlike the librarian whose job is very familiar to those who use libraries, information scientists are rather a rare sight. They are more likely to be working in specialist libraries such as biomedical, pharmaceutical or legal libraries and less likely in national, public and university libraries, which are more open to more members of the public. Typically information scientists are primarily involved in creating, retrieving, organizing or disseminating information, and their work involves much use of computer technology. Georgia Institute of Technology, in Atlanta, began teaching information science in 1963.

304.
First university in the U.K. to offer
an extensive program in information science

In early 1961 City University School of Informatics in London, became the first university in the world to train professional information scientists. Over the years more than half of all qualified information scientists in the UK who reside in London studied at City University, including the author of *Library World Records*.

City University in London. It was the first university in the world to offer courses in Information Science.

311.
Most prestigious award for U.K.
and European information scientists

Each year the U.K. Institute for Information Scientists awards the Jason Farradane Award to an individual or organization for an outstanding contribution to the information field or in recognition of an advancement in the field of information science. It is named after one of the founding fathers of information science in the U.K. who taught at City University in London and was the first person in the U.K. to be recognized academically as an information scientist. Past winners include the librarians who developed the popular BUBL (Bulletin Board for Libraries), in 1989. BUBL is probably the most visited library website by librarians in the U.K.

312.
First full-time paid librarian in the U.K.

Richard Johnson in 1653 was appointed by Chetham Library in Manchester and given a salary of £15 per annum. The library itself claims to be the oldest still-existing public library in the U.K. and indeed the English-speaking world.

313.
6 libraries with over 800 staff members
and their annual budgets

1. Library of Congress, Washington, D.C. U.S. 4,360 staff / $400 million.

2. Russian State Library, Moscow. 2,500 staff / $12 million*

3. British Library, London. 2,410 staff / $185 million*

4. National Library of France, Paris. 1,900 staff / $172 million*

5. National Library of China, Beijing. 1,600 staff / $15 million*

6. National Library of Japan, Tokyo. 860 staff / $190 million*

Notes. The largest annual library budget is the U.S. National Security Agency Library budget of about $900 million. The university library with the largest budget is Harvard University Library at $140 million, while the New York Public Library has the largest public library budget, around $97 million a year. For centuries, the rich, members of royal families, politicians, and others have made generous donations of books or money to *libraries. In terms of the largest financial donations made to libraries by billionaires to date, two individuals have given grants of more than $220 million combined up to 2001. George Soros (through* *his Soros Foundation Network) and Bill Gates (through the Bill & Melinda Gates Foundation).*

*Based on 2001 local currency exchanges rates for the U.S. dollar.

314.
212 largest and most important libraries

This list focuses only on the largest and most important libraries, in each country, with 2 or more million books.

Omissions: both Russia and the U.S. have dozens of academic, research, special and public libraries with more than 2 million books. This list of largest libraries has thus excluded the following: U.S. university libraries with fewer than 7 million books, and public libraries with fewer than 5 million books, and Russian university, research and special libraries with fewer than 2.5 million books.

Two other omissions include Ukrainian special libraries and Chinese provincial and special libraries, with less than 3 million books.

Rank	Name	Location	Volume of books (millions)
1.	Library of Congress	Washington, D.C.	25
2.	The British Library	London	18
3.	Russian State Library	Moscow	17
4.	Harvard University Library	Cambridge, Massachusetts, U.S.	13.6
5.	National Library of France	Paris	13
6.	New York Public Library	U.S.	12
7.	National Library of Russia	St. Petersburg	11.8
8.	National Library of Germany	Frankfurt and Leipzig	11.3
9.	National Library of Canada	Ottawa and Montreal	10.2
10.	Russian Academy of Sciences Library	St. Petersburg	10
11.	National Library of Ukraine	Kiev	10
12.	Yale University Library	New Haven, Connecticut, U.S.	9.9
13.	Cincinnati & Hamilton County Public Library	Ohio, U.S.	9.6
14.	Berlin State Library	Germany	9.4
15.	National Library of Japan	Tokyo	9.2
16.	Chicago Public Library	U.S.	9.2
17.	Queens Borough Public Library	New York, U.S.	9.1
18.	National Library of China	Beijing	9
19.	Romanian Academy Library	Bucharest	8.9
20.	University of Illinois Library, Urbana-Champaign	U.S.	8.6
21.	University of California Library	Berkeley, U.S.	8.4
22.	Philadelphia Public Library	Pennsylvania, U.S.	8.1
23.	National Library of Italy	Rome and Florence	8.1

Rank	Name	Location	Volume of books (millions)
24.	Shanghai Library	China	8
25.	Bavarian State Library	Munich, Germany	8
26.	Lomonosov State University Library	Moscow, Russia	8
26.	Tokyo University Library	Japan	7.7
27.	Toronto Public Library	Ontario, Canada	7.6
28.	Boston Public Library	Massachusetts, U.S.	7.4
29.	Los Angeles County Public Library	California, U.S.	7.4
30.	National Library of Australia	Canberra	7.3
31.	University of Texas Library	Austin, U.S.	7.2
32.	University of California Library	Los Angeles, U.S.	7.2
33.	University of Michigan Library	Ann Arbor, U.S.	7.1
34.	Stanford University Library	California, U.S.	7
35.	Columbia University Library	New York, U.S.	7
36.	Vernadsky Central Scientific Library	Kiev, Ukraine	7
37.	Brooklyn Public Library	New York, U.S.	6.8
38.	National Library of Romania	Bucharest	6.4
39.	National Library of Kazakhstan	Almaty	6.5
40.	Bodleian Library, Oxford University	U.K.	6.5
41.	Beijing University Library	China	6.5
42.	Berlin Free University Library	Germany	6.4
43.	National Library of the Czech Republic	Prague	6.3
44.	University of Paris, I-XIII Libraries	France	6.3
45.	Carnegie Library of Pittsburgh	Pennsylvania, U.S.	6.3
46.	Nanjing University Library	China	6.3
47.	University of Toronto Library	Ontario, Canada	6.2
48.	National Library of Scotland	Edinburgh, U.K.	6
49.	Nanjing Library	China	6
50.	National Library of Georgia	Tbilisi	6
51.	National Library of Austria	Vienna	6
52.	Cambridge University Library	U.K.	5.8
53.	Los Angeles Public Library	California, U.S.	5.7
54.	Kyoto University Library	Japan	5.5
55.	National Library of Lithuania	Vilnius	5.5
56.	National Library of Spain	Madrid	5.4
57.	University of London Libraries	U.K.	5.4
58.	National Library of Bulgaria	Sofia	5.4
59.	Vilnius University Library	Lithuania	5.2
60.	Zhdanov State University Library	St. Petersburg, Russia	5.1
61.	National Library of Latvia	Riga	5.1
62.	National Library of Belgium	Brussels	5.1
63.	Houston Public Library	Texas, U.S.	5.1
64.	National Library of Turkmenistan	Ashkhabad (Ashgabat)	5
65.	National Library of Medicine	Bethesda, Maryland, U.S.	5
66.	Kazan State University Library	Russia	4.9
67.	John Rylands University Library	Manchester, U.K.	4.8
68.	Hanover Technical University Library	Germany	4.8
69.	Chinese Academy of Sciences Library	Beijing, China	4.7
70.	McGill University Library	Montreal, Canada	4.7
71.	National Library of Sweden	Stockholm	4.6

Rank	Name	Location	Volume of books (millions)
71.	National Library of Denmark/ Copenhagen University Library		4.6
72.	Martin Luther University Library	Halle-Wittenberg, Germany	4.6
73.	National Library of India	Calcutta	4.5
74.	Mitchell Library	Glasgow, U.K.	4.5
75.	Oslo University Library	Norway	4.5
76.	Leipzig University Library	Germany	4.5
77.	National University Library	Strasbourg, France	4.5
78.	National Library of New Zealand	Wellington	4.4
79.	National Library of Poland	Warsaw	4.4
80.	CISTI Library	Ottawa, Ontario, Canada	4.3
81.	Russian Library for Foreign Literature	Moscow	4.3
82.	Waseda University Library	Tokyo, Japan	4.3
83.	Sydney University Library	Australia	4.3
84.	Utrecht University Library	The Netherlands	4.2
85.	Lund University Library	Sweden	4.1
86.	Metropolitan London Borough Libraries	London, U.K.	4.1
87.	George August University Library	Göttingen, Germany	4.1
88.	Hebrew University Library/Israel National Library	Jerusalem	4
89.	Vienna University Library	Austria	4
90.	Lvov State Scientific Library	Ukraine	4
91.	Dresden University Library	Germany	4
92.	Florence University Library	Italy	4
93.	National Library of Hungary	Budapest	4
94.	Amsterdam University Library	The Netherlands	4
95.	National Library of Wales	Cardiff, U.K.	4
96.	Buenos Aires University Library	Argentina	4
97.	Central House of the Russian Army Library	Moscow	4
98.	Frankfurt University Library	Germany	4
99.	Russian Central Epidemiology Institute	Moscow	4
100.	National Library of Mongolia	Ulan Bator	4
101.	Estonian Academic Library	Tallinn	4
102.	Russian State Medical Library	Moscow	3.9
103.	Jagiellonian University Library	Kraków, Poland	3.9
104.	Beijing Society of Library Science Capital Library	China	3.9
105.	Irkutsk University Library	Russia	3.8
106.	Hampshire County Public Libraries	Winchester, U.K.	3.8
107.	Zhejiang Provincial Library	Hangzhou, China	3.8
108.	São Paulo Federal University Library	Brazil	3.7
109.	INION Library	Moscow, Russia	3.6
110.	Leuven Catholic University Library	Belgium	3.6
111.	Kyushu University Library	Fukuoku, Japan	3.6
112.	Babes-Bolyai University Library	Cluj-Napoca, Romania	3.5
113.	Kent County Public Libraries	Maidstone U.K.	3.5
114.	Mickiewicz University Library	Poznan Poland	3.5
115.	Tomsk University Library	Russia	3.5

Rank	Name	Location	Volume of books (millions)
116.	Fudan University Library	Shanghai, China	3.5
117.	Sichuan Provincial Library	Chengdu, China	3.5
118.	Hubei Provincial Library	Wuhan, China	3.4
119.	National Library of the Netherlands	Amsterdam	3.4
120.	National Library of Switzerland	Bern	3.4
121.	Shandong Provincial Library	Jinan, China	3.3
122.	Waterloo University Library	Canada	3.3
123.	Heidelberg University Library	Germany	3.3
124.	Swiss Federal Institute of Technology Library	Zürich	3.3
125.	Charles University Library	Prague, Czech Republic	3.3
126.	Humboldt University Library	Berlin, Germany	3.3
127.	Birmingham Public Library	U.K.	3.3
129.	National Parliamentary Library	Kiev, Ukraine	3.3
130.	Odessa University Library	Ukraine	3.3
131.	National Library of Mexico/ NAU Library	Mexico City	3.3
132.	Montpellier University Libraries	France	3.3
133.	Tartu University Library	Estonia	3.2
134.	Munich City Library	Germany	3.2
135.	Tbilisi State University Library	Georgia	3.2
135.	Berlin Central Library	Germany	3.1
136.	National Library of Argentina	Buenos Aires	3
137.	University of British Columbia Library	Vancouver, Canada	3
138.	National Library of Estonia	Tallinn	3
139.	Saratov University Library	Russia	3
140.	Georgian Academy of Sciences Central Library	Tbilisi	3
141.	National Library of Greece	Athens	3
142.	Lancashire County Public Libraries	Preston, U.K	3
141.	Melbourne University Library	Australia	3
142.	Graz University Library	Austria	3
143.	Liverpool Public Library	U.K.	3
144.	Hunan Provincial Library	Changsha, China	3
145.	Hokkaido University Library	Sapporo, Japan	3
146.	Trinity College Library, Dublin University	Ireland	2.9
147.	Jena University Library	Germany	2.9
148.	Rome "La Spienza" University Library	Italy	2.9
149.	University of Alberta Library	Edmonton, Canada	2.9
150.	Kobe University Library	Japan	2.9
151.	Rostov State University Library	Russia	2.8
152.	Wurzburg University Library	Germany	2.8
153.	Essex County Public Libraries	Chelmsford, U.K.	2.8
154.	Center for Research Library	Chicago, U.S.	2.8
155.	National Library of Finland / Helsinki University Library		2.8
156.	National Library of Venezeula	Caracas	2.7
157.	U.S. National Agricultural Library	Washington, D.C.	2.7
158.	Edinburgh University Library	U.K.	2.7
159.	Nagoya University Library	Japan	2.7

Rank	Name	Location	Volume of books (millions)
160.	Madrid Autonomous University Library	Spain	2.7
161.	Turin University Library	Italy	2.6
162.	Basel University Library	Switzerland	2.6
163.	Hamburg Public Library	Germany	2.6
164.	National Library of Portugal	Lisbon	2.6
165.	Air University Library, MAF	Alabama, U.S.	2.6
166.	National Library of Cuba	Havana	2.6
167.	Cologne University Library	Germany	2.6
168.	Bucharest University Library	Romania	2.5
169.	Russian State Public Historical Library	Moscow	2.5
170.	Seoul National University Library	South Korea	2.5
171.	Eotvos Lorand University Library	Budapest, Hungary	2.5
172.	Stockholm University Library	Sweden	2.5
173.	National Library of Korea	Seoul, South Korea	2.5
174.	Leeds University Library	U.K.	2.5
175.	Dusseldorf University Library	Germany	2.5
176.	Chongqing Library	China	2.5
177.	Lyons University Library	France	2.4
178.	Leiden State University Library	the Netherlands	2.4
179.	National Library of Norway	Oslo	2.3
180.	National Library of Greece	Athens	2.5
181.	Nankia University Library	Tianjin, China	2.3
182.	Munich University Library	Germany	2.3
183.	Birmingham University Library	U.K.	2.3
184.	Uppsala University Library	Sweden	2.3
185.	Heidelberg University Library	Germany	2.2
186.	Stockholm City and County Library	Sweden	2.2
187.	Malaya University Library	Kuala Lumpur, Malaysia	2.2
188.	New South Wales University Library	Sydney, Australia	2.2
189.	Pyongyang Academy of Sciences Library	North Korea	2.1
190.	Tübingen University Library	Germany	2.1
191.	Latvia University Library	Riga	2.1
192.	Wuhan University Library	China	2.1
193.	Osaka University Library	Japan	2.1
194.	Korolenko State Scientific Library	Kharkov, Ukraine	2.1
195.	Dublin City Library	Ireland	2.1
196.	Toulouse University Library	France	2.1
197.	National Library of Egypt	Cairo	2
198.	Aristotle University of Thessaloniki Library	Greece	2
199.	National Library of Vietnam	Hanoi and Ho Chi Minh City	2
200.	Rio de Janeiro Federal University Library	Brazil	2
201.	National Library of Taiwan	Taipei	2
202.	National Library of Thailand	Bangkok	2
203.	Lyons Municipal Library	France	2
204.	Louvain Catholic University	Belgium	2
205.	Complutense University Library	Madrid, Spain	2
206.	Bern University Library	Switzerland	2
207.	Coimbra University Library	Portugal	2

Rank	Name	Location	Volume of books (millions)
208.	Malmö City Library	Finland	2
209.	National Library of Belarus	Minsk	2
210.	Rotterdam Municipal Library	the Netherlands	2
211.	National University of Ireland Library	Dublin	2
212.	National University of Uzbekistan	Tashkent	2

These 212 libraries have a grand total of over 900 million books.

Abbreviations

CISTI. Canada Institute for Scientific and Technical Information.

INION. Institute for Scientific Information on Social Sciences Library.

MAF. Maxwell Air Force Base.

NAU. National Autonomous University.

N.B.: The figure for the National Library of Canada in Ottawa, includes that of the National Library of Quebec in Montreal.

315.
95 oldest libraries

This list focuses only on the oldest significant libraries (founded up to about mid-16th century, and excluding private libraries) that are still in existence today. For information on the earliest libraries in the world (but which no longer exist intact), see list **124**. World records on the oldest library buildings are at list **194**.

Rank	Name and Location	Year founded (AD)
1.	Al-Qarawiyin University Library, Fez, Morocco	circa 859
2.	Al-Azhar University Library, Cairo, Egypt	985
3.	Al-Nizamiyah University Library, Baghdad, Iraq	1070
4.	Bologna University Library, Italy	1088
5.	Padua University Library, Italy	1122
6.	Modena University Library	1160
7.	Hacettepe University Library, Ankara, Turkey	1206
8.	Vicenza University Library, Italy	1204
9.	Salamanca University Library, Spain	1218
10.	Sorbonne University of Paris Library, France	1230
11.	Montpellier University Library, France	1240
12.	Perugia University Library, Italy	1243
13.	Sienna University Library, Italy	1245
14.	Piacenza University Library, Italy	1248
15.	Arezzo University Library, Italy	1252
16.	Parma University Library, Italy	1255
17.	Salerno University Library, Italy	1265
18.	Vercelli University Library, Italy	1270
19.	Valladolid University Library, Spain	1290

Rank	Name and Location	Year founded (AD)
20.	Macerata University Library, Italy	1290
21.	Coimbra University Library, Portugal	1290
22.	Lisbon University Library, Portugal	1291
23.	Toulouse University Library, France	1292
24.	Complutense University Library, Madrid, Spain	1293
25.	Seville University Library, Spain	1295
26.	Naples University Library, Italy	1297
27.	Valencia University Library, Spain	1298
28.	Rome University Library, Italy	1304
29.	Orleans University Library, France	1306
30.	Florence University Library, Italy	1321
31.	Grenoble University Library, France	1339
32.	Cahor University Library, France	1342
33.	Pisa University Library, Italy	1343
34.	Angers University Library, France	1345
35.	Cambridge University Library, U.K.	1347
36.	Charles University, Prague, Czech Republic	1348
37.	Perpignan University Library, France	1350
38.	Pavia University Library, Italy	1361
39.	Avignon University Library, France	1363
40.	Jagiellionian University Library, Kraków, Poland	1364
41.	Vienna University Library, Austria	1365
42.	Orange University Library, France	1365
43.	National Library of the Czech Republic, Prague	1366
44.	Pécs University Library, Hungary	1367
45.	National Library of Austria, Vienna	1368
46.	Rupert-Charles University Library, Heidelberg, Germany	1386
47.	Cologne University Library, Germany	1388
48.	Ferrara University Library, Italy	1391
49.	Erfurt University Library, Germany	1392
50.	Würzburg University Library, Germany	1402
51.	Turin University Library, Italy	1404
52.	Leipzig University Library, Germany	1409
53.	St. Andrews University Library, U.K.	1410
54.	Aix-Marseille University Library, France	1413
55.	Rostock University Library, Germany	1419
56.	Besançon University Library, France	1422
57.	Louvain (Leuven) Catholic University Library, Belgium	1425
58.	Barcelona University Library, Spain	1430
59.	Caen University Library, France	1431
60.	Poitiers University Library, France	1432
61.	Bordeaux University Library, France	1441
62.	Catania University Library. Italy	1444
63.	Vatican Library, Rome, Vatican City	1451
64.	Glasgow University Library, U.K.	1451
65.	Istanbul University Library, Turkey	1455
66.	Greifswald University Library, Germany	1456
67.	Freiburg University Library, Germany	1457
68.	Basel University Library, Switzerland	1460
69.	Rennes University Library, France	1461
70.	Marciana National Library, Venice, Italy	1468

Rank	Name and Location	Year founded (AD)
71.	Aberdeen University Library. U.K.	1494
72.	Munich University Library, Germany	1472
73.	Eichstatt-Ingolstadt Catholic University Library, Germany	1472
74.	Mainz University Library, Germany	1476
75.	Uppsala University Library, Sweden	1477
76.	Tübingen University Library, Germany	1477
77.	National Library of France, Paris	1480
78.	Saragossa University Library, Spain	1480
79.	Copenhagen University Library, Denmark	1482
80.	Martin Luther University Library, Halle-Wittenberg, Germany	1502
81.	Royal College of Surgeons Library, Edinburgh , U.K.	1505
82.	Madrid Autonomous University Library of Library, Spain	1510
83.	Frankfurt University Library, Germany	1511
84.	Royal College of Physicians Library, London, UK	1518
85	Zürich University Library, Switzerland	1523
86.	Latvian Academic Library, Riga,	1524
87.	Lyons Municipal Library, France	1527
88.	Bern University Library, Switzerland	1528
89.	Granada University Library, Spain	1533
90.	Santo Domingo Autonomous University Library, Dominican Republic	1538
91.	National University Library, Strasbourg, France	1540
92.	St. Nicholas of Hidalgo Michoacan University Library, Morelia, Mexico	1549
93.	Mexico National Autonomous University Library, Mexico City, Mexico	1551
94.	San Marcos National University Library, Lima, Peru	1552
95.	Pontifical Gregorian University Library. Rome, Vatican City	1553

Notes. *Cambridge University (#31) was originally founded in the 13th century. The Bodleian Library at Oxford University does not make this list because it was re-founded in 1602, even though the library was originally founded in 1320. Palencia University Library in Spain was founded in 1210, but it was closed near the end of the 13th century because of the prominence of Salamanca University, so it has been excluded. Also excluded from this list is Kaliningrad University, which was founded as Königsberg University in 1544, but was destroyed in the Second World War. Avignon University (#39) was originally founded in the 13th cen-tury. The Vatican Library (#63) original founding date goes back to the 14th century. Istanbul University (#65) was founded as Constantinople University in AD 430. Some book collections of the National Library of France (#77) date back to 1368. The libraries of Copenhagen University (#79) and Mexico National Autonomous University Library (#88) are also part of the national library in those countries. Several other significant old library collections, such as religious libraries (e.g. libraries in cathedrals, monasteries and mosques), still exist today, some dating back to the 5th century AD. See entries **68**, **124** and **194** for more details.*

Saint Jerome, the Librarian's Patron Saint

St. Jerome is the patron saint for librarians and libraries. He was a passionate lover of books and apart from being ordained a priest, he also worked for some time in Rome as a prolific translator of the Bible from Hebrew to Latin.

In fact one of his major translations of the Bible finished in the 4th century AD is the vulgate edition of the Bible, which is the basis for the Bible used in Roman Catholic churches today.

One of St. Jerome's most remarkable feats was to seek solitary refuge in Syria's Chalcis desert for five years, just reading, praying and fasting!

GODFREY OSWALD'S 18 GREATEST TEXTS OF ALL TIME

Thank you for reaching the end of *Library World Records*. During my two-year research for this book, I came across several extraordinary texts in different forms such as stone or clay inscriptions, and manuscripts and books made from leaves, papyrus parchment, paper, etc. Many of these texts have had a tremendous influence on the progress of humanity. From my research notes, here is my list of the 18 all time greatest texts of the world, my own personal world records for this book. They are presented alphabetically for want of a better arrangement. I have also given in parentheses the entry numbers in this book that provide information about them. For yet more information consult the index.

The Bible (125)

Nicolaus Copernicus' book (58)

Charles Darwin's *Origin of Species* (46)

The Dead Sea Scrolls (125)

Encyclopaedia Britannica, printed version (166)

Albert Einstein's journal publications (50)

Ancient Egyptian hieroglyphics (125)

Classical Greek texts (124 and 125)

King Hammurabi's *Code of Laws* (124)

I Ching (125)

The Koran (128)

Karl Marx's *Das Kapital* (122)

Claudius Ptolemy's *Geographia* (91)

The *Tablets of the Law*, given to Moses (152)

Sumerian cuneiform inscriptions (125)

The *Vedas* (125)

The *Tripitaka Canon* at the Kuthodaw Pagodas (168)

Leonardo da Vinci's notebooks, including the *Codex Hammer* (172) and the *Codex Atlanticus* (26)

BIBLIOGRAPHY

Abdulrazak, F. *Arabic Historical Writing: An Annotated Bibliography of Books in History from All Parts of the Arab World*. London: Mansell Information Publishing, 1976.

American Library Directory. 52nd ed. New York: Bowker, 1999.

Bartz, B., H. Opitz, and E. Richter, eds. *World Guide to Libraries*. 13th ed. Munich: K. G. Saur, 1997.

Casson, L. *Libraries in the Ancient World*. New Haven, Connecticut: Yale University Press, 2001.

Columbia Encyclopedia. 6th ed. New York: Columbia University Press, 2000.

Coulmas, F. *The Blackwell Encyclopedia of Writings Systems*. Oxford: Blackwell Publishers, 1999.

Edwards, E. *Memoirs of Libraries*. London: Trübner & Co., 2 vol., 1859, repr. 1964.

Encyclopædia Britannica. 15th ed. Chicago: Encyclopædia Britannica Inc., 1994.

Faerber, M. *Gale Directory of Databases 2000*. London: Gale Research, 1999.

Feather, J., ed. *International Encyclopedia of Information and Library Science*. London: Routledge, 1997.

Harris, M. H. *History of Libraries in the Western World*. 4th ed. Metuchen, New Jersey: Scarecrow, 1995.

Hutchinson Encyclopedia 2002 (CD-ROM). 10th ed. Oxford: Helicon, 2001.

Irwin, R. *Origins of the English Library*. London: Allen & Unwin, 1958, repr. 1981.

Jiangzhong, W., ed. *New Library Buildings of the World*. Shanghai: Kexue-Jishu Wenxian-Chubanshe, 1999.

Thomas, L., ed., *Encyclopedia of Librarianship*. 3rd ed. New York: Hafner Publishing Co., 1966.

McMurtrie, C. *The Book: The Story of Printing and Bookmaking*. New York: Oxford University Press, 1962.

Microsoft Encarta Encyclopedia 98 (CD-ROM). Richmond, Washington: Microsoft Corp., 1997.

Nakanishi, A. *Writing Systems of the World: Alphabets, Syllabaries, Pictograms*. Rutland, Vermont: C. E. Tuttle Co., 1995.

Savage, E. A. *The Story of Libraries and Book-collecting*. London: Routledge, 1909, repr. 1969.

Tolzmann, D. H., ed., et al. *Memory of Mankind: The Story of Libraries Since the Dawn of History*. New Castle, Delaware: Oak Knoll, 2001.

Schottenloher, K. *Books and the Western World: A Cultural History*. Jefferson, North Carolina: McFarland, 1989.

Stam, D., ed. *International Dictionary of Library Histories*. Chicago: Fitzroy Dearborn, 2 vols., 2001.

Stern, M. B., and L. Rostenberg. *Bookman's Quintet: Five Catalogues about Books, Bibliography, Printing History, Booksellers, Libraries, Presses, Collectors*. Newark, Delaware: Oak Knoll, 1980.

UNESCO Statistical Yearbooks. Paris: UNESCO Press, 2000.

Wedgeworth, R., ed. *ALA World Encyclopedia of Library and Information Services*. 2nd ed. Chicago: American Library Association, 1986.

Wiegand, W., and D. Davis, eds. *Encyclopedia of Library History*. New York: Garland, 1994.

Winckler, P. *History of Books and Printing: A Guide to Information Sources*. Detroit: Gale Research, 1979.

World Book Encyclopedia. Chicago: World Book, Inc., 2001.

The World of Learning. 51st ed. London: Europa Publications, 2001.

Periodicals and Newspapers
(past issues mostly via databases such as LISA)

Library History
Library Journal
Archives
American Libraries
The Library
Liber Quarterly
*Journal of the American Medical Library
    Association*
IFLA Journal
The New York Times
School Library Journal
Publishers Weekly
Bookseller

Libri
The Library Quarterly
Online
Managing Information
Library Record
The Boston Globe
*Journal of the American Society for Information
    Science*
Journal of Information Science
Information Today
Information World Review
Searcher

INDEX

References are to entry numbers.

Aachen palace library 122
AACR2 207
Aberdeen University Library 69
ABI / Inform database 252
Abudarham 152
academic libraries, largest and old-
    est 44–77, 315
The Academy 66, 67
acid in books 136
Adelaide University Library 62
Adolf Marx 186
Adonis 292
advertisement, worst depicting
    libraries 121
Advis pour dresser une bibliothèque
    162
AFNOR cataloging rules 207
Africa: collections on 104; first
    book printed in 152 *see also*
    African languages; largest and
    oldest public libraries 2, 41;
    largest and oldest university
    libraries 65, 77; largest book fair
    193; largest book publishers *see*
    book publishers; largest book-
    stores *see* bookstores; most
    expensive library building 1,
    205; national archives, oldest
    116; oldest handwritten book
    134; oldest libraries *see* oldest;
    oldest printing press 152
African languages, oldest texts 125,
    134, 152
Agricola database 261
agriculture: largest databases 261;
    largest libraries 97, 99
Agris database 261
The Ahiram Inscriptions 125
Aichi Prefectural Library 19
air travel, largest schedules 274
Air University Library 100
airline reservations, largest database
    274
Aix-Marseille University Library
    47
Akademibokhandeln 185
Akateeminen Kirjakauppa 185
Akbar, Jalalal-Din 122
Akkadian texts, oldest 125
Al-Akhawayn University 66
Al-Aqsa Mosque 194

Al-Azhar University Library
    66
Al-Hakem II, caliph 124
Al-Hasan al-Basri 128
Al-Khwarizmi 122
Al-Mamun, caliph 122, 124
Al-Mutawakki Mosque 109
Al-Nizamiyah University Library
    66
Al-Qarawiyin University Library
    66
Al-Zahiriyah Library 122
Albatross Books 161
Albert I, king of Belgium 1
Alberta University Library 59
Albrecht III, archduke 1
Albrecht V, duke 1
Alexandria Library 1, 91, 117, 122,
    124, 171, 205
Alexander the Great 124
Alexandria University 1, 66
Alfred, king of Britain 132
Algeria: largest and oldest univer-
    sity library 65, 77; oldest texts
    134
Algeria University Library 65, 77
Allen, Paul 297
AllTheWeb search engine 289
Almaktabah 185
alphabets, largest, oldest, smallest
    125
Alsted, Johann 166
Alta Vista search engine 290
Altair 297
Amadeus 274
Amazon online bookstore 179
Ambrosian Library 26, 117, 122
American Bible Association 109
American Chemical Society 235
American Dental Association
    Library 80
American Economic Association
    252
American Geographical Society
    Library 91
American Institute for Chemical
    Engineers 93
American Institute for Mechanical
    Engineers 93
American Library Association 23,
    122, 299, 306

American Psychological Associa-
    tion 271
American Society for Civil Engi-
    neers 93
American Society for Information
    Science 310
American Society for Mechanical
    Engineers 93
American Type Culture Collection
    263
American University, Beirut 92
American University Library,
    Beirut, 64, 66
Americas: largest book publishers
    see book publishers; largest
    bookstores *see* bookstores;
    largest libraries *see* largest; oldest
    libraries *see* oldest
Amharic, oldest texts 134, 152
Amr Mosque 194
Amsterdam University Library 53,
    74
Analysis of Judaica 233
Ancestry PLUS databases 272
Andronicus, Livius 125
Anglo-American Cataloging Rules
    2 *see* AACR2
Anglo-Saxon Chronicle 132
Angola: oldest public library 41;
    oldest texts 135
Angus & Robertson Bookshop 185
Antonius, Marcus 124
antiquarian bookseller, largest 179
Antwerp Central Public Library 7
Apostol 144
Apple Macintosh 221
Arabic: oldest encyclopedia 166;
    oldest printed books 137; oldest
    texts 128
Arabic Legislations Encyclopedia
    168
Arba'ah Turim omf 150
Archimedes 1
Archives, oldest 112–116
Ariel 161
Argentina: largest and oldest uni-
    versity libraries 63, 76; largest
    bookstore 185; oldest public
    library 33
Aristophanes 122
Aristotle 67

Ark of the Convenant 152
Armenian, first printed book 147
art libraries, largest 104
Arturo, Allesandi 122
Ashmolean Museum 125
Asia Books 185
Asia-Pacific region largest book
    publishers see book publishers;
    largest bookstores see book-
    stores; largest libraries see
    largest; oldest libraries see oldest
Asian languages (including Middle
    East), oldest texts 125, 128, 129,
    133, 136, 137, 147–150, 153
Asher, Jacob Ben 150
Ashurbanipal 122, 124
ASLIB 307
Asoka, King of India 125
Association of College and
    Research Libraries 44
Association of Research Libraries 44
Assyria, oldest texts 124, 125
astronomy, largest library 106
Athenaeum Boekhandel 185
Atreya Sumhita 135
Attalus I 124
Auckland University Library 62
Audubon, James John 168, 172
Austen, Jane 170
Australia: first printed book in
    153; largest and oldest book-
    stores 185; largest and oldest
    university library 62, 75; largest
    book publisher 186; oldest pub-
    lic library 39
Australian National University Co-
    op 185
Australian National University
    Library 62
Austria: largest and oldest univer-
    sity libraries 50, 74; largest
    bookstores 185; largest public
    library 7; oldest newspaper 156
Austrian Library Association 307
Avery Architectural & Fine Arts
    Library 104
Avicenna 122
Avignon papal library 26
Axel Springer 186
Ayasofya Library 122

Babylonian texts, oldest 124, 125
Bacon, Francis 171
Baegun 137
Baer, Karl Ernst von 122
Baghdad University Library 64
The Bahamas, oldest public library
    34
Bailey, Nathaniel 173
Baird, John Logie 297
Baker & Taylor 295
ban on books, longest 171
Bangladesh, largest book publisher
    186
Baquerizo, Alfredo 122

Barbados, oldest public library 34
Barcelona Cathedral 68
Barcelona Public Library 7
Barcelona University Library 51
Barnes & Noble Bookstores 178,
    185
Barnet borough public libraries 8
Basel University Library 50, 74
Basque, oldest texts 131, 142
Bath University Library 46
Battle of Talas River 136
Bavarian State Library 1, 2, 117, 154
Bay Psalm Book 140
Baybars I, sultan of Egypt and
    Syria 122
Bayt-al-Hikmah 124
BBC Library 96
BCA see Book Club Associates
Bede, Venerable 132
Beijing University Library 61, 122
Beilstein, Friedrich 265
Beilstein database 265
Beinecke Rare Book and Manu-
    script Library 203
Belgian Library Association 307
Belgian Ministry of Foreign Affairs
    African Library 105
Belgique Loisirs 185
Belgium: largest and oldest uni-
    versity libraries 53, 74; largest
    bookstore 185; largest public
    library 7; oldest newspaper 156;
    Belize libraries 117
Bell & Howell 238
Ben Gurion University Library 64
Benedictine Rules 122
Beowulf 132
Berkeley Public Library 205
Berlin Central Library 7, 15
Berlin Free University Library 45
Berlin Papyrus 135
Berlin public libraries 15
Berlin State Library 1, 2, 117, 202
Berlin University 171
Berlioz, Hector 122
Berman National Library 64
Bern Convention 155
Bern Public Library 26
Bern University Library 50, 74
Berners-Lee, Tim 290
Bertelsmann 177, 186
Bessarione, cardinal 1
Beyazit State Library 40
Bezos, Jeff 179
The Bible 109, 125, 171
Biblia Pauperum 172
Biblio-Globus 185
Bibliographic Retrieval Services
    227
Bibliotheca Alexandrina 1, 205
Bibliothèque de l'Alliance Israélite
    109
biggest books see books
biggest libraries see largest
    libraries

biggest library buildings see
    library buildings
Bild-Zeitung 156
Bill & Melinda Gates Foundation
    313
Billings, John 122, 258
biological databases, largest 257,
    260, 262, 263
biomedical databases see medicine
biomedical libraries see medicine
Biosciences Information Service
    see BIOSIS
BIOSIS database 262
Biotechnobase 262
biotechnology database, largest
    262
Birchalls Bookshop 185
Birds of America 168, 172
Birmingham Central Public
    Library 7, 8, 12
Birmingham University Library 46
Blackwell's Bookshop 185
BLAISE database host 224
BLISS Classification 206
block-printing of books, earliest
    137
Bloomberg 246
Boccaccio 171
Bodleian Library see Oxford Uni-
    versity
Bodley, James 69
Bokia Bokhandel 185
Bokkilden Bokhandel 185
Bokus.com 185
Boleyn, Anne 24
Bolivia: largest and oldest univer-
    sity library 76; oldest public
    library 33
Bologna University Library 49, 68
Bolton Public Library 28
Bonaparte, Napoleon 4, 26, 100,
    117, 168
Bonfire of the Vanities 171
Bonnier Group 186
book, definition of 2
book ban, longest 171
book-burning rituals, first and
    largest 171
book classification, oldest and most
    popular 206
Book Club Associates 177
book clubs, largest and oldest 177
Book Expo of America 189
book fairs, largest 188–193
book fines, biggest 169; see also
    book stealing
Book House 185
Book of Change 125
Book of Common Prayer 146
Book of Kells 146
Book of the Dead 125
book preservation 136
book publishers: largest 186; old-
    est 186
book reading day, largest 131

book stealing, biggest 119; *see also* book fines
BookBank 245
Bookfinder.com 179
books and manuscripts: biggest, smallest, heaviest, tallest 168; largest number of readers 24, 187; most expensive 168, 172; most overdue library book 169; most read in public libraries 170; oldest 125–153, 166, 173; rare and out-of-print 179
Books etc. 185
Books in Print 245
bookstores: largest 178–184, 185; oldest 175, 176, 185
Boots Pharmaceutical Research Library 86
Bordeaux Municipal Library 14
Borders Bookstore 185
Borges, Jorge Luis 122
Borromeo, Federico 122
Borsippa Library 124
Boston Athenaeum 119
Boston Public Library 6, 32, 219
botanical library, largest 99
Bowker-Saur 245, 275
Brahmi script 125
Brainerd, Paul 137
Branches *see* library branches
Brazil: largest and oldest university libraries 63, 76; largest bookstores 182, 185; largest public libraries 20; tallest public library building 196
Brazilian Library Association 306
Briand, Joseph 140
Bridgetown Public Library 34
Brisbane Public Library 40
Bristlecone pine tree 125
Britain *see* U.K.
British Broadcasting Corporation Library *see* BBC library
British Columbia University Library 59
British Copyright Act 155
British Council libraries 118
British Dental Association Library 80
British Film Institute Library 96
The British Library 1, 2, 28, 54, 94, 117, 121 122, 125, 136, 137, 139, 168, 197, 202, 209, 224, 284, 313
British Library Document Supply Center 291
British Library of Political and Economic Science 90
British Medical Association Nuffield Library 85
British Museum 125, 134, 238
British Museum Library 2, 28, 195, 202
British National Bibliography 209, 224

Brooklyn Public Library 6
BRS Online 227
Bruciotto, Giacinto 134
Bruna Boekhandel 185
Brussels Free University Library 53
BUBL 311
Bucharest City Library 7
Bucharest University Library 58, 73, 117
Budapest Metropolitan Library 7
Budapest Synagogue Library 109
Budapest University Library 73
Buddhism, oldest texts 125, 136
Buddhist libraries, largest 109
Budgets *see* library budgets
Budshah, Zanulabin 136
Buenos Aires Public Library 33
Buenos Aires University Library 63
Buffalo & Eire County Public Library 32
building and consruction, largest database 267
buildings *see* library buildings
Bulletin Board for Librarians 311
Burgrave, Thomas 76
Burma, oldest texts 133
burning of books, biggest and oldest 171
burning of libraries 117, 171
Burns, Robert 175
Busck, Arnold 185
Bush, Laura 122
busiest libraries 11, 12
business, largest databases 246–252
business data, largest providers 246
Butterworths database 255
Byzantium Imperial Library 124

Cadamosto, Alvise de 134
Cadaverous 121
Caesar, Julius 117, 132
Cairo University Library 64
Calcutta Book Fair 190
Calcutta University 45, 75
Calgary University Library 196
California state public libraries 17
California State University Library 210
California University Library, Berkeley 44, 210
California University Library, Irvine 200, 210
California University Library, Los Angeles 44, 96, 121, 210, 290
Caligula 171
Callimachus 1, 122
Calpurnius, Lucius 124
Cambodia, oldest texts in Khmer 133
Cambridge Public Library 28
Cambridge Scientific Abstracts 269

Cambridge University Library 45, 54, 69, 125, 169, 203
Cambridge University Press 186
Canada: first book printed in 140; first papermill 136; largest and oldest public libraries 6, 35, 36; largest and oldest university libraries 59, 76; largest book publisher 186; largest bookstores 185; largest library building 198; most expensive library building 203; tallest library building 196
Canada Institute for Scientific and Technical Information 79, 292
Canadian Library Association 306
Canterbury Cathedral 194
Canterbury Public Library 28
The Canterbury Tales 139, 172
Cape Town City Library 22
Cape Town Provincial Library Service 22
Cape Town University Library 65, 77
Cappelen 186
Carboni, Raffaello 153
Carnegie Library of Pittsburgh 6
Carnegie Public Library 34
Carrie 121
Carroll, Lewis 241
Carte Topographique de l'Egypt 168
CAS databases 265
CAS Registry System 265
Casa de Libro 185
Casanova, Giovanni 122, 171
cataloging of books, see AACR2
catalogs *see* library catalogs
Catchword 292
Catechism 140
cathedral libraries 44, 194
Catherine the Great, empress 2, 29
caveman paintings, oldest 125
Cawdrey, Robert 173
Caxton, William 138, 139, 178
CD-ROM disk, books on 166, 242, 297
Census Bureau database 221
CERN 290
Cervantes, Miguel de 101
La Chanson de Roland 130
Chapters Bookstore 185
Charlemagne 122, 125 130
Charles I, king of Spain 76
Charles II, king of Britain 168
Charles IV, king of the Czech Republic 1
Charles V, king of France 1
Charles University 1; Library 58, 73
Charlie's Angels 121
Chaucer, Geoffrey 139, 172
Chemical Abstracts Service 265, 286, 292
chemical engineering, largest library 93

Chemical Titles 235
chemistry: largest databases 265, 286; largest libraries 93
Chester Beatty Library 125, 205
Chetham Library 27, 312
Chicago Medical Library 200
Chicago Public Library 6, 16, 32, 117
Chie, Wang 136
Chihuahua Public Library 33
China: first book printed in 136, 137; largest book publisher 186; largest bookstores 181, 185; largest library building 197, 199; largest public libraries 6, 19; largest university libraries 61; oldest libraries 124; oldest library building 194; oldest texts in Chinese 125; tallest library building 196
China Publishing Group 186
Chinese Academy of Agricultural Science Library 97
Chinese Academy of Sciences Library 61
Chinese University of Hong Kong 72
Chin-kang Ching 136
Christian libraries, oldest and largest 109
Christianity, oldest texts 125
Christie's 172
Church of St. Mary Zion 152
CIA library 120, 268
Cincinnati & Hamilton County Public Library 6, 32, 199
cinema *see* film
citation indexes, first and largest 232–235
Cite 186
City of Angels 121
City University School of Informatics 304, 311
civil engineerng, largest database 267; *see also* engineering
CLAIMS database 285
classification of books, most popular and oldest 206
Clement Classification 206
Cleopatra, Queen 117, 124
Cleveland Public Library 32
Club 185
Cluj-Napoca Lucian Blaga University Central Library 58
Cockeram, Henry 173
Code of Laws 124
Codex Atlanticus 26
Codex Hammer 172
Codex Leicester 172
Codex Sinaiticus 125
Codex Vaticanus 26, 125
Coimbra University Library 47, 74
coins commerating libraries, first 42
Cold War and libraries 23

College of Physicians of Philadephia 82
Collins 186
Cologne University Library 71
Colombia, oldest public library 33
Colon Classification 206
Coloquios dos Simples e drogas he da India 149
Columbia University, library school 102, 298
Columbia University Library 44
Columbus, Christopher 72, 76, 91
Comenius Library 107
company information *see* Business
EI Compendex database, 266
Complutense University Library 51, 72
Compton's Encyclopedia 242
Computer Library Systems 219
Confucius 125, 171, 204
Congress of Vienna 1, 26
Consortium of University Research Libraries 211
Constantine, Roman emperor 124
Constantinople University 66
The Constitution 2
construction and building, largest database 267
Cookson, Catherine 170
COPAC 211
Copenhagen University, library school 300
Copenhagen University Library 1, 52, 74, 117
Copernicus, Nicolaus 58, 171
Coptic Museum 125
Coptic texts, oldest 125, 134
copyright, earliest important dates 155
Corante 156
Corbis Collection 282
Corbis Picture Experience 282
Córdoba University Library 76
Cornaro Missal 172
Cosmographia see *Geographia*
Cuesta 185
Cujas Library 103
cuneiform inscriptions, oldest 124, 125
Current Contents database 236
Current Drugs 259
Croatia, oldest university library 73
cybercafes, largest 290
Czech Republic: largest and oldest university libraries 58, 73; largest public library 7

Da Gama, Vasco 91
Dallas Public Library 121, 122
Dancer, John 220
Dante 171
Dar Al Ma'aref 186
Darby Library Company 31
Darius I, king of Persia 125

Darwin, Charles 46
database: first 221; largest 283
databases and database hosts, largest and oldest 221–288
Dataphasc 217, 219
DataStar database host 244, 228
David Lubin Memorial Library 97
Day, Stephen 140
The Day of the Jackal 121
dBASE 221
De Oratore 142
Dead Sea Scrolls 2, 125, 152
deafness, largest library on 89
De Agostini 186
Deakin University, Library 217
The Declaration of Independence 2
Defoe, Daniel 101
Delphion 283
Demetrius 1
demotic script 125
Denmark: largest and oldest bookstores 185; largest and oldest university libraries 52, 74; largest book publishers 186; oldest texts in Danish 133
dental libraries, oldest and largest 80
Derby Central Library 204
Derwent Information 284, 286
Descartes, René 171
Desk Top Publishing *see* DTP
De Slegte Boekhandel 185
destruction of books and libraries, with fire, largest 117, 171
Deutches Wörterbuch 173
Dewan Bahasa dan Pustaka 186
Dewey, Melvil 44, 206, 298, 306
Dewey Decimal Classification 206
DGSE library 120
The Dharani Sutra 136
DIALOG database host 244, 222
Dialogus Creatururum Moralizatus 145
The Diamond Sutra 136
diary, oldest existing 129
Diaz de Santos 185
Dickens, Charles 170, 202
Dictes and Sayings of the Philosophres 139
dictionaries, oldest and largest 173
digital images, largest database 282
Digital Millennium Copyright Act 155
DIMDI database host 225
Diocletian, Roman emperor 124
DK Books 185
DNA Databank of Japan 260
DNA databases, largest 260
Doc Deliver 292
Doctrina Christiana 153
document delivery/supply services, largest 291, 292
Domesday Book 132

Dominican Republic: largest bookstore 185; oldest newspaper 156; oldest public library 34; oldest university library 76
Dominican Republic Public Library 34
donations, largest to libraries *see* library, donations
Dong-Eui University Library 205
Donner Boekhandel 185
D'Orta, Garcia 149
Double Jeapardy 121
Dow Jones Interactive 246
Dracon 125
Dragon, René 220
Dresden Technical University Library 48
Drexel University library school 305
drug database, largest 259
DTP, invention of 137
Dublin City Library 7
Dublin University *see* Trinity College
Dun & Bradstreet database 246
Dunya Kitapevi 185
Dupré, Dupré 141
Durie, John 162
Dutch, oldest texts 133
DVD-ROM disk 297
Dymocks 185
Dyna Book 221

e-books 137, 155, 241, 290
Eadfrith 132
earliest books *see* books
earliest libraries *see* oldest libraries
Eason and Sons Bookshop 185
Eastman-Kodak 220
easyInternetCafé 290
Ebers Papyrus 135
Eberhart, George 163
EBSCO 24, 241, 244, 294
EBSCO Business Source Premier database 252
Ecclesiastical History of the English People 132
EconLit database 252
economics: largest databases 252; largest libraries 90; *see also* business
Ecuador, oldest university library 76
Edinburgh Circulating Library 27
Edinburgh University Library 46, 69
Edipresse 186
Edison, Thomas 96, 195
Éditions de Luxe 141
education: largest databases 273; largest libraries 107
Educational Resources Information Center 273
Edward VI, king of Britain 69

Edward Kardelja University Library 73
Egmont 186
Egypt: earliest libraries 124; largest and oldest university libraries 64, 66; largest book publisher 186; largest bookstore 185; oldest handwritten book 134; oldest texts 125
Egyptian Coptic Psalter 134
Egyptian Library Association 309
Einstein, Albert 50
electrical engineering, largest database 268; *see also* engineering
electricity, first library to use 195
electronic books *see* e-books
Electronic Information for Libraries Direct 293
electronic journals, largest collections 241, 237; *see also* full-text databases
electronic library, largest 241
electronics, largest database 268; *see also* engineering
Eleftheroudakis 185
Elsevier Science 241, 259
EMBASE 259
EMBL DNA database 260
Eminescu, Mihail 122
Encyclopædia Britannica 166, 171, 242
Encyclopédie Français 167
encyclopedias, largest and oldest 166, 167
Enderun Kitabevi 185
endnote 277
engineering: largest databases 266–269; largest libraries 93
Engineering Index 266
Engineering Information 266
Engels, Fredrich 122
England *see* U.K.
English: earliest texts 132, 138, 139, 140; largest book databases 245; oldest dictionaries 173; oldest encyclopedia 166
ENIAC 221
Ensemble database 259
Eotvos Lorand University Library 73
The Epic of Gilgamesh 125
Equifax 246
Eratosthenes 122
Erbauliche Monaths-Unterredungen 157
Erfurt University Library 71
ERIC database 273
Erwin Szabo Library 7
ESA-IRS database host 229
Escape from Alcatraz 121
Escorial Library 122
Eslite 185
Essex county public libraries 9
O Estado de São Paulo 156
Estelle Doheny Collection 172

Estonia, largest university library 58
Ethiopia: earliest texts 134; first printed book 152
Eton College 69
Etruscan alphabet 125
Euclid 1
Eumenes II 124
Europe: largest book publishers *see* book publishers; largest bookstores *see* bookstores; largest libraries *see* largest; oldest libraries *see* oldest
European Bioinformatics Institute 260
European Information Network Services 229
European languages, oldest texts 125, 126, 130–134, 136–146, 150
European Space Agency's Information Retrieval Service *see* ESA-IRS
Evans, Arthur 125
Excerpta Medica 259
Exclusive Books 183
expensive books and manuscripts, most *see* books
expensive libraries, most 120, 313
expensive library budget, most 120, 313; *see also* library buildings
Experian 246

Factiva 246
Fahasa 185
famous librarians 122
Farewell to Arms 161
Farnsworth, Philo 297
Farsi, oldest texts printed in 147
FAST search engine 289
Fast Search and Transfer 289
Fatal Attraction 121
Fatih Library 122
Faxon 292
FBI 23, 122, 119, 260
Fedorov, Ivan 144
Feltrinelli 186
Fillmore, Abigail Powers 122
film libraries, largest 96
films featuring libraries 121
financial data, largest providers 246; *see also* business
FIND/SVP 276
fines *see* book fines
fingerprint database, largest 260
Finland: first book printed in 145; largest and oldest bookstores 185; largest book publisher 186; largest public library 204; largest university libraries 52; oldest handwritten book 134; oldest texts in Finnish 125
fire, destruction of libraries and books with 117, 171

First Edition 296
first Jewish revolt 2
First World War, destruction of
    libraries in 117
Firstandsecond.com 185
FirstSearch database 241
FIZ Karlsruhe 265
Flora Fountain bookshops 185
Flora Lamson Hewlett Library 109
Florence Medical School Library 81
Florence University Library 49
Folger, Clay, Henry 111
Folger Shakespeare Library 111
Fontana, Domenico 194
food science, largest database 261
Forsyth, Fredrick 121
Fort Knox 2
Foul Play 121
Fourah Bay College Library 77
Foyles Bookshop 185
France: first book printed in 141;
    first papermill 136; first printing
    press 137; largest and oldest
    bookstores 185; largest and old-
    est public libraries 15, 26;
    largest and oldest university
    libraries 45, 47, 68, 70; largest
    book publisher 186; largest
    library building 197; military
    libraries, largest 100; oldest texts
    in French 130
Francis Countway Medical Library
    78, 200
Frankfurt International Book Fair
    188, 279
Frankfurt University Library 48
Franklin, Benjamin 31, 122, 165
Franklin Public Library 31
Fraunhofer Informationszentrum
    267
Frederick II, Holy Roman emperor
    138
Frederick III, king of Denmark 1
Freedom of Information Act 120
The French Constitution of 1791
    130
French Library Association 307
French National Center for Sci-
    entific Research 223
French National Institute for Sci-
    entif and Technical information
    292
French, oldest texts in 130, 141
French Patent and Trademark
    Office 286
French Union Catalog 212
Fudan University Library 61
Fukagawa Library 121
Fulda Monastry 68
full-text catalogs, first 2
full-text databases, first and largest
    237; see also electronic journals

Gacon, Samuel 143
Gaelic, oldest texts 132

Gale Group 243, 244
Galileo database 274
Galileo Galilei 171
Gallica catalog 2
Gandhran Buddhist Scrolls 125
Garfield, Eugene 234
Garzanti 186
Gates, Bill 172, 282, 297, 313
Gaylord 219
Geac 214, 215, 216, 218, 219
GEC GAD 185
Ge'ez, oldest texts 134, 152
GenBank database 260
genealogy, largest database 272
General Theological Seminary 125
Geneva University 260
Genios database host 249
Genizah 171
The Gentleman's Magazine 157
George I, king of Britain 48
George III, king of Britain 202
George Augustus University,
    library school 300
George Augustus University
    Library 48
Georges Pompidou Center Library
    12, 14
Georgia, largest university library
    58
Georgia Institute of Technology
    303
Geographia 91
geography, largest library 91
German Book and Writing
    Museum 174
German Institute for Medical
    Documentation and Informa-
    tion 225
German Library Association 307
German Museum of Science and
    Technology Library 174
German National Library of Medi-
    cine 78
Germany: first book printed in
    137; first papermill 136; first
    printing press 137; largest and
    oldest public libraries 7, 15, 26,
    30; largest and oldest university
    libraries 45, 48, 71; largest book
    publishers 186; largest book-
    stores 185; oldest texts in Ger-
    man 126; tallest library building
    196
Getty, Paul 172
Geuchmatt 155
Ghana Library Board Act 41
Ghana University Balme Library
    65
Ghota, Bartholemeus 145
Ghostbusters 121
Ginsberg, Allen 122
Gigas Librorum 168
Gladstone, William 28
Glasgow University Library 46, 69
Glasgow Women's Library 110

GlaxoSmithKline Libraries 86
Glydenhal 186
Goa University 83
Godfry, Thomas 114
Goebbels, Joseph 171
Goethe, Johann Wolfgang von 48,
    122
Goethe-Institut 118
Golda Meir Library 91
Goldeneye 121
Gondishapur University 61
Google search engine 290
Gordon Memorial University
    Library 66
The Gospel Book of Henry the Lion
    172
Gotfried van Os 145
Government Printing Office
    259
The Graduate 121
Grainger Engineering Library and
    Information Center 23, 200
Gramedia 185, 186
Grant & Cutter 185
Graz University Library 50
Great Chicago Fire 117
Great Fire of Turku 1, 117
Greece: earliest libraries 124; first
    book printed in 150; largest and
    oldest university libraries 55,
    66, 67; largest book publisher
    186; largest bookstores 185; old-
    est encyclopedia 166; oldest
    public libraries 26; oldest texts
    in Greek 125
Grenoble University Library 70
Grimm, Wilhelm 173
Grolier Electronic Encyclopedia 242
Guadalajara University Library 63
Guatemala, oldest texts 127
Guelph University Library 214
guillotine 130
The Guinness Book of World Records
    125, 203
Gustavus I, king of Sweden 1
Gutenberg, Johannes 137, 172, 297
Gutenberg Bible 137, 162, 172

Habsburg Dynasty 1
Hacettepe University Library 66
Hadrian's Wall 132
The Hague Public Library 204
Haifa University Library 64
Haji-Ioannou, Stelios 290
Haldimand, Frederick 35
Hamburg City Library 15
Hamburg University Speersort
    Library 117
Hammurabi, king of Babylonia
    124
Hampshire county public libraries
    9, 290
Handelsblatt Publishing Group
    249
Handley Public Library 204

Hangul 129
Hanover Technical University Library 48
hard of hearing libraries *see* hearing loss
Hardayal Municipal Public Library 38
Harlequin 186
The Harley Latin Gospels 125
Harold Washington Library Center 6, 199, 204
HarperCollins 186
The Harris Papyrus 168
Harry Potter and the Philosopher's Stone 121
Hart, Michael 241
Hartford Seminary Library 109
Harvard, John 44
Harvard University Law Library 102
Harvard University Library 44, 76, 117, 120, 137, 210, 220, 313
Harvard University Medical School Library 78, 200
Hausa, oldest texts 134
Havas 186
Hayes, Rutherford B. 122
hearing loss, largest library on 89
heaviest books *see* books
Hebrew: first book printed in 148; oldest texts 125, 148
Hebrew University, library school 302
Hebrew University Library 64, 66, 109
Heidelberg University Library 71, 117
Helsingborgs City Library 204
Helsinki University Library 1, 52, 117
Hemingway, Ernest 122, 161
Henriques, Henrique 149
Henry III, king of Britain 132
Henry VI, king of Britain 69
Henry VII, king of Britain 2
Henry VIII, king of Britain 24
Hereford Cathedral Library 103
Hesiod 125
hieratic script 125
Higginbothams' Bookshop 185
Hildebrandslied 126
Hildesheim Cathedral 68
Hindi, first printed book 149
Hinduism, oldest texts 125
Hiragana 125, 129
Historia Naturulis 166
History of King Boccus 155
Hitler, Adolf 101
Hittite texts, oldest 125
Ho Ti, emperor of China 136
Hodder Headline 186
Hodges Figgis Bookshop 185
Hoffman Tablet 125
Hokkaido University Library 60
Hollywood 121
Holtzbrinck 186

Homer 1, 125, 171
Homo sapiens sapiens 125
Hong Kong, largest university library 62
Hong Kong Book Fair 190
Hoover, J. Edgar 122
Hoover's 246
horticulture library, largest 99
Hours and Psalter of Elizabeth de Bohun 172
House of Wisdom 122, 124
Houston Public Library 6, 32, 122
Huaisheng Mosque 194
Huang, Qin Shih 171
Hugendubel Buchhandlung 185
Hugo, Victor 168, 171
Hulagu Khan 52
Hull University Library 122, 216
The Human Genome Project 260
Humboldt University 45
Hume, David 122
Hungary: first book printed in 144; largest public library 7; oldest university library 73; oldest public libraries 26
Huntington Library 121
hurricane, destruction of libraries 117
Hutchinson Electronic Encyclopedia 242
Hypatia 122

I Ching 125
Iaşi University Library 122
Ibadan University Library 65
IBM patent database 283
Ibn-al-As, Amr 117
Ibn Battutah 134
Ibn Ishaq, Hunayn 124
Ibn Nahmias, David 150
Ibn Nahmias, Samuel 150
Ibn Qutayba 166
Ibn Sina 122
ICC Information 248
Iceland 24
ICONDA 267
IDdb³ 259
IDG 186
IDT 280
IFI/Plenum Data Corporation 285
IFLA 205, 306
IHS Engineering databases 269
The Iliad 125
incunabula, largest collection 62
Index Libroram Prohibitorum 171
Index Medicus 122, 258
Index of Prohibited Books 171
An Index to Periodical Literature 232
India: first book printed in 149; first papermill 136; largest and oldest public libraries 19, 38; largest and oldest university libraries 62, 66, 75; largest bookstores 185; oldest texts in Sanskrit, and Hindi 125

Indian National Scientific Documentation Center 292
Indiana Jones and the Last Crusade 121
Indiana University, library school 305
Indiana University Library 198
Indonesia: largest book publisher 186; largest bookstore 185; oldest texts 133; oldest university library 75
Indus Valley texts, oldest 125
Infobase 279
information brokers, oldest service 276
information science, first university courses 303, 304
information science, largest database 275
information services, largest providers 239
Information Services for the Physics and Engineering Communities *see* INSPEC
InfoTorg database host 231
InfoTrac 288
Ingenta 241
Innerpeffray Library 28
The Inquisition 26, 112, 125, 171
INSPEC database 268
Institut Français 118
Institute for Electrical and Electronic Engineering 93
Institute for Scientific Information 234
Institute of Education Library 107
Institution of Civil Engineers Library 93
Institution of Electrical Engineers 268
Institution of Royal Engineering Library 100
Integrum-Techno database host 226
intelligence agency libraries, most secure 120
inter-library loans, largest service 291
International Bibliography of the Social Sciences 90
International Construction Database 267
international digital copyright treaty 155
International Federation for Documentation 310
International Federation of Library Associations and Institutes *see* IFLA
International Food Information Service 261
International Paper 136
International Seminar on Library Buildings 205
The Internet 137, 289, 297

The Internet Archive 290
Internet Bookstore 180
Internet cafes, largest 290
Internet Database Service 269
Internet Explorer 290
Investigational Drug Database 259
Iran, first printed book 147
Iraq: largest and oldest university
  library 64, 66; oldest texts 125
Ireland: first book printed in 146;
  largest and oldest university
  library 54; largest bookstores
  185; largest public library 7;
  oldest texts in Irish 132
An Irish Alphabet and Catechism
  146
Irkutsk University Library 47
ISI Document Solution 292
Islam, oldest texts 128
Islamic libraries 66, 109, 124,
  194
Islamic University of Imam
  Muhammad Ibn Saud Library
  64
Ismael, Abdul Kassam 124
Israel: first book printed in 148;
  largest and oldest bookstores
  185; largest and oldest university
  libraries 64, 66; largest book
  publisher 186; largest public
  libraries 21; oldest texts in
  Hebrew 125
Israel Institute of Technology
  Library 64
Israel Museum 125
Istanbul Technical University
  Library 66
Istanbul University Library 66
Italian, oldest text printed in 142
Italian Library Association 307
Italy: first book printed in 142;
  first papermill 136; first printing
  press 137; largest and oldest
  public libraries 7, 26; largest
  and oldest university libraries
  49, 68; largest book publisher
  186; largest bookstores 185; old-
  est paper document 136; oldest
  library buildiing 194
Ivan Franko State University
  Library 73

Jagiellonian University Library 58,
  73
James Bond, gadgets in libraries
  120
Jāna Rozes Bookstore 185
Japan: first book printed in 153;
  largest and oldest bookstores
  185; largest and oldest university
  libraries 44, 60, 75; largest book
  publisher 186; largest library
  building 197; largest public
  libraries 19; oldest texts in Japanese 129

Japan Information Center for Sci-
  ence and Technology 264, 292
Japan Library Association 308
Jareer 185
Jarrow Monastery 68
Jason Farradane Award 311
Javanese, oldest texts 133
Jena University Libary 122
Jerusalem City Public Library 21
Jesuit College Library 76
Jesuit University of St. Joseph
  Library 66
Jesuits 1, 75, 137
Jewish libraries, largest 109
Jewish National and University
  Library see Hebrew University
  Library
Jewish Theological Seminary of
  America Library 109
Jikji Simgyeong 137
Johannes Walberg-Wolfegg-Wald-
  see Library 208
Johannesburg Public Library 22
John I, king of Britain 132
John Rylands University Library
  46, 211
John Smith & Sons Bookstore 175
Johnson, Richard 312
Johnson, Samuel 173
Johnson, Samuel, Jr. 173
Joint Services Command and Staff
  College Library 100
Journal du Palais 159
Journals, oldest 158–160; see also
  electronic journals
Journals@Ovid 241
Judaism, oldest texts 125
Junkodo 185
Juta Bookshop 186

Kahoun Papyrus 135
Kaliningrad University 73, 122
Kanda Book Town 185
Kanji 125, 129
Kant, Immanuel 122
Das Kapital 122
Karolinska Institute Library 88
Katakana 125, 129
Kazan State University Library 57
Keio University Library 75
Kent county public libraries 9
Kersey, John 173
Key Word in Context indexing
  235
KGB library 120
Khach'atur 147
Khedieval Palace Library 5
Khmer, oldest texts 133
Khomeini, Ayatollah 171
Khon Konchog Gylapo 109
Kidderminster Public Library 28
Kiel Institute of World Economics
  90
Kiel University 90
Kiepert Buchhandlung 185

King, Stephen 121, 137
King Fahd University of Petroleum
  and Minerals Library 92
King Saud University Library 64
King's College Library 45, 205
King's Library 202
Kinokuniya 185
Kirkwell Library 28
Kleukens, C.H. 220
Knight-Ridder Information 222
Kobe University Library 60
Kobzar of Tara Shevchen Ko 168
Kodansha 186
Kojiki 129
Komjáti, Benedek 144
Kompass database 246
Königsberg University see Kalin-
  ingrad University
Koprulu, Pasha 66
Koprulu Library 40, 66
Koran 128, 137, 171
Korea: first book printed in 137;
  largest bookstore 185; largest
  public library 19; largest univer-
  sity library 62; largest university
  library building 205; oldest
  texts in Korean 129, 136
Kukai 129
Kulturkaufhaus Dussmann Buch-
  handlung 185
Kuthodaw Pagodas 168
KWIC indexing 235
Kyobo 185
Kyoto Public Library 38
Kyoto University Library 60
Kyushu University Library 60

Lachish Palace 125
Lagardère 186
Lancashire county public libraries
  9
Lancaster University Ruskin
  Library 203
Lane, Allen 161
languages, most published books
  187
La Paz Municipal Library 33
La Plata National University
  Library 63
largest book clubs 177
largest book fairs 183–193
largest book publishers 186
largest books and manuscripts see
  books
largest bookstores 178–184, 185
largest databases see databases
largest libraries: in Africa 5, 22,
  65; in the Americas 2, 4, 6, 20,
  44, 59, 63, 78, 79, 91, 94, 97,
  100, 102, 109, 111; in the Asia-
  Pacific region 2, 3, 6, 19, 44,
  60–62; in Europe 2, 7, 8–10,
  13–15, 44–58, 78, 85–108; in
  the Middle East 5, 21, 64, 92,
  106; worldwide 315

largest library buildings *see* library buildings
Larkin, Philip 122
Latin: largest university library collection in 55; oldest texts 125
Latin America: largest book publishers *see* book publishers; largest bookstores *see* bookstores; largest libraries *see* largest; oldest libraries *see* oldest
Latvia: first book printed in 144; largest bookstore 185
Laurentian Library 26, 205
law libraries, oldest and largest 102–103; *see also* legal databases
Lawtel databases 255
Leardo, Giovanni 91
Leatherhead Information Services 261
Lebanon: largest and oldest university library 64, 66; largest bookstore 184; oldest texts 125
Lectorum Bookstore 185
Leeds University Library 46
Lefevre, Raoul 138
legal databases, largest 253–256; *see also* law libraries
legal libraries *see* law libraries
Lehmanns Fachbuchhandlung 185
Leibniz, Gottfried von 122
Leiden Papyrus 135
Leiden State University Library 53, 74, 103
Leignton Library 28
Leipzig University 195
Leipzig University, library school 300
Leipzig University Library 48, 71
Lektüre Buchhandlung 185
Lenin, Vladimir Ilyich, 2, 57, 202
Lenin State Library of the USSR 2
Leo III, emperor of Byzantium 124
Leonardo da Vinci 26, 172, 241
Leopold II, king of Belgium 105
Leuven Catholic University Library *see* Louvain Catholic University
Lewis, Sinclair 122
Lexis-Nexis databases 233, 237, 244, 254
Librairie Decitre 185
Librairie FNAC 185
Librairie Gallimard 185
Librairie La Procure 185
Librairie Le Furet du Nord 185
Librairie Mollat 185
librarians, first 2, 44, 45, 122, 124, 312
librarians, notable people as 122
Librarian's Yellow Pages 275
The Librarie-Keeper 162
libraries *see* busiest, expensive, largest, oldest
library, translated in 40 languages 123

Library and Information Science Abstracts 275
library and information science exhibitions, largest 278–281
library and information science, largest database 275
library associations, largest and oldest 306–309
Library Awareness Program 23
library branches, most worldwide 118
library budgets, largest 6, 16, 17, 120, 313
library buildings: largest 197–200; most expensive 2, 120, 205; most fascinating 201–205; oldest 66, 124, 194, 315; tallest 196
library catalogs: first full-text 2; largest 208–213; oldest computerized *see* OPAC
library classification 206
Library Company of Philadelphia 31
library consortium, largest 293
library donations, largest 313
library handbook, oldest and most popular 162, 163
Library Journal 164
library journal, oldest 164
library network, largest 293
Library of Congress 2, 42, 117, 120, 121, 122, 137, 154, 168, 194, 197, 202, 208, 224, 313
Library of Congress Classification 206
Library of Congress Music Division 94
Library of the Faculty of Advocates 1, 122
library schools: best in the U.S. 305; oldest 298–301
library serial, first in the U.S. 166
library staff, largest 313
library subscription services, largest and oldest 294, 295
Library Tower 195
Librería ABC
Librería de Cristal 185
Libreria Editrice Vaticana 185
Libreria Feltrinelli 185
Libreria Flaccovio 185
Librería Gandhi 185
Librería Jovellanos 185
Librería Lectura 185
Libreria Marzocco 185
Librería Porrúa 185
Libreria Rizzoli 185
Libya, earliest texts 152
Liège University Library 53
Lincoln's Inn Law Library 103
Linda Hall Library 93
Lindisfarne Gospels 132
Linear A script 125
Linear B script 125
Linen Hall Library 27

Linklater, Eric 161
linotype machine 137
LISA database 275
Lisbon University Library 74
literacy rate 24
Lithuania: first book printed in 144; largest and oldest university library 58, 73
Little Red Book 125
Liverpool Public Library 8, 28
Livraria Barata 185
Livraria Bertrand 185
Livraria Cultura 182
Livraria La Selva 185
Livraria Lojas Saraiva 185
Livraria Nobel 185
Livraria Siciliano 185
Ljubljana University Library 73
Lockheed Missile and Space Corporation 222
Lomonosov State University Library 44, 57, 117, 195
London Book Fair 188
London Guildhall University 110
London Hospital Medical Library 84
London Library 13, 27
London public libraries 8
London School of Economics and Political Science 90, 108
London Undergrond (Metro) 197
London University libraries 45
London University School of African and Oriental Studies 105
London University Senate House Library 45
Lord of Aratta 125
Lord's Prayer 158
Loreto College Library 117
Los Angeles County Public Library 6, 16
Los Angeles Public Library 6, 32, 122, 121, 196
Louis XI, king of France 1
Louvain Catholic University 53, 74, 117
Louvre Museum 124, 125
Luanda Municipal Library 41
LuEsther T. Mertz Library 99
Luhn, Hans Peter 235
Lun Ts'al 136, 297
Lund University Library 52
Luther, Martin 71
Luthy Buchhandlung 185
Luxeuil Monastery 68
Lvov University Library 73
The Lyceum 66, 67
Lyons Municipal Library 14, 26
Lyons University Library 47

M.D. Gunasena 186
Macedonia, largest university libraries 58

Machine Readable Cataloging *see* MARC
Macleish, Archibold 122
Macmillan Computer Publishing 186
Madbouli Bookshop 185
Madras University Library 75
Madrasahs 66
Madrid Autonomous University Library 51
magazines, oldest 157
Magdeburg Public Library 26
Magellan, Ferdinand 91
Magna Carta 132
Mahakal Temple 117
Mahmud I, Ottoman sultan 122
Mainz Psalter 137
Malatesta Library 194
Malaya University Library 62
Malaysia: largest book publisher 186; largest bookstores 185; largest university library 62; oldest public library 37; oldest texts in Malay 133
Malian Empire 75
Malmö City Library 7, 204
Manchester Public Library 28
manuscripts, largest, most expensive, oldest *see* books
Mao Zedong (Tse-tung) 61, 122, 125
MARC 214
Marciana National Library 1
Maria, Verge 143
Marnix, Philip von 172
Marsh Public Library 27
Marsiliana Tablet 125
Martin Luther University Library 48
Maruzen 185
Marx, Karl 122, 202
Maryland University Dental School Library 80
Masjids 66
Massachusetts Institute of Technology 92
Maurois, André 161
Maya, oldest texts 127
Maximilian, duke of Bavaria 71
Mazarin Library 26, 122, 137, 162
McDonald's restaurants 23
McGill University Library 59
McNally Robinson Bookstore 185
mechanical engineering, largest library 93
medical libraries, largest, oldest *see* medicine
medical texts, oldest 135
medicine: databases, largest 257–260; libraries, largest and oldest 78–88
MEDLARS database host 224, 257
MEDLINE 122, 224, 257

Meir, Golda 122
Melbourne Public Library 40
Melbourne University Library 62
MELVYL catalog 44, 210
Memory of the World Register 137
Mencius 171
Mendoza, Juan de Palafox 194
Menelik I, emperor of Ethiopia 152
Menelik II, emperor of Ethiopia 125
Mercure Galant 157
Mercury Rising 121
Merged Markush Services 286
Mergenthaler, Otto 137
Mesopotamia, ancient libraries 124
Methuselah 125
Metropolitan Bookshop 185
Mexican International Book Fair 191
Mexico: first book printed in 151; first papermill 136; first printing press 137; largest and oldest public libraries 20, 33; largest and oldest university libraries 63, 76; largest bookstores 185; oldest texts 127
Mexico National Autonomous University 4, 45
Mexico National Autonomous University Library 63, 76, 203
Mexico Public Library 20
MI6 librarry 120
Miami Book Fair International 189
Mickiewicz University Library 58
Microbial Strain Data Network 263
microbiological databases, largest 263
microfiche 220, 238
microfilm 112, 220, 238, 297
MicroPatent 283
Microsoft Encarta Encyclopedia 242
Middle East: largest book publishers *see* book publishers; largest bookstores *see* bookstores; largest libraries *see* largest; oldest libraries *see* oldest
Mihalopoulos 185
Milan University Library 49
military libraries, largest 100
Minas Gerais Federal University Library 63
Minoan texts, oldest 125
Miscellanea Curiosa Ephermeridium Medico Physicorum Germanorum 160
Les Misérables 168
Missale Aboense 145
Mr. Magoo 121
Mitchell Library 7
Mladinska Knjiga 185
MMS *see* Merged Markush Services

Moabite stone 125
Modena University Library 68
Molodaya Gvardia 185
Monash University Library 62
monastic libraries 68, 109, 194, 315
Mondadori, Arnoldo 186
Monrovia University Library 77
Monte Cassino Monastry 68, 122
Montpellier University Library 47, 68, 70
Monuments Blau 125
Moody's 246
Moravian Bookstore 176
Morocco: oldest texts 134; oldest university library 66
Mosaic web browser 137
Moscow City Public Library 7
Moses 125, 152
mosque libraries 66, 122, 124 194
Mossad library 75
Mount Sinai Arabic Codex 128
movies *see* films
MPH 185
Mumbai University Library 75
Munich City Library 7, 15
Munich University library school 300
Musa, Mansa, king of Mali 77
museum libraries, oldest and largest 174
Mushaf of Othman 128
music libraries, largest 94
Muslim libraries *see* Islamic libraries

Nalanda University 66
Nancy City Library 91
Nankai University Library 61
Nanjing Library 6
Nanjing University Library 61
Naqada culture 125
NARA 2, 122
Narodna Knjiga 185, 186
NASA 222
Nash Papyrus 125
Nasional Pers 186
Nassau Public Library 34
National Agricultural Library 97, 261
National and Kapodistrian University Library 55
National Archaeological Museum 124
National Archives and Records Administration *see* NARA
National Archives of Angola 116
National Archives of Argentina 113
National Archives of Egypt 114
National Archives of France 112
National Archives of India 115
National Archives of Mexico 113
National Archives of the U.S. *see* NARA
National Art Library 104

National Center for Biotechnology Information 260
National Defense University Library, Fort McNair 100
National Health University 85
National Institute of Medical Research Library 85
National Institutes of Health 260
national libraries, largest and oldest 1–5
National Library of Algeria 5, 117
National Library of Argentina 1, 4, 122
National Library of Australia 3
National Library of Austria 1, 202
National Library of Belgium 1
National Library of Brazil 4
National Library of Bulgaria 1
National Library of Cambodia 117
National Library of Canada 2
National Library of Chile 122
National Library of China 3, 197, 313
National Library of Croatia 1
National Library of Cuba 4
National Library of the Czech Republic 1, 202
National Library of Denmark 1, 52, 202
National Library of Education 107
National Library of Egypt 5, 205
National Library of Finland 1, 52, 117
National Library of France 1, 2, 122, 125, 137, 202, 206, 212, 220, 313
National Library of Germany 2, 219
National Library of India 1, 3
National Library of Israel 1, 5, 64
National Library of Italy 1
National Library of Japan 3, 197, 202, 313
National Library of Macedonia 1, 58
National Library of Malaysia 202
National Library of Malta 1
National Library of Medicine 78, 224, 257, 260, 292
National Library of Mexico 1, 4, 63
National Library of New Zealand 3
National Library of Papua New Guinea 3
National Library of the Philippines 1
National Library of Quebec 2
National Library of Russia 1, 2
National Library of Sarajevo 117
National Library of Scotland 1, 2, 54, 122
National Library of Singapore 1, 38
National Library of South Africa 5
National Library of Sweden 1

National Library of Taiwan 202
National Library of Tunisia 5
National Library of Turkey 5, 197
National Library of the U.K. see British Library
National Library of Ukraine 2
Naitonal Library of the U.S. see Library of Congress
National Library of Venezuela 4
National Library of Wales 1, 2, 54
National Marine Biological Library 98
National Online Meeting 281
National Postal Museum Library and Research Center 43
National Register of Historic Places 194
National Security Agency Library 120, 121, 205, 313
National Sound Archives 94
National Technical Information Service 268
National Union Catalog 208
National University of Ireland Library 54
natural disasters, libraries destroyed in 117
Naudé, Gabriel 162
Navarre University Library 51
Nazi regime, treatment of books 171
Neanderthals 125
Necrologium Lundense 133
Nedivot, Sameul 152
Nehru, Jawaharlal 101
Nero, Roman emperor 125
The Netherlands: first printing press 137; largest and oldest public libraries 7, 26; largest and oldest university libraries 53, 74; largest bookstores 185; oldest texts in Dutch 133
Netscape Navigator 137, 290
New Delhi Public Library 19
New Delhi University Library 62
New Delhi World Book Fair 190
New England Journal of Medicine 160
New Orleans Public Library 32
New South Wales Standing Order 153
New South Wales University Library 62
New York Academy of Medicine Library 78
New York Botanical Gardens Library 99
New York Public Library 6, 11, 12, 16, 32, 43, 120, 121, 136, 137, 214, 313
New York state public libraries 17
New York Times 220
New York University Bobst Library 121, 146

New Zealand: largest bookstore 185; largest university library 62
Newark Public Library 204, 219
NewsBank 244
newspaper databases 243, 244
newspapers: largest circulation 156; largest databases 240, 241, 244; oldest 156; oldest database coverage 243
Newton, Helmut 168, 172
Niepce, Joseph 212
Nieuwe Tijdinghen 156
NIFTY-Serve database host 230
Nigeria: largest university libraries 65; oldest texts 134
Nigeria University Library 65
Nihon Shoki 129
Nikkei Economic Electronic Database 251
Nile & Euphrates 184
Nineveh Library 122, 124
The Ninth Gate 121
Nippon Cataloging Rules 207
Nolit 185
Norfolk and Norwich Millennium Library 205
Norli Bokhandel 185
North Carolina University library school 305
North Dakota state public libraries 18
The Northumberland Bestiary 172
Norway: largest book publisher 186; largest bookstores 185; largest public library 7; largest university library 52; oldest texts in Norwegian 133
Norwich City Library 28
Norwich Public Library 28
Notre Dame Cathedral 194
Notre Dame University Library 196
NSA see National Security Agency
Nubian, oldest texts 134
nutrition, largest database 262
Nyströms Bokhandel 185

OAG 274
Oaxaca Public Library 33
Obeikan 185
Obres Otrobes la Hors dela 143
OCLC 213, 293
Odessa University Library 58
The Odyssey 125, 171
Ogham aphabet 132
Ohio Bar Association 253
Ohio State University Library 215
oil exploration, largest library 92
Old King Cole 168
Old Nubian Miracle of Saint Menas 134
oldest book club 177
oldest book publisher 186
oldest books and manuscripts see books

oldest bookstores 175, 176, 185
oldest databases *see* databases
oldest libraries: in Africa 1, 41, 66,
    77, 124; in the Americas 31–36,
    76, 80, 82, 119; in the Asia-
    Pacific region 37–39, 75, 83; in
    Europe 1, 26–30, 67–74, 81, 84,
    110; in the Middle East 40, 66,
    124; worldwide 124, 314
oldest library buildings *see* library
    buildings
Olmec civilization 127
Omar I, caliph 117
Online Information 278
Online Public Access Catalogs *see*
    OPAC
Het Onze Vader 168
OPAC 206; oldest 214–219
OPAC 97 209
Open Society Institute 293
Open University 46
Oporto Public Library 7
oracle bones 125
Oracle database 221
Orange Free State University
    Library 77
Orell Fussli Buchhandlung 185
Orleans University Library 70
Osaka Prefectural Library 19
Osasso Public Library 205
Osgoode Hall Law School Library
    102
Oslo Deichman Public Library 7
Oslo University Library 52
Otava 186
Othman, caliph 128
Otlet, Paul 310
Ottoman Empire libraries 122
out-of-print bookseller, largest
    179
overdue books, longest 169
Ovid 171
Ovid Technologies 227, 241, 287
Oxford English Dictionary 173
Oxford Public Library 28
Oxford University Bodleian Law
    Library 103
Oxford University Bodleian
    Library 1, 45, 54, 69, 121, 122,
    203
Oxford University Press 137, 186
Oxford University Sacker Library
    205

Pablos, Juan 151
Padjadjaran University Library 75
Padua University Library 68
PageMaker 137
Pakistan, oldest texts 125
Palacky University Library 73
Palafox Library 194
Palencia University Library 68, 72
Palestine, oldest texts 125
Palestrina 125
Palmart, Lambert 143

Panaji Medical School Library 83
Panchatantra 124
Panini 125
Panizzi, Antonio 122
Panizzi Municipal Library 7
Pannartz, Arnold 142
paper: invention of 136; largest
    database 270; largest manufac-
    turer 270; oldest handwritten
    books 122, 136; oldest printed
    books 137–154
paperbacks, first 161
Paperbase 270
papermills, earliest 136
papyrus: first use of 125; longest
    document 168; oldest document
    125
Papyrus 53 125
parchment, first use of 124
Parikh, Bhimjee 149
Paris City Library 14
Paris Conservatoire library 122
Paris public libraries 14
Paris University 49
Paris University Library 45, 68,
    70, 103
Pasadena Public Library 121,
    204
Pascal, Blaise 171
PASCAL database 223
patent databases, largest 283–286
Patriotic Act 23
Paul, Apostle 125
Pavlov, Ivan 45
PC-Van database host 230
PDA 137, 290
Pearson 186
Peckham Public Library and Media
    Center 204
Pécs University Library 73
The Pelican Brief 121
Pelotas University Library 76
Penang Library 37
Penguin Books 161
Penguin Putnam 186
Penny Black 43
Pergamum Library 124
Peripatetic School Library 67
Pernambuco Federal University
    Central Library 63
Persae of Timotheus 125
Persian, oldest texts 125, 147
Personal computer, invention of
    297
Personal Digital Assistant *see* PDA
Peru: oldest newspaper 156; oldest
    university library 76
Perugia University Library 68
Peter I, Tsar of Russia 44
Peterboro Public Library 32
Peterhouse College Libray 68
Petrie, Flinders 125
petroleum exploration, largest
    library 92
Petronas Twin Towers 196, 202

Pfizer 86
pharmaceutical databases, largest
    257, 259
pharmaceutical libraries, largest 86
Philadelphia Public Library 6, 32,
    121
Philip II, king of Spain 122
Philippines: first book printed in
    153; largest and oldest university
    library 62, 75; largest bookstore
    185; oldest newspaper 156
Philippines University Library 62
Philosophical Transactions 158
Phoenician texts, oldest 125
Phoenix Central Public Library
    204
Phönix-Montanus Buchhandlung
    185
photocopying, invention of 297
photography, largest database 282
Pinakes 1, 122, 207
Pinochet, Augusto 171
PIR database 260
Pisistratus Public Library 26
Piso Library 124
Planeta Actimedia 186
Plato 67, 171
Pliny the Elder 166
Poblet Monastery 194
Pocket Book 161
pocketbooks *see* paperbacks
Poema del Cid 131
poetry, largest library 95
Poet's Pub 161
Pol Pot 117
Poland: first book printed in 144;
    first papermill 136; largest and
    oldest university libraries 58,
    73; largest book publisher 186;
    largest public library 7
political science, largest library 90
Politikens Boghallen 185
Pollio, Gaius Asinius 26
Polo, Marco 91, 101
Poole, William 232
Pontifical Gregorian University
    Library 55, 74
Pontifical Lateranese University
    Library 55
Pontifical Santo Tomás University
    Library 75
Pope Agapetus 109
Pope Benedict XIV 171
Pope Clement V 26
Pope Damascus I 109, 112
Pope Gregory XI 26
Pope Gregory XV 71
Pope Leo XIII 112
Pope Nicholas V 26, 122
Pope Pius XI 122
Pope Sixtus V 194, 205
Popol Vuh 127
Popular Bookshop 185
popular libraries 20
Port of Spain Public Library 34

Portrait of Dr. Gachet 172
Portugal: first book printed in 143; first printing press 137; largest and oldest university libraries 51, 74; largest bookstores 185; largest public library 7; oldest texts in Portuguese 131
postage stamps commemorating libraries, first 43
Powell, Humphrey 146
Powell, Samuel 176
Powell's Bookstore 185
Power, Eugene 238
Prague Municipal Library 7
Pratt Institute School of Information & Library Science 299
presidential libraries, U.S. 122
Presstorg 185
Pretoria University Library 65
Priestley, Joseph 122
Princeton University 92
printing presses, earliest 137
prison libraries, largest and oldest 101
Prison Service College Library 101
Prisse Papyrus 125
private libraries, oldest 119
Privilegii 155
ProCite 277
Project Gutenberg 241
ProQuest Information and Learning 238, 252
Prosveta 186
protein sequence database, largest 260
Prous Science 259
Provisions of Oxford 132
Proxis 185
Prussian State Library 1
psychology, largest databases 271
PsycINFO 271
Ptolemy, Claudius 91
Ptolemy, Philadelphus 124
Ptolemy I, king of Egypt 1, 122, 124
Ptolemy XIII 117
Pu Yi, Henry 122
public libraries, busiest 11, 12
public libraries, largest and oldest 6–41
Public Library Day 25; *see also* book reading day
publishers, largest and oldest *see* book publishers
Puebla Autonomous University Library 63, 76
Puerto Rico, oldest public library 134
Pusan Civil Library 19

QuarkXpress 137
Quebec City Library 35
Queen Mary's School of Medicine and Dentistry Library 84

Queens Borough Public Library 6, 16
Queensland University Library 62
Questel-Orbit database host 222, 223, 283
QuickLaw 256
Quito Central University Library 76
Quixote, Don 171
Quran see Koran

R.R. Bowker 240
Raffles, Stamford 37
Raiders of the Lost Ark 152
railway travel, largest schedules 274
RAK cataloging rules 207
Ralegh, Walter 101
Rama V, king of Thailand 122
Ramesseum Papyrus 135
Ramses II library 124
Random House 186
Ranganathan, Shiyali Ramamrita 194
rare bookseller, largest 179
Reader's Guide to Periodical Literature 232
Reader's World 185
Reading Prison 122
Reagan, Ronald 23
Recuyell of the Histories of Troye 138
Red Dragon 121
Reed Elsevier 177, 237, 262
Reference Manager 277
ReferenceUSA 247
relational database 131
religious libraries, largest and oldest 109
residential library, oldest 28
Reuters 246
Riding the Bullet 137
Rig Veda 125
Rio de Janeiro Federal University Library 63
Rio Grande Public Library 20
Roberts, Ed 297
Robo Cop 121
Roger I, king of Sicily 136
Roman Empire libraries 124
Romania: first book printed in 144; largest and oldest university libraries 44, 45, 58, 73; largest public library 7
Romanian Academy Library 44
Rome University Library 49
Rosetta Stone 125
Rostov State University Library 57
Rothschild Prayer Book 172
Rotterdam Municipal Library 7, 26, 204
Rouen Cathedral 68
Round Reading Room 202
Rowling, J.K. 121
Royal Botanical Gardens Library 99

Royal College of Physicians Libraries 84, 85
Royal College of Surgeons Libraries 84, 85
Royal Military Academy Sandhurst Library 100
Royal Military College Library 100
Royal National Institute for the Deaf Library 89
Royal Society of Medicine Library 85
royalties, first 155
Rumyantsev, Nickolai 2, 122
Runic inscriptions 126
Rupert-Charles University Library 71
Russia: first book printed in 141; first printing press 137; largest and oldest public libraries 7, 29, 44; largest and oldest university libraries 44, 45, 57, 73; largest book publisher 186; largest bookstores 185; largest library building 197; military library, largest 100; oldest texts in Russian 133; tallest university library building 196
Russian Academy of Sciences Institute for Scientific Information on Social Sciences 108
Russian Academy of Sciences Library 44, 117, 122
Russian Army Central House Library 100
Russian Central Epidemiology Institute 78
Russian Central Scientific Agricultural Library 97
Russian Institute of Scientific and Technical Information 265
Russian State Library 2, 196, 313
Russian State Medical Library 78
Rutgers University library school 305
Rylands Papyrus 124
Ryukoku University Library 75
RZK database 265

SABINET 229
SABRE 274
St. Andrews University Library 69
St. Augustine 132
St. Benedict 68, 122
St. Clement Ohridski National and University Library 58
St. Columbas Monastery 146
St. Deiniol's Library 28
St. Frumentius 134
St. Gallen Monastery 68, 109
St. George's Day 131
St. Honorat Island Monastery 194
St. John of Jerusalem 1
St. Joseph County Public Library 290
St. Mark 125

St. Mary's University 76
St. Maurice Monastery 194
St. Nicholas of Hidalgo Michoacan University Library 76
St. Patrick 132
St. Petersburg University Library 45
St. Thomas Aquinas Pontifical University Library 55
Saka no Sono 121
Sakya Buddhist Monastery 109
Salamanca University Library 68, 72
Salerno Medical School Library 81
Salford Public Library 28
Saltykov-Shchedrin State Public Library 2, 29, 44
San Antonio Public Library 199
San Carlos University Library 75
Sancho I, king of Portugal 131
Sandeido 185
San Francisco Public Library 121, 204
San Francisco Xavier Royal Pontifical University Library 76
Sankore University 77
San Marcos National University Library 76
Sanskrit texts, oldest 125
Santa Fe Public Library 33
Santo Domingo Autonomous University Library 76
São Paulo Federal University Library 63
São Paulo Municipal Library 20, 195
Saragossa University Library 51
Saratov State University Library 57
Sartre, Jean Paul 171
The Satanic Verses 171
Saudi Arabia: largest bookstores 185; largest petroleum library 92; largest university library 64
Scandinavia: first book printed in 145; oldest texts 133
Scheltema Holkema Vermeulen Boekhandel 185
Schiller-Anstalt Library 122
Scholastic 186
schools *see* library schools
ScienceDirect 241
search engines, largest 289–290
secondhand bookseller, largest 179
Second World War, destruction of libraries in 73, 117
Sejong, king of Korea 129
Sema InfoData 231
Semitic alphabet 125
Send Inscription 125
Sennacherib 124
Seoul National Museum 136
Seoul National University Library 62
septentrionalium 169

Serapeum Library 124
Serbo-Croat, oldest texts 133
Shah Faisal Mosque 109
Shakespeare, largest book collection on 111
Shakespeare, William 111, 124, 170, 241
Shanghai Book City 185
Shanghai Library 6, 196, 199, 204
Sheng, Pi 137
Sherbone Missal 172
Shepard's Citations 233
Shotoku, empress of Japan 136
Shrine of the Book 125
Siddhanta 124
Siena University Library 68
Sierra Leone, oldest university library 77
Silesian University Library 205
Silos Missal 136
SilverPlatter SPIRS 287
Singapore: largest bookstores 185; largest library building 205; largest university library 62; oldest library 37
Singapore National University Library
Slovenia: largest bookstore 185; largest university library 73
smallest book *see* books
Smithsonian Institution 43
social sciences library, largest 91, 108
Solomon, king of Israel 152
Solzhenitsyn, Alexander 122
Somali, oldest texts 134
Somerset County Public Library 218
Sorbonne University Library 68
Soros, George 313
Soros Foundation Network 293, 313
Sotheby's 172
sound recordings, largest collection in a library 94, 96
South Africa: first printing press 152; largest and oldest university libraries 65, 77; largest book publisher 186; largest bookstores 183, 185; largest public library 22, 41; oldest newspaper 156
South Africa Library Association 309
South Africa University Library 65
South Caroliniana Library 194
Southern California University Doheny Library 121
Soyinka, Wole 101
Spain: first book printed in 143; first papermill 136; first printing press 137; largest and oldest university libraries 51, 68, 72; largest book publisher 186; largest bookstores 185; largest

public library 7; oldest library building 194; oldest paper document 136; oldest texts in Spanish 131, 143
Spangenberg, Augustus 176
special libraries, largest and oldest 78–111
Special Libraries Association 306
specialty libraries *see* special libraries
Speusippus 166
SPIRS 287
Spofford, Ainsworth 122
spy agency libraries, most secure 120
SQL database 221
Sri Lanka: first book printed in 149; largest book publisher 186; oldest texts in Tamil 125
Stalin, Josef 122, 171
stamps commerating libraries, first 43
Standard & Poor's 246
Standard Boekhandel 185
Stanford University Library 44
The Star 156
State University of New York 44, 45, 102, 227
Statue of Anne 155
Stauffacher Buchhandlung 185
Steele, Danielle 170
Steimatzky's Bookstore 185
Stein, Aurel 136
Stemzky 186
Step Pyramid 194
STN database host 265
Stockholm City Library 7
Stockholm University Library 52
Stoddard, Solomon 44
Strasbourg National University Library 47
Strasbourg Oath 130
Stratford Public Library 205
Strindberg, John 122
Sturgis Library 194
subscription libraries, largest and oldest 6–41
Sudan: oldest texts 134; oldest university library 66
Suleymaniye Mosque 109, 122
Sumeria, ancient libraries and texts 124, 125
Sumo 168, 172
Sung Document 91
Suomalainen Kirjakauppa 185
The Super Book 168
SVP 276
Sweden: first book printed in 145; first papermill 136; largest and oldest university library 52, 74; largest bookstores 185; largest book publishers 186; largest public library 7; oldest texts in Swedish 133

Swedenborg, Emanuel 171
Swedish Chancery Archives 112
Sweet & Maxwell legal database 255
Sweetest Thing 121
Sweinheim, Konrad 142
Swets 292
Swets Blackwell 294
Swiss Co-operative Movement 177
Swiss Federal Institute of Technology Library 50, 284
SWISS PROT database 260
Switzerland: largest and oldest university library 50, 74; largest book publishers 186; largest bookstores 185; oldest public library 26
Sydney Subscription Library 39
Sydney University Library 62, 75
Syllabic writing systems 125
Syracuse University library school 305
Syria, oldest texts 125

Tablets of the Law 152
Ta-chao, Li 122
Taipei International Book Exhibition 190
Taiwan: largest book publisher 186; largest bookstores 185; largest university library 62
Taiwan National Palace Museum 125
Taiwan National University Library 62
Takshila University 66
Talis 219
tallest books *see* books
tallest library buildings *see* library buildings
Tamaulipas Autonomous University Library 63
Tamerlane 66
Tamil: first book printed in 149; oldest texts 125
Tamkang University Library 203
Tanum Bokhandel 185
Tartu University Library 58
Tasmania University Library 217
Tbilisi State University Library 58
Tehran International Book Fair 192
Tehran University Library 64
Teikoku Databank 250
Tel Aviv Central Public Library 21
Tel Aviv University Library 64
Telesytemes-Questel database host 223
Television, invention of 297
Television libraries, largest 96
Temasek Polytechnic Library 205
Temple Mount 152
Temple of Literature 66
Tesfatsion, Abba 152

Texas University, library school 305
Texas University Library 44, 219
Thailand: largest bookstores 185; oldest texts in Thai 134
Thalia 185
Thambiran va Nakkam 149
theft of books, largest 119
Theodosius I, Roman emperor 124
Thomas Nelson 109
Thomson 222, 228, 234, 239
Thomson & Thomson 283
Thomson Directories Database 247
Thomson Financial Services 246
Tianyi Library 194
Tibet, oldest texts in Tibetan 133
Time Warner Books 186
The Times 243
Titus, Roman emperor 2
Tokyo Metropolitan Central Library 19
Tokyo University Library 44, 60
Toledo Cathedral 194
Toledo translation school 124
Tomsk State University Library 57
Topkapi Museum Library 122
Torah 125, 148
Toronto Public Library 6, 36
Toronto University Library 59, 196, 198, 203
Tosa Nikki 129
Toulouse Municipal Library 14
Toulouse University Library 47, 70
Trademark Scan 283
trademarks, largest databases 283
Trajan, Marcus, Roman emperor 122, 124
Transportation information, largest database 274
Transportation Research Information Services 274
The Travels of Marco Polo 101
Trinidad and Tobago, oldest public library 34
Trinity College, Dublin University Library 54, 146, 203
Tripitaka Canon 168
TRIS database 274
Ts'ai, Lun 136
Tse-tung, Mao *see under* Mao
Tsinghua University Law School Library 103
Tsurayuki, Ki 129
Tuareg alphabet 134
Tunisia, oldest texts 134
Turin University Library 49
Turkey: first book printed in 150; largest bookstores 185; largest library building 197; oldest newspaper 156; oldest public library 40; oldest university library 66
Turkish Book Fair 192
Turkish Scientific and Technical

Research Council Documentation Center 292
Twelve Monkeys 121
24-hour university library, first 46
21 North Main 179
Tyndale, William 125
Tzu, Lao 122, 124, 171

Ukraine: first book printed in 144; largest and oldest university libraries 44, 45, 58, 73
Ukrainian National Academy of Sciences Library 44
Ulfilas 126
Ullstein Heyne List 186
Ulpian Library 124
Ulrich's International Periodical Directory 240
Umayyad Mosque 194
UMI 238
UnCover 292
UNESCO 1, 2, 117, 122, 137, 187
Union of Kalmar 1
United Kingdom: first book printed in 138, 139; first library building to use electricity 195; first newspaper 156; first papermill 136; first printing press 137; largest and oldest book publishers 186; largest and oldest bookstores 175, 180, 185; largest and oldest public libraries 7, 8, 9, 10, 28; largest and oldest university libraries 44, 45, 69; largest library building 197; military libraries, largest 100; oldest texts in English 132
United Kingdom Library Association 307
United Kingdom Museums Act 28
United Kingdom Public Lending Right 170
United Kingdom Public Library Act 28
United Nations Educational, Scientific and Cultural Organization *see* UNESCO
United Nations Food and Agricultural Organisation 97, 261
United Nations World International Book Day 1, 131
United States: first book printed in 140; first newspaper 156; first papermill 136; first printing press 137; largest and oldest bookstores 176, 178, 179, 185; largest and oldest public libraries 6, 32; largest and oldest university libraries 44, 76; largest book publishers 186; largest library buildings 197, 198, 199, 200; military libraries, largest 100; oldest library build-

Index

...ing 194; tallest library buildings 196, 203
United States Naval Observatory 106
United States Patent and Trademark Office 285
Universal Decimal Classification 206
University College, library school, London 300
University College Library, London 45, 89
University of Chicago Library 198
University of Illinois, library school 305
University of Illinois Library 44, 93, 290
University of Massachusetts W.E.B. Du Bois Library 196, 203
University of Memphis Library 196
University of Michigan, library school 305
University of Michigan Library 44, 203
University of Pennsylvania Medical School Library 82
University of Pennsylvania Museum of Archaeology and Anthropology 125
University of Pittsburgh 195
University of Pittsburgh, library school 305
University of South Carolina Library 194
University of Wisconsin–Milwaukee, Golda Meir Library 91
university libraries, largest and oldest 44–77, 315
University Microfilms, Inc. 238
UPL 186
Uppsala University Library 74
Ussher, John 146
Utrecht University Library 53

vakif libraries 66, 122
Valencia University Library 72
Valladolid University Library 72
Vancouver Public Library 121, 204
Van Gogh, Vincent 172
Vasa, Gustavus 1
Vatican Archives, 26, 112
Vatican City: largest and oldest university library 55, 74; largest bookstores 185; oldest public library 26
Vatican Library 26, 71, 91, 122, 125, 194, 205
Vedas 125
vellum, first use of 124
Venetian Republic 1, 155
Venetian Republic National Library 1
Venezuela, largest bookstore 185

Vespucci, Amerigo 208
Vicenza University Library 68
Vienna Public Library 7, 42, 290
Vienna University Library 50, 74
Vietnam: largest bookstore 185; oldest texts in Vietnamese 133; oldest university library 66
Vietnam National University Library 66
Vikramshila University 66
Vilnius University Library 58, 73
VINITI see Russian Institute for Scientific and Technical Information
Volksbibliotheken 30

W.E.B. Du Bois Library 196, 203
Wachtendonk Psalm 133
Waldenbooks Bookstore 185
Waldsemüller, Martin 208
Wall Street Journal 156
Walpole, Robert 169
Wang Fu Jing 185
WAP sites, first public library 290
War Games 121
War of 1812 117
Warrington Public Library 28
Warsaw Public Library 7
Waseda University Library 60, 203
Waterloo University Library 59, 214
Waterstone's Bookshop 185
Watterson, George 2
Way-Back-Machine search engine 290
Webb, Sydney 90
websites 3, 289, 290
Webster, Noah 173
Weltbild 186
Werner Soderstrom Oyi 186
West Publishing 253
Westinghouse, George 195
Westminster borough public libraries 8, 10
Westlaw 253
Whitaker Information Services 245
Whitcaullis and Bennetts 185
WHO Library 155
Whole Library Handbook 163
WHSmith 180, 185
Wiener Zeitung 156
Wilde, Oscar 101, 122
William, Frederick 1
William & Mary College 76
William the Conqueror 132
Winchester Public Library 28
Wings of Desire 121, 202
Wisconsin University library school 305
Witwatersrand University Library 65
Women's Library 110
World Bank 117
World Book Encyclopedia 242

World Data Center for Microorganisms 263
World Health Organization Library 87
World Intellectual Property Organization 155
World International Book Day 1, 131
World War II, destruction of libraries 73, 117
WorldCat 213
World's Biggest Bookstore 185
World's Smallest Book 168
Worldspan 274
Wren, Christopher 203
writing 124, 125
Wsip 186
Wuhan University library school 301
Würzburg University Library 71

X.25 database access 222
Xerox 297
Xerox Star 221
Xi, Fu 125
Xinhua 181, 185
Xuan Thu 185

Yahoo search engine 290
Yale University Library 44, 137, 140, 203
Yale University Medical School Library 78
Yamani, Ahmed 92
Yellow Emperor's Classic of Internal Medicine 135
Yeongpung 185
Yomiuri Shimbun 156
Yonsei University Library 62
York Cathedral 68
York University 102
Younis, Mohammed 168
You're a Big Boy Now 121
Yucatan University Library 76
Yugoslavia: largest book publisher 186; largest bookstores 185

Zagreb National and University Library 1, 73
Zambia University Library 65
Zaydan, Shafif 122
Zedong, Mao see under Mao
Zenodotus 1, 122
Zhdanov State University Library 45, 57
Zimbabwe International Book Fair 193
Zimbabwe University Library 65
zoological libraries, largest 98
Zoological Record database 263
Zoological Society of London Library 98, 263
zoology, largest database 263
Zumarraga, Juan de 151
Zürich University Library 50, 74